CW01301774

JOEL AND OBADIAH

The Old Testament Library

GENESIS, A Commentary. Revised Edition. BY GERHARD VON RAD
THE BOOK OF EXODUS, A Critical, Theological Commentary. BY BREVARD S. CHILDS
LEVITICUS, A Commentary. BY ERHARD S. GERSTENBERGER
NUMBERS, A Commentary. BY MARTIN NOTH
DEUTERONOMY, A Commentary. BY RICHARD D. NELSON
DEUTERONOMY, A Commentary. BY GERHARD VON RAD
JOSHUA, A Commentary. BY RICHARD D. NELSON
JUDGES, A Commentary. BY SUSAN NIDITCH
JUDGES, A Commentary. BY J. ALBERTO SOGGIN
RUTH, A Commentary. BY KIRSTEN NIELSEN
I & II SAMUEL, A Commentary. BY HANS WILHELM HERTZBERG
I & II KINGS, A Commentary. BY MARVIN A. SWEENEY
I & II CHRONICLES, A Commentary. BY SARA JAPHET
EZRA-NEHEMIAH, A Commentary. BY JOSEPH BLENKINSOPP
ESTHER, A Commentary. BY JON D. LEVENSON
THE BOOK OF JOB, A Commentary. BY NORMAN C. HABEL
THE PSALMS, A Commentary. BY ARTUR WEISER
PROVERBS, A Commentary. BY RICHARD J. CLIFFORD
ECCLESIASTES, A Commentary. BY JAMES L. CRENSHAW
SONG OF SONGS, A Commentary. BY J. CHERYL EXUM
ISAIAH, A Commentary. BY BREVARD S. CHILDS
ISAIAH 1–12, A Commentary. Second Edition. BY OTTO KAISER
ISAIAH 13–39, A Commentary. BY OTTO KAISER
ISAIAH 40–66, A Commentary. BY CLAUS WESTERMANN
LAMENTATIONS, A Commentary. BY ADELE BERLIN
JEREMIAH, A Commentary. BY LESLIE C. ALLEN
EZEKIEL, A Commentary. BY WALTHER EICHRODT
DANIEL, A Commentary. BY NORMAN W. PORTEOUS
HOSEA, A Commentary. BY JAMES L. MAYS
JOEL AND OBADIAH, A Commentary. BY JOHN BARTON
AMOS, A Commentary. BY JAMES L. MAYS
THE BOOK OF AMOS, A Commentary. BY JÖRG JEREMIAS
JONAH, A Commentary. BY JAMES LIMBURG
MICAH, A Commentary. BY JAMES L. MAYS
NAHUM, HABAKKUK, AND ZEPHANIAH, A Commentary. BY J. J. M. ROBERTS
HAGGAI AND ZECHARIAH 1–8, A Commentary. BY DAVID L. PETERSEN
ZECHARIAH 9–14 AND MALACHI, A Commentary. BY DAVID L. PETERSEN

EXILE AND RESTORATION: A Study of Hebrew Thought of the Sixth Century B.C. BY PETER R. ACKROYD
A HISTORY OF ISRAELITE RELIGION IN THE OLD TESTAMENT PERIOD, Volumes I and II. BY RAINER ALBERTZ
INTRODUCTION TO THE OLD TESTAMENT. Third Edition. BY J. ALBERTO SOGGIN
JEWISH WISDOM IN THE HELLENISTIC AGE. BY JOHN J. COLLINS
OLD TESTAMENT THEOLOGY, Volumes I and II. BY HORST DIETRICH PREUSS
OLD TESTAMENT THEOLOGY, Volumes I and II. BY GERHARD VON RAD
THEOLOGY OF THE OLD TESTAMENT, Volumes I and II. BY WALTHER EICHRODT

John Barton

JOEL AND OBADIAH
A Commentary

WJK WESTMINSTER
JOHN KNOX PRESS
LOUISVILLE · KENTUCKY

© 2001 John Barton

14 15 16 17 18 19 20 — 10 9 8 7 6 5 4 3 2

All rights reserved. No part of this book may be reproduced or transmitted in any form or by any means, electronic or mechanical, including photocopying, recording, or by any information storage or retrieval system, without permission in writing from the publisher. For information, address Westminster John Knox Press, 100 Witherspoon Street, Louisville, Kentucky 40202–1396. Or contact us online at www.wjkbooks.com.

Book design by Jennifer K. Cox

Library of Congress Cataloging-in-Publication Data is on file at the Library of Congress, Washington, D.C.

ISBN: 978-0-664-21966-6 (hardback)

ISBN: 978-0-664-23726-4 (paperback)

∞ The paper used in this publication meets the minimum requirements of the American National Standard for Information Sciences—Permanence of Paper for Printed Library Materials, ANSI Z39.48-1992.

This book is dedicated with love
to my daughter Katie and her fiancé.

CONTENTS

Preface	ix
Abbreviations	xi
Select Bibliography for Joel	xiii
Select Bibliography for Obadiah	xix
The Book of Joel	1
Introduction	3
Commentary on Joel	37
Superscription: Joel 1:1	39
First Lament Cycle: Joel 1:2–20	40
Second Lament Cycle: Joel 2:1–17	66
The Divine Response: Joel 2:18–27	84
Oracles of Salvation: Joel 2:28–3:21	92
The Book of Obadiah	113
Introduction	115
Commentary on Obadiah	131
Superscription: Obadiah 1a	133
First Oracle against Edom: Obadiah 1b–4	134
Second Oracle against Edom: Obadiah 5–7	139
Third Oracle against Edom: Obadiah 8–11	142
Fourth Oracle against Edom: Obadiah 12–14, 15b	147
An Oracle against the Nations: Obadiah 15a, 16–18	150
An Oracle about the Restoration of Israel: Obadiah 19–21	154

ACKNOWLEDGMENTS

Warm thanks are due to many colleagues and students from whom I have learned much about the biblical prophets and their interpretation. I am specially indebted to Ms. Susan Lake and her colleagues at the Oxford Theology Faculty Library for help in tracking down books and articles. I am grateful to Westminster John Knox Press and to the editors of the Old Testament Library for inviting me to contribute this volume on two books of the Bible that deserve to be more widely studied than they are.

PREFACE

In modern times the study of the twelve Minor Prophets has been uneven. Amos, Hosea, and Micah have been in the forefront of attention, because of their deep engagement with the moral life of Israel, their penetrating analysis of the ills of the society in which they lived, and their conviction that these ills would result in divine judgment. The Old Testament Library has long included volumes on these three prophets, and in the case of Amos no fewer than three commentaries have been published in this series. Those Minor Prophets whom modern scholarship judges to have been involved in the Israelite cult, especially in Second Temple times, have attracted far less interest.[1] Joel and Obadiah have been particularly affected by this relative neglect. There are indeed many monographs, commentaries, and articles about them, but students study them much more rarely than the "big three," and pastors seldom preach about them. As so often with neglected subjects, closer study reveals much of interest, however, and my hope is that this commentary may stimulate readers to concern themselves more with these lesser-known books of the Old Testament.

One factor that has also contributed to the neglect of these books (and of some other Minor Prophets) is the comparative lack of information available about their life and times. Traditionally, commentators have been confident in reconstructing the setting and historical background of Amos and Hosea, but with Joel and Obadiah this task is much harder. Even their dating is unclear, with proposals ranging from the early monarchic to the late postexilic age. Where so much is uncertain, it has been hard to feel that the contents of the books can be analyzed with confidence, since we so often do not know what they are alluding to.

Of course, one may make a virtue of necessity by arguing that the business of critics is not to attempt historical reconstructions of any book's original setting and meaning but simply to read "what is there" in a synchronic and holistic way or as part of the "canon of scripture"—perhaps drawing on the interpretations

---

1. See R. J. Coggins, "An Alternative Prophetic Tradition?" in *Israel's Prophetic Tradition: Essays in Honour of Peter Ackroyd*, ed. R. J. Coggins, M. A. Knibb, and A. Phillips, Cambridge 1982, pp. 77–94.

of past, "precritical" commentators. This kind of commentary is in vogue at the moment. I comment on possible readings in these modes both in the introductions to Joel and Obadiah and in the course of the commentaries. But my conviction is that commentaries should seek the original location of the book so far as is possible and then record honest uncertainty. Holistic readings need to justify themselves by pointing to elements of unity and cohesion within the text itself, rather than by imposing unity *a priori* on literary or religious grounds. And the history of the text's interpretation is (I believe) a different, though also intensely interesting, question, best handled outside the context of a verse-by-verse commentary. (In the case of Joel, the work of Adalbert Merx already provides a very substantial basis for such a study.)[2]

In other words, these commentaries aim to stand in the so-called historical-critical tradition. This does not imply blindness to "literary" questions, since the books of Joel and Obadiah are unquestionably literature and raise throughout questions of unity, coherence, and meaning; a "historical" critic is concerned not simply with history but with the text—a piece of literary art—in its historical setting. Nor does it imply an absence of interest in the texts' theological message: on the contrary, it is precisely in order to try to discover this message that one must take so much trouble over seeking the context of any biblical book. It is also important to see that, whatever the original setting of the prophet—or of other authors who may have contributed to the book—there also exists an end product, the completed book of Joel or Obadiah; and it makes perfectly good sense to ask about its context, too. Historical criticism is concerned not only with original components of biblical books but also with the books themselves, which have their own historical setting, usually in Judaism of the Second Temple period. We shall try to pay attention to the contribution made by individual passages to the finished books, and hence to the contribution both the passages and the complete books make to biblical theology.

In preparing my translation of these books, I have used the New Revised Standard Version (NRSV) as a basis but have departed from it in the interest of a more "literal" rendering of the Hebrew—even though this sometimes makes for less elegant English—and where my decisions on textual matters need to be reflected in the translation.

---

2. A. Merx, *Die Prophetie des Joel und ihre Ausleger von den ältesten Zeiten bis zu den Reformatoren*, Halle 1879.

ABBREVIATIONS

AASOR	Annual of the American Schools of Oriental Research
ABD	*Anchor Bible Dictionary* (ed. D. N. Freedman)
ATA	Alttestamentliche Abhandlungen
ATAT	Arbeiten zu Text und Sprache im Alten Testament
ATD	Das Alte Testament Deutsch
BASOR	*Bulletin of the American Schools of Oriental Research*
BDB	F. Brown, S. R. Driver, and C. A. Briggs, *Hebrew and English Lexicon of the Old Testament*
BEATAJ	Beiträge zur Erforschung des Alten Testaments und des Antiken Judentums
BH	Biblical Hebrew
BHS	*Biblia hebraica stuttgartensia*
BZAW	Beihefte zur *Zeitschrift für die alttestamentliche Wissenschaft*
CAT	Commentaire de l'Ancien Testament
CBC	Cambridge Bible Commentary
CBQ	*Catholic Biblical Quarterly*
CTA	*Corpus des tablettes en cunéiformes alphabétiques découvertes à Ras Shamra-Ugarit de 1929 à 1939.* Edited by A. Herdner
E	Elohist source
ETR	*Etudes théologiques et religieuses*
EvTh	*Evangelische Theologie*
GK	*Gesenius' Hebrew Grammar.* Edited by E. Kautzsch. Translated by A. E. Cowley, 2d. ed. Oxford, 1910
HAT	Handbuch zum Alten Testament
IB	*Interpreter's Bible*
ICC	International Critical Commentary
JBL	*Journal of Biblical Literature*
JNES	*Journal of Near Eastern Studies*
JSOT	*Journal for the Study of the Old Testament*
JSOTSup	Journal for the Study of the Old Testament—Supplement Series
JTS	*Journal of Theological Studies*
KAT	Kommentar zum Alten Testament

L	Leningrad codex
LXX	Septuagint
MSS	manuscripts
MT	Masoretic Text
NEB	New English Bible
NICOT	New International Commentary on the Old Testament
NRSV	New Revised Standard Version
OTL	Old Testament Library
OTS	*Oudtestamentische Studiën*
P	Priestly source
PEQ	*Palestine Exploration Quarterly*
RB	*Revue biblique*
REB	Revised English Bible
RSR	*Recherches de science religieuse*
RSV	Revised Standard Version
SJOT	*Scandinavian Journal of the Old Testament*
SOTSMS	Society for Old Testament Studies Monograph Series
TDOT	*Theological Dictionary of the Old Testament* (ed. G. J. Botterweck and H. Ringgren)
THAT	*Theologisches Handwörterbuch zum Alten Testament.* Edited by E. Jenni, with assistance from C. Westermann. 2 vols., Stuttgart, 1971–1976
UUÅ	Uppsala universitetsårsskrift
VT	*Vetus Testamentum*
VTSup	Vetus Testamentum Supplements
WMANT	Wissenschaftliche Monographien zum Alten und Neuen Testament
ZAW	*Zeitschrift für die alttestamentliche Wissenschaft*

SELECT BIBLIOGRAPHY FOR JOEL

I. Commentaries

Allen, L. C. *The Books of Joel, Obadiah, Jonah and Micah.* NICOT 13/2. Grand Rapids 1976.

Bewer, J. A. *A Commentary on Obadiah and Joel.* ICC, pp. 49–146 of J. M. P. Smith, W. H. Ward, and J. A. Bewer, *A Critical and Exegetical Commentary on Micah, Zephaniah, Nahum, Habakkuk, Obadiah, and Joel.* Edinburgh 1911.

Bič, M. *Das Buch Joel.* Berlin 1960.

Credner, K. A. *Der Prophet Joel übersetzt und erklärt.* Halle 1831.

Crenshaw, J. L. *Joel: A New Translation with Introduction and Commentary.* Anchor Bible. New York 1995.

Keller, C. A. *Joël.* Pp. 99–155 in E. Jacob, C. A. Keller, and S. Amsler, *Osée, Joël, Amos, Abdias, Jonas.* CAT XIa. Geneva 1965. 2d ed. Geneva 1982.

Mason, R. A. *Zephaniah, Habakkuk, Joel.* Old Testament Guides. Sheffield 1994.

Merx, A. *Die Prophetie des Joel und ihre Ausleger von den ältesten Zeiten bis zu den Reformatoren.* Halle 1879.

Ogden, G. S., and R. R. Deutsch. *A Promise of Hope: A Call to Obedience (Joel and Malachi).* Grand Rapids 1987.

Robinson, T. H., and F. Horst. *Die zwölf kleinen Propheten.* HAT 14. 3d ed. Tübingen 1964.

Rudolph, W. *Joel-Amos-Obadja-Jona.* KAT 13:2. Gütersloh 1971.

Schmalohr, J. *Das Buch des Propheten Joel, übersetzt und erklärt.* ATA 7:4. Münster 1922.

Sellin, E. *Das Zwölfprophetenbuch.* KAT 12:1. 3d ed. Leipzig 1930.

Watts, J. D. W. *The Books of Joel, Obadiah, Jonah, Nahum, Habakkuk, and Zephaniah.* CBC. Cambridge 1975.

Weiser, A. *Das Buch der zwölf kleinen Propheten.* ATD 24:1. 3d ed. Göttingen 1959.

Wellhausen, J. *Die kleinen Propheten übersetzt und erklärt.* Skizzen und Vorarbeiten 5. 3d ed. Berlin 1898. Reprint, 1963.

Wolff, H. W. *Joel and Amos.* Hermeneia. Philadelphia 1977. Translation of *Dodekapropheton 2 Joel and Amos.* Neukirchen-Vluyn 1969. 2d ed., 1975.

II. Monographs and Other Studies

Abegg, M., P. Flint, and E. Ulrich. *The Dead Sea Scrolls Bible: The Oldest Known Bible Translated for the First Time into English.* San Francisco 1999.

Ahlström, G. *Joel and the Temple Cult of Jerusalem.* VTS 21. Leiden 1971.

Barker, M. *The Gate of Heaven: The History and Symbolism of the Temple in Jerusalem.* London 1991.

──────. *The Older Testament: The Survival of Themes from the Ancient Royal Cult in Sectarian Judaism and Early Christianity.* London 1987.

Barton, J. *Oracles of God: Perceptions of Ancient Prophecy in Israel after the Exile.* London 1986. New York 1988.

Bergler, S. *Joel als Schriftprophet.* BEATAJ 16. Frankfurt am Main 1988.

Blenkinsopp, J. A. *A History of Prophecy in Israel from the Settlement in the Land to the Hellenistic Period.* London 1984.

Buber, M., and F. Rosenzweig. *Bücher der Kundung.* Cologne 1958.

Clements, R. E. *Isaiah and the Deliverance of Jerusalem: A Study in the Interpretation of Prophecy in the Old Testament.* JSOTSup 13. Sheffield 1980.

Clifford, R. J. *The Cosmic Mountain in Canaan and the Old Testament.* Harvard Semitic Monographs 4. Cambridge, Mass. 1972.

Driver, S. R. *Einleitung in die Literatur des Alten Testaments.* Translated and annotated by J. W. Rothstein. Berlin 1896.

Eissfeldt, O. *The Old Testament: An Introduction.* New York 1965. Translated from *Einleitung in das Alte Testament unter Einschluß der Apokryphen und Pseudepigraphen sowie der apokryphen- und pseudepigraphenartigen Qumran-Schriften.* Neue Theologische Grundrisse. 3d ed. Tübingen 1964.

Fuller, R. E. "The Minor Prophets Manuscript from Qumran, Cave IV." Ph.D. dissertation, Harvard University, 1988.

Goldfajn, T. *Word Order and Time in Biblical Hebrew Narrative.* Oxford 1998.

Grabbe, L. L. *Judaism from Cyrus to Hadrian.* London 1994.

Hanson, P. D. *The Dawn of Apocalyptic: The Historical and Sociological Roots of Apocalyptic Eschatology.* Philadelphia 1975.

House, P. R. *The Unity of the Twelve.* JSOTSup 97. Sheffield 1990.

Hvidberg, F. F. *Weeping and Laughter in the Old Testament.* Leiden 1962.

Jacobsen, T. *The Harps That Once....* London and New Haven 1987.

Johnson, A. R. *The Cultic Prophet in Ancient Israel.* Cardiff 1944.

──────. *The Cultic Prophet and Israel's Psalmody.* Cardiff 1979.

Kaiser, O. *Isaiah 13—39.* OTL. London 1974. Translation from *Der Prophet Jesaja/Kap. 13–39.* ATD 18. Göttingen 1973.

Kapelrud, A. S. *Joel Studies.* UUÅ 1948:4. Uppsala 1948.

Koch, K. *Die Profeten.* Stuttgart 1978. 3d ed., 1995. English translation: *The Prophets.* 2 vols. London 1982–83.

Loretz, O. *Regenritual und Jahwetag im Joelbuch: Kanaanäischer Hintergrund; Kolometrie, Aufbau und Symbolik eines Prophetenbuches.* Ugaritisch-biblische Literatur 4. Altenberge 1986.

Mowinckel, S. *He That Cometh.* Oxford 1959. English translation of *Han som kommer.* Copenhagen 1951.

———. *The Psalms in Israel's Worship.* Oxford 1962. English translation of *Offersang og Sangoffer.* Oslo 1951.

Nogalski, J. *Literary Precursors to the Book of the Twelve.* BZAW 217. Berlin 1993.

———. *Redactional Processes in the Book of the Twelve.* BZAW 218. Berlin 1993.

Plöger, O. *Theocracy and Eschatology.* Richmond, Va. 1968. Translation of *Theokratie und Eschatologie.* WMANT 2. Neukirchen-Vluyn 1959.

Prinsloo, W. S. *The Theology of the Book of Joel.* BZAW 163. Berlin 1985.

Simkins, R. *Yahweh's Activity in History and Nature in the Book of Joel.* Ancient Near Eastern Texts and Studies 10. Lewiston, Queenston, and Lampeter 1991.

Tov, E. *Textual Criticism of the Hebrew Bible.* Minneapolis 1992.

Vatke, W. *Die biblische Theologie wissenschaftlich dargestellt: I. Die Religion des Alten Testaments.* Berlin 1835.

Vernes, M. *Le Peuple d'Israël et ses espérances relatives à son avenir depuis les origines jusqu'à l'époque persane (Ve siècle avant J. C.).* Paris 1972.

von Rad, G. *Holy War in Ancient Israel.* Grand Rapids 1991. English translation of *Der heilige Krieg im alten Israel.* 3d ed. Göttingen 1958.

III. Articles

Albertz, R., and C. Westermann. "*rûah* Geist." *THAT* 11 (1979): 726–53.

Andiñach, P. R. "The Locusts in the Message of Joel." *VT* 42 (1992): 433–41.

Baumgärtel, F. "Die Formel *ne'um jahwe*." *ZAW* 73 (1961): 277–90.

Baumgartner, W. "Joel 1 and 2." In *Karl Budde zum 70. Geburtag.* Edited by K. Marti. BZAW 34. Berlin 1920, pp. 10–19.

Bergman, J., H. Ringgren, and M. Tzevat. "*betûlâ, betûlîm.*" *TDOT* 2 (1975): 338–43.

Bourke, J. "Le Jour de Yahvé dans Joël." *RB* 66 (1959): 5–31 and 191–212.

Brongers, H. A. "Bemerkungen zum Gebrauch des adverbialen *we'attah* im Alten Testament." *VT* 16 (1965): 289–99.

———. "Fasting in Israel in Biblical and Post-Biblical Times." In *Instruction and Interpretation.* Edited by A. S. van der Woude. OTS 20. Leiden 1977, pp. 1–21.

Carroll, R. P. "Eschatological Delay in the Prophetic Tradition?" *ZAW* 94 (1982): 47–58.

_____. "Joel." In *A Dictionary of Biblical Interpretation*. Edited by R. J. Coggins and J. L. Houlden. London 1990, pp. 357–58.
Cathcart, K. "Day of Yahweh." *ABD* 2 (1992): 84–85.
Childs, B. S. "The Enemy from the North." *JBL* 68 (1959): 187–98.
Clements, R. E. "Patterns in the Prophetic Canon." In *Canon and Authority: Essays in Old Testament Religion and Theology.* Philadelphia 1977, pp. 42–55. Also in Clements, R. E. *Old Testament Prophecy: From Oracles to Canon.* Louisville 1996, pp. 191–202.
Clines, D. J. A. "Was There an *'bl* II 'be dry' in Classical Hebrew?" *VT* 42 (1992): 1–10.
Coggins, R. J. "An Alternative Prophetic Tradition?" In *Israel's Prophetic Tradition: Essays in Honour of Peter Ackroyd.* Edited by R. J. Coggins, M. A. Knibb, and A. Phillips. Cambridge 1982, pp. 77–94.
_____. "Interbiblical Quotations in Joel." In *After the Exile: Essays in Honour of Rex Mason.* Edited by J. Barton and D. J. Reimer. Macon, Ga. 1996, pp. 75–84.
_____. "The Minor Prophets—One Book or Twelve?" In *Crossing the Boundaries: Essays in Biblical Interpretation in Honour of Michael D. Goulder.* Edited by S. E. Porter, P. Joyce, and C. E. Orton. Leiden 1994, pp. 57–68.
Crenshaw, J. L. "The Expression *mî yôdea'* in the Hebrew Bible." *VT* 36 (1986): 274–88.
_____. "Who Knows What Yahweh Will Do? The Character of God in the Book of Joel." In *Fortunate the Eyes That See: Essays in Honor of David Noel Freedman in Celebration of His Seventieth Birthday.* Edited by A. B. Beek, A. H. Bartelt, and C. A. Franke. Grand Rapids 1995, pp. 185–96.
Deist, F. E. "Parallels and Reinterpretation in the Book of Joel: A Theology of the Yom Yahweh?" In *Text and Context: Old Testament and Semitic Studies for F. C. Fensham.* JSOTSup 48. Sheffield 1988, pp. 63–79.
Dennefeld, L. "Les problèmes du livre de Joël." *RSR* 4 (1924): 555–75; 5 (1925): 35–37, 591–608; 6 (1926): 26–49.
Dentan, R. C. "The Literary Affinities of Exodus XXXIV 6f." *VT* 13 (1963): 34–51.
Dozeman, T. B. "Inner-Biblical Interpretation of Yahweh's Gracious and Compassionate Character." *JBL* 108 (1989): 207–23.
Driver, G. R. "Linguistic and Textual Problems. Minor Prophets. III. Joel." *JTS* 39 (1938): 400–402.
_____. "Studies in the Vocabulary of the Old Testament VI." *JTS* 34 (1933): 378.
Duhm, B. "Anmerkungen zu den Zwölf Propheten." *ZAW* 31 (1911): 161–204.
Duval, Y.-M. "Jérôme et les prophètes: Histoire, prophétie, actualité et actuali-

Select Bibliography for Joel xvii

sation dans les commentaires de Nahum, Michée, Abdias et Joël." *Salamanca Conference Volume*. Edited by J. A. Emerton. VTSup 36. Leiden 1985, pp. 108–31.

Elliger, K. "Ein Zeugnis aus der jüdischen Gemeinde im Alexanderjahr 322 v. Chr." *ZAW* 62 (1950): 63–115.

Ellul, D. "Introduction au livre de Joël." *ETR* 54 (1979): 426–37.

Eslinger, L. "Inner-Biblical Exegesis and Inner-Biblical Allusion: The Question of Category." *VT* 42 (1992): 47–58.

Everson, J. "The Days of Yahweh." *JBL* 93 (1974): 329–37.

Firmage, E. "Zoology." *ABD* 6 (1992): 1109–67.

Fox, M. V. "The Identification of Quotations in Biblical Literature." *ZAW* 92 (1980): 416–31.

Frankfort, T. "Le כי de Joël I 12," *VT* 10 (1960): 445–49.

Hillers, D. R. "A Convention in Hebrew Literature: The Reaction to Bad News." *ZAW* 77 (1965): 86–90.

Horst, F. "Zwei Begriffe für Eigentum (Besitz): *nahalâ* und *ahuzzâ*." In *Verbannung und Heimkehr: Beiträge zur Geschichte und Theologie Israels im 6. und 5. Jahrhundert vor Chr. (Festschrift für Wilhelm Rudolph)*. Edited by A. Kuschke. Tübingen 1961, pp. 135–56.

Hulst, A. R. "*Kol basar* in der priesterlichen Fluterzählung." In *Studies on the Book of Genesis*. OTS 12. Leiden 1958, pp. 28–66.

Hurowitz, V. A. "Joel's Locust Plague in Light of Sargon II's Hymn to Nanaya." *JBL* 112 (1993): 597–603.

Jeppesen, K. "The Day of Yahweh in Mowinckel's Conception Reviewed." *SJOT* 2 (1988): 42–55.

Jepsen, A. "Kleine Beiträge zum Zwölfprophetenbuch." *ZAW* 56 (1938): 86–96.

Kedar-Kopfstein, B. "The Hebrew Text of Joel as Reflected in the Vulgate." *Textus* 9 (1981): 16–35.

Kutsch, E. "Die Wurzel 'sr im Hebraischen," *VT* 2 (1952): 57–69.

Lambert, W. G. "Destiny and Divine Intervention in Babylon and Israel." *The Witness of Tradition*. Edited by A. S. van der Woude. OTS 17. Leiden 1972, pp. 65–72.

Leeuwen, R. C. van. "Scribal Wisdom and Theodicy in the Book of the Twelve." In *In Search of Wisdom*. Edited by L. G. Perdue, B. B. Scott, and W. J. Wiseman. Philadelphia 1993, pp. 31–49.

Mallon, E. D. "A Stylistic Analysis of Joel 1:10–12." *CBQ* 45 (1983): 537–48.

Marcus, D. "Non-recurring Doublets in the Book of Joel." *CBQ* 56 (1994): 56–67.

Müller, H.-P. "Prophetie und Apokalyptik bei Joel." *Theologia Viatorum* 10 (1966): 231–52.

Myers, J. M. "Some Considerations Bearing on the Date of Joel." *ZAW* 74 (1952): 177–95.

Ogden, G. S. "Joel 4 and Prophetic Responses to National Laments." *JSOT* 26 (1983): 97–106.
Raitt, T. M. "The Prophetic Summons to Repentance." *ZAW* 83 (1971): 30–49.
Redditt, P. L. "The Book of Joel and Peripheral Prophecy." *CBQ* 48 (1986): 225–40.
Reimer, D. J. "The 'Foe' and the 'North' in Jeremiah." *ZAW* 101 (1989): 223–32.
Roth, C. "The Teacher of Righteousness and the Prophecy of Joel." *VT* 13 (1963): 91–95.
Schmidt, W. H. "*safôn* Norden." *THAT* 2 (1976): 575–82.
Simkins, R. "God, History and the Natural World in the Book of Joel." *CBQ* 55 (1993): 435–52.
Soggin, J. A. "*sûb* zurückkehren." *THAT* 2 (1976): 886–88.
Stephenson, F. R. "The Date of the Book of Joel." *VT* 19 (1969): 224–29.
Thompson, J. A. "Joel's Locusts in the Light of Near Eastern Parallels." *JNES* 14 (1955): 52–55.
———. "The Use of Repetition in the Prophecy of Joel." In *On Language, Culture, and Religion: In Honor of Eugene A. Nida*. Edited by M. Black and W. A. Smalley. The Hague and Paris 1974, pp. 101–10.
Treves, M. "The Date of Joel." *VT* 7 (1953): 149–56.
Wanke, G. "*nahalâ* Besitzanteil." *THAT* 2 (1979): 55–59.
———. "Prophecy and Psalms in the Persian Period." In *The Cambridge History of Judaism*. Edited by W. D. Davies and L. Finkelstein. Cambridge 1984, vol. 1, pp. 174–77.
Wenham, G. J. "*Betûlah*. 'A Girl of Marriageable Age.'" *VT* 22 (1972): 326–48.

SELECT BIBLIOGRAPHY FOR OBADIAH

1. Commentaries

Allen, L. C. *The Books of Joel, Obadiah, Jonah, and Micah.* NICOT 5. London and Grand Rapids 1976.

Ben Zvi, E. *A Historical-Critical Study of the Book of Obadiah.* BZAW 242. Berlin 1996.

Coggins, R. J., and S. Paul. *Israel among the Nations (Nahum, Obadiah, Esther).* International Theological Commentary. Grand Rapids and Edinburgh 1985.

Mason, R. *Micah, Nahum, Obadiah.* Old Testament Guides. Sheffield 1991.

McComiskey, T., ed. *The Minor Prophets: An Exegetical and Expository Commentary.* Vol. 2: *Obadiah, Jonah, Micah, Nahum, and Habakkuk.* Grand Rapids 1993.

Raabe, P. R. *Obadiah: A New Translation with Introduction and Commentary.* AB 24D. New York 1996.

Thompson, J. A. "The Book of Obadiah." In *IB* 6. New York 1956, pp. 855–67.

Wellhausen, J. *Die Kleinen Propheten übersetzt und erklärt.* 4th ed. Berlin 1963. 3d ed., 1898.

Wolff, H. W. *Obadiah and Jonah: A Commentary.* Minneapolis 1986. English translation of *Obadja und Jona.* Neukirchen-Vluyn 1977.

2. Monographs and Special Studies

Barton, J. *Amos' Oracles against the Nations.* SOTSM 6. Cambridge 1980.

_____. *Isaiah 1—39.* Old Testament Guides. Sheffield 1995.

Carroll, R. P. *Jeremiah: A Commentary.* OTL. London 1986.

Glueck, N. *The Other Side of the Jordan.* New Haven 1940.

Wehrle, J. *Prophetie und Textanalyse: Die Komposition Obadja 1–21 interpretiert auf der Basis textlinguistischer und semiotischer Konzeptionen.* ATAT 28. St. Ottilien 1987.

3. Articles

Ackroyd, P. R. "Obadiah." *ABD* 5 (1992): 2–4.
Barr, J. "Is Hebrew קן 'nest' a Metaphor?" In *Semitic Studies in Honor of Wolf Leslau*. Edited by A. S. Kaye. Wiesbaden 1991, vol. 1, pp. 150–61.
Bartlett, J. R. "The Brotherhood of Edom." *JSOT* 4 (1977): 2–27.
———. "Edom and the Fall of Jerusalem." *PEQ* 114 (1982): 13–24.
Barton, J. "Ethics in the Book of Isaiah." In *Writing and Reading the Scroll of Isaiah: Studies of an Interpretive Tradition*. Edited by C. C. Broyles and C. A. Evans. VTSup 70. 2 vols. Leiden 1997, vol. 1, pp. 67–77.
———. "Ethics in Isaiah of Jerusalem." *JTS* 32 (1981): 1–18.
———. "Natural Law and Poetic Justice in the Old Testament." *JTS* 30 (1979): 1–14.
Beit-Arieh, I. "New Data on the Relationship between Judah and Edom toward the End of the Iron Age." In *Recent Excavations in Israel: Studies in Iron Age Archaeology*. Edited by S. Gitin and W. G. Dever. AASOR 49. Winona Lake 1989, pp. 125–31.
Ben Zvi, E. "Twelve Prophetic Books or 'the Twelve': A Few Preliminary Considerations." In *Forming Prophetic Literature: Essays in Isaiah and the Twelve in Honour of John D. W. Watts*. Edited by J. D. W. Watts and P. R. House. JSOTSup 235. Sheffield 1996.
Bič, M. "Zur Problematik des Buches Obadja." *Congress Volume Copenhagen 1953*. VTSup 1 (1953): 11–25.
Carroll, R. P. "Obadiah." In *A Dictionary of Biblical Interpretation*. Edited by R. J. Coggins and J. L. Houlden. London 1990, pp. 496–97.
Coggins, R. J. "An Alternative Prophetic Tradition?" In *Israel's Prophetic Tradition: Essays in Honour of Peter Ackroyd*. Edited by R. J. Coggins, M. A. Knibb, and A. Phillips. Cambridge 1982, pp. 77–94.
———. "The Minor Prophets—One Book or Twelve?" In *Crossing the Boundaries: Essays in Biblical Interpretation in Honour of Michael D. Goulder*. Edited by S. E. Porter, P. Joyce, and C. E. Orton. Leiden 1994, pp. 57–68.
Cresson, B. C. "The Condemnation of Edom in Post-Exilic Judaism." In *The Use of the Old Testament in the New and Other Essays (Studies in Honor of William Franklin Stinespring)*. Edited by J. M. Efird. Durham, N.C. 1972, pp. 125–48.
Davies, G. I. "A New Solution to a Crux in Obadiah 7." *VT* 27 (1977): 484–87.
de Vaux, R. "Téman, ville ou région d'Edom?" *RB* 76 (1969): 379–85.
Dick, M. B. "A Syntactic Study of the Book of Obadiah." *Semitics* 9 (1984): 1–29.
Dupont-Sommer, A. "Une inscription araméenne inédite d'époque perse trouvée à Daskyléion." *Comptes rendus de l'Académie des Inscriptions et Belles-Lettres* (1966): 44–57.

Select Bibliography for Obadiah

Fohrer, G. "Die Sprüche Obadjas." In *Studia biblica et semitica T. C. Vriezen dedicata*. Wageningen 1966, pp. 81–93.

Glazier-McDonald, B. "Edom in the Prophetical Corpus." In *You Shall not Abhor an Edomite for He Is Your Brother: Edom and Seir in History and Tradition*. Edited by D. V. Edelman. Archaeology and Biblical Studies 3. Atlanta 1995, pp. 23–32.

Gray, J. "The Diaspora of Israel and Judah in Obad. 20." *ZAW* 65 (1953): 53–59.

House, P. R. *The Unity of the Twelve*. JSOTSup 97. Sheffield 1990.

Huffmon, H. B. "Lex Talionis," *ABD* 4 (1992): 321–22.

Kornfeld, W. "Die jüdische Diaspora in Ab., 20." In *Mélanges bibliques rédigés en l'honneur de André Robert*. Paris 1957, pp. 180–86.

Lipiński, E. "Obadiah 20." *VT* 23 (1973): 368–70.

McCarter, P. Kyle. "Obadiah 7 and the Fall of Edom." *BASOR* 221 (1976): 87–91.

Myers, J. M. "Edom and Judah in the Sixth–Fifth Centuries B.C." In *Near Eastern Studies in Honor of W. F. Albright*. Edited by H. Goedicke. Maryland 1971, pp. 377–92.

Neiman, D. "Sefarad: The Name of Spain." *JNES* 22 (1963): 128–32.

Nogalski, J. *Literary Precursors to the Book of the Twelve*. BZAW 217. Berlin 1993.

_____. *Redactional Processes in the Book of the Twelve*. BZAW 218. Berlin 1993.

Ogden, G. S. "Prophetic Oracles against Foreign Nations and Psalms of Communal Lament: The Relationship of Psalm 137 to Jeremiah 49:7–22 and Obadiah." *JSOT* 24 (1982): 89–97.

Otto, E. "Die Geschichte der Talion im Alten Orient und in Israel." In *Ernten, was man sät: Festschrift für Klaus Koch zu seinem 65. Geburtstag*. Edited by D. R. Daniels, U. Glessmer, and M. Rösel. Neukichen-Vluyn 1991, pp. 101–30.

Robinson, R. B. "Levels of Nationalization in Obadiah." *JSOT* 40 (1988): 83–97.

Rudolph, W. "Obadja." *ZAW* 8 (= 49) (1931): 222–31.

Snyman, S. D. "Cohesion in the Book of Obadiah." *ZAW* 101 (1989): 59–71.

Wolff, H. W. "Obadja—Ein Kultprophet als Interpret." *EvTh* 37 (1977): 273–84.

THE BOOK OF JOEL

INTRODUCTION

"Our Joel is the problem-child of Old Testament exegesis," wrote Adalbert Merx in his important monograph on the book and the history of its interpretation.[1] And indeed, it has proved difficult for commentators to arrive at any consensus on this short and vivid book. It has been dated anywhere between the ninth and second centuries B.C.E. It has been regarded as a tightly composed unity but also as an almost random collection of disparate oracles. Joel has been thought of as a prophet like the preexilic prophets, with a message of imminent divine intervention, but also as a purely literary compilation of stock eschatological themes with no message of immediate relevance to anyone. In Christianity the promise that God will "pour out [God's] spirit on all flesh" (Joel 2:28) has been seen as fulfilled on the day of Pentecost (Acts 2:1–21), but the rest of the book has scarcely had a distinctive profile among the Minor Prophets. And then there are the locusts: are they real or symbolic, bringers of a literal famine or harbingers of the last days, or all these things at once? It has proved difficult to get any real purchase on the message of this enigmatic prophet. Indeed, commentators cannot even agree on the unity of the book of Joel, with powerful voices defending an essentially single work and others thinking in terms of two separate collections, 1:1–2:27 and 2:28–3:21, possibly deriving from quite different periods.

The reason for such confusions is clear enough: there is simply too little evidence for most of these issues to be resolved definitively. Joel is a complex book, about which we do not possess enough information to come to firm conclusions. This may sound like a counsel of despair, but it is better to be clear at the outset that the best we can hope for are reasonable and defensible hypotheses, not any kind of certainty. That being said, this commentary like all others will defend one possible reading of the book, rather than remaining in a state of suspended judgment. But the reader needs to realize at the beginning that such a reading represents only a best guess and depends throughout on various prior beliefs about the likely development of Hebrew prophecy and the growth of the Old Testament corpus of literature.

1. Merx, *Die Prophetie des Joel*, pp. iii–iv.

My main discussion partners in the body of the commentary have been the most important commentaries of recent times, H. W. Wolff[2] and J. L. Crenshaw.[3]

1. The Canon and Text

In the "Book of the Twelve" in the Hebrew Bible, Joel takes the second place, after Hosea and immediately before Amos. This led early interpreters to think that Joel, like these other two, was a preexilic prophet, even though the book offers no overt indications of date. In the tradition represented by the Septuagint, however, Joel appears later, with Obadiah and Jonah, after Hosea, Amos, and Micah. Here, too, it is unclear whether any chronological judgment is implied, though the compilers of the Greek Bible do seem to have been more interested in chronology than those of the Hebrew, and perhaps their arrangement of Hosea, Amos, and Micah together reflects the awareness that these three were preexilic but that Joel was not.

The truth is that we do not know what considerations weighed in arranging the books in order, nor do we know for certain how they were arranged in the period before manuscripts of either the Hebrew or the Greek Bible are extant. In recent years it has been suggested that there may be some rhetorical intention in arranging the books in the Hebrew canon.[4] Certainly, there may be deliberate intention in placing Joel next to Amos, with which it shares the phrase "YHWH roars from Zion, and utters his voice from Jerusalem" (Joel 3:16a = Amos 1:2a). This may have caused editors to place Joel immediately before Amos. Amos and Joel end with similar oracles, and both contain the phrase "the mountains shall drip sweet wine" (Joel 3:18 = Amos 9:13). Either or both of the oracles in question may be secondary additions to either or both books, however, so they do not offer a secure basis for explaining the way in which the books are now arranged.

There are no complete manuscripts of Joel older than the Cairo codex of the prophets (C: ninth century C.E.), the Aleppo Codex (A or א: tenth century), and the Leningrad Codex (L: eleventh century), from the last of which modern

---

2. H. W. Wolff, *Joel and Amos* (Hermeneia), Philadelphia 1977, translation of *Dodekapropheton 2 Joel und Amos,* Neukirchen-Vluyn 1969, 2d ed. 1975.

3. J. L. Crenshaw, *Joel: A New Translation with Introduction and Commentary* (Anchor Bible), New York 1995.

4. Cf. J. Nogalski, *Literary Precursors to the Book of the Twelve* (BZAW 217), Berlin 1993; idem, *Redactional Processes in the Book of the Twelve* (BZAW 218), Berlin 1993; P. R. House, *The Unity of the Twelve* (JSOTSup 97), Sheffield 1990; R. J. Coggins, "The Minor Prophets—One Book or Twelve?" in *Crossing the Boundaries: Essays in Biblical Interpretation in Honour of Michael D. Goulder,* ed. S. E. Porter, P. Joyce, and D. E. Orton, Leiden 1994, pp. 57–68; R. C. van Leeuwen, "Scribal Wisdom and Theodicy in the Book of the Twelve," in *In Search of Wisdom,* ed. L. G. Perdue, B. B. Scott, and W. J. Wiseman, Philadelphia 1993, pp. 31–49.

Introduction 5

printed Bibles such as *BHS* derive (though the Hebrew University Bible project takes A as its basis). But fragments have been found among the Dead Sea Scrolls (4Q78; 4Q82; and Mur88, the *Minor Prophets Scroll* from Wadi Muraba'at). Joel is not found in the Greek *Minor Prophets Scroll* from Nahal Hever (8HevXIIgr).[5]

The text of Joel is generally coherent and seems well preserved, though there are several *hapax legomena* and a number of textual cruces, which do not greatly affect the sense of the whole work. The LXX sometimes helps in resolving difficulties but seems in general to be translated from a text close to the MT as we have received it.

There is a particular problem about the division of Joel into chapters. Chapter divisions go back only to Stephen Langton's work on the Vulgate in about 1205 C.E., and these correspond to the division found in English Bibles, where there are three chapters: 1:1–20, 2:1–32, and 3:1–21. During the fourteenth century this division was also introduced into the Septuagint and into the Hebrew text, where it appears in the first (printed) Rabbinic Bible of 1516–17. The second Rabbinic Bible (1524–25), however, redivided the work into four chapters, as follows:

Vulgate, LXX, 1st Rabbinic Bible	*2d Rabbinic Bible*
1:1–20	1:1–20
2:1–32	2:1–27
	3:1–5
3:1–21	4:1–21

The effect of this rearrangement is simply to create a fresh chapter out of 2:28–32. This corresponds to the intuition of many commentators that the book of Joel divides into two parts at 2:28 (3:1), and for many purposes the four-chapter model is thus more satisfactory. It has become the normal division for modern printed Hebrew Bibles. Since this commentary assumes that readers will tend to refer to English translations, however, references will be to the three-chapter division throughout.

2. The Unity and Structure of the Text

1. The book of Joel appears to describe the effects of a plague of locusts (1:1–12) combined with a drought (1:10, 12). This is followed by a call to a

---

5. See E. Tov, *Textual Criticism of the Hebrew Bible,* Minneapolis 1992, on the ancient manuscripts in general; also R. E. Fuller, "The Minor Prophets Manuscript from Qumran, Cave IV" Ph.D. diss., Harvard University, 1988; M. Abegg, P. Flint, and E. Ulrich, *The Dead Sea Scrolls Bible: The Oldest Known Bible Translated for the First Time into English,* San Francisco 1999.

ceremony of lamentation (1:13–14) and its execution (1:15–20). Then comes a further description of devastation, again possibly caused by locusts but this time described as "the day of YHWH" (2:1–11). The response is again a liturgy of lamentation (2:12–17). There follows what is apparently a description of YHWH's response to the people's laments (2:18–27), in which YHWH promises to remove "the northerner" (2:20) and to restore the nation's prosperity after the depredations of the locusts. After this there follow a number of prophecies of the endtime, beginning with the pouring out of God's spirit on "all flesh" (2:28) and continuing with heavenly portents (2:30–31), the restoration of a remnant of the people (2:32), judgment on foreign nations (3:1–14), again accompanied by heavenly signs (3:15). YHWH then promises that his presence will be with his people to save them from attack by foreign armies (3:16–18). Judah will enjoy miraculous fruitfulness (3:18), while Egypt and Edom are punished for their violence (3:19–21).

2. But commentators have long been uncertain about the overall coherence of the book. M. Vernes initiated this discussion in 1872, arguing that Joel consists of two distinct collections of prophecies, 1:1–2:27 and 2:28–3:21—in other words, 1–2 and 3–4 in the conventional Hebrew division into four chapters.[6] B. Duhm, in his influential article of 1911, argued that whereas the first part of the book (which for him ended at 2:17) derived from an early postexilic prophet, the second was an addition ("eine Ergänzerarbeit") from as late as the Maccabean period.[7] The same hand added the references to the day of YHWH in the first half (i.e., 1:15a; 2:1c; and 2:11c).

Essentially the same position can be found in the writings of J. A. Bewer, T. H. Robinson, O. Eissfeldt, and O. Plöger.[8] It is still defended by J. A. Blenkinsopp.[9] In Plöger's work, it is linked to his theory that postexilic Judaism was marked by a division between a "theocratic" and an "eschatological" party. The theocrats, who are represented in the Old Testament by the work of the Chronicler and the P strand in the Pentateuch, believed that the present order of things in the small province of Judah—rule by a priestly elite—was intended by God

---

6. M. Vernes, *Le Peuple d'Israël et ses espérances relatives à son avenir depuis les origines jusqu'à l'époque persane (Ve siècle avant J. C.)*, Paris 1972. This position was endorsed by J. W. Rothstein in his German edition of Driver's *Introduction to the Literature of the Old Testament*: see S. R. Driver, *Einleitung in die Literatur des Alten Testaments*, trans. and annotated by J. W. Rothstein, Berlin 1896, pp. 333–34.

7. B. Duhm, "Anmerkungen zu den Zwölf Prophcten," ZAW 31 (1911): 161–204.

8. J. A. Bewer, *A Commentary on Obadiah and Joel* (ICC), Edinburgh 1911 = pp. 49–146 of J. M. P. Smith, W. H. Ward, and J. A. Bewer, *A Critical and Exegetical Commentary on Micah, Zephaniah, Nahum, Habakkuk, Obadiah, and Joel*; T. H. Robinson and F. Horst, *Die zwölf kleinen Propheten* (HAT 14), 3d ed., Tübingen 1964; O. Eissfeldt, *The Old Testament: An Introduction*, New York 1965; O. Plöger, *Theocracy and Eschatology*, Richmond, Va. 1968.

9. J. A. Blenkinsopp, *A History of Prophecy in Israel from the Settlement in the Land to the Hellenistic Period*, London 1984.

to be permanent; they did not look for any intervention by God that might change the status quo (from which they themselves greatly profited).

Against them, it is said, were ranged a number of more sectarian groups, who in due time developed into the apocalyptists, authors of such books as Daniel. These people hoped for a radical change to the present order, when YHWH would intervene in power to overthrow the ruling class and replace them with his own rule over Israel, and indeed, over all the world.[10] According to Plöger, one action of these eschatological groups was the editing of the book of Joel, in which they took an older (maybe even preexilic) text and supplemented it, realigning it with their own program of radical change by adding 3:1–21, which speaks of a great transformation of the world order. Later still, 2:28–32 was added to emphasize that the beneficiaries of the new order would not be everyone, even in Israel, but only those who "call on the name of YHWH" (2:32)— a special "remnant." Plöger's theory has not commanded universal support, and it seems to stand or fall with the general theory of theocracy versus eschatology. But it does bring out the difference in tone between the two halves of Joel, however this is to be explained. We shall build on this perception to develop a theory according to which the two halves come from different situations in postexilic Judaism, and we even propose the term *Deutero-Joel* for the second half.

3. In contrast, there have been significant defenders of the book's unity. The backlash against a division of the text began with the work of L. Dennefeld in 1924,[11] and his defense of the unity of Joel has led to what is probably now the majority view.[12] Even defenders of the book's essential unity are ready, in most cases, to see evidence of secondary additions and redactional interpolations, but it can be said that Joel is now most commonly seen as essentially the work of one author, not a compilation from diverse materials.

4. In fact, the arguments supporting a division within the book are more complicated than the simple contrast between 1:1–2:27 and 2:28–3:21. This basic

---

10. This theory was developed further by P. D. Hanson, *The Dawn of Apocalyptic: The Historical and Sociological Roots of Apocalyptic Eschatology*, Philadelphia 1975.

11. L. Dennefeld, "Les Problèmes du livre de Joël," *RSR* 4 (1924): 555–75; 5 (1925): 35–37, 591–608; 6 (1926): 26–49. In a scholarly discipline so dominated by German scholarship as Old Testament studies, it is interesting that both major theories about the origins of Joel go back to a work in French!

12. It is supported by such scholars as A. Jepsen, "Kleine Beiträge zum Zwölfprophetenbuch," *ZAW* 6 (1938): 86–96; A. S. Kapelrud, *Joel Studies* (UUÅ 1948:4), Uppsala 1948; A. Weiser, *Das Buch der zwölf kleinen Propheten* (ATD 24:1), 3d ed. Göttingen 1959; G. Ahlström, *Joel and the Temple Cult of Jerusalem* (SVT 21), Leiden 1971; C. A. Keller, *Joël*, pp. 95–155 of E. Jacob, C. A. Keller, and S. Amsler, *Osée, Joël, Amos, Abdias, Jonas* (CAT 11a), Geneva 1965, 2d ed., 1982; W. Rudolph, *Joel-Amos-Obadja-Jona* (KAT 13:2), Gütersloh 1971; L. C. Allen, *The Books of Joel, Obadiah, Jonah, and Micah* (NICOT 13/2), Grand Rapids 1976; and given the seal of approval in the most important modern commentary, that of Wolff.

division rests on the observation that a new section begins with the words "Then afterward" (*wĕhāyāh 'aḥărê kēn*), which many scholars regard as a typical mark of the addition of eschatological material to earlier prophetic oracles. Whereas what precedes this point of division is a relatively well-ordered complex of oracles in time of trouble, heavily modeled on liturgical prototypes by someone who was perhaps a "cult prophet," the material that follows is a more random set of prophecies looking forward to various salient events of the "last days," possibly in no particular order. This establishes a basic division within the book.

But even 1:1–2:27 shows possible signs of composite origins. For one thing, the material can be divided into two *parallel* prophecies in time of locust plague and/or drought: 1:2–20 and 2:1–17, each describing the parlous state of the country and then calling the hearers to a liturgical lamentation. It would clearly be possible to argue that only one of these represented the authentic words of Joel (though it is hard to decide which). Then 2:18–27 represents the divine response to either or both of the people's laments. Furthermore, it can be suggested that the second of the cycle of oracles, 2:1–17, represents a different perspective from the first. Whereas 1:2–20 describes a literal locust invasion, it may be said, 2:1–17 treats locusts as symbols of the coming eschatological adversaries of Judah on the day of YHWH, which is an event that far surpasses in gravity any purely physical locust plague and is rather to be compared with the great battle against Gog of Magog in Ezekiel 38–39 (thus Wolff).

5. Pressing a detailed analysis further still, one may think that 1:2–20 is already a composite. Duhm argued that there were three different afflictions referred to in this passage: an invasion of locusts in 1:4, 5, 8, 10, 12c, and 16b (also in 2:1–11); an invasion by a human army in 1:2, 3, 6, 7, 9, 11, and 12ab; and a drought in 1:13–20 (omitting 16c). All these were perfectly "this-worldly" disasters, which had occurred during the early postexilic period and had called forth the prophet's oracles bidding the people to lamentation and intercession. An editor, however, was responsible for weaving them together to produce a speciously unified text. The idea that all or any of these disasters were harbingers of the last days was not at all present in the mind of the prophet: such an interpretation was imposed on the oracles when they were joined with 2:28–3:21 to complete the book.[13] There was originally no difference in the understanding of the locust plague between 1:2–2:20 and 2:1–17; the eschatological overtones of the second chapter derive from its juxtaposition with 2:28–3:21, rather than being inherent in the description of the "day of YHWH" in 2:1–2.

---

13. A process which, as we saw, Duhm believed took place no earlier than the Maccabean period of the second century B.C.E.

Introduction 9

Vernes and Duhm argued (and their ideas have been taken up by Plöger) that the original prophet's message of imminent judgment had been transformed, in the process of editing, into an apocalyptic scheme through the addition of 1:15; 2:1b–2a; and 2:11b, the passages referring to the day of YHWH. These had not originally been part of Joel's proclamation of judgment and salvation. The possibility that at least 2:1b might be a gloss designed to redirect the emphasis of the original prophecy has been canvassed more recently by R. P. Carroll. Carroll suggests that at least the phrase "for the day of the LORD is coming, it is near" might be a gloss "from a later writer who wished to deny that the day of Yahweh had actually come in Joel's time, in order to protect the prophetic expectation from having been falsified by subsequent events. Or the intention of the gloss could have been to indicate that although the day of darkness and gloom had indeed come the salvation aspect of the day of Yahweh awaited another day."[14] As Carroll observes, that such an apparently central idea as the day of YHWH is a gloss in this book cannot be proved but is possible.

6. Some scholars have accepted that the book of Joel came into being in several stages but have not thought it necessary to postulate more than one author, preferring to see Joel himself as responsible for both the original oracles and their redaction. This is the position, for example, of H.-P. Müller. He thinks[15] that Joel originally called the people to repentance and lamentation much as other (especially cultic) prophets would have done, and that the core of 1:2–2:27 is accordingly oral in origin. Only 1:2–4 (an introduction to the already completed book) and 2:18 (recording YHWH's intervention) are of purely literary origin. Joel 2:28–3:21 is then a literary compilation of *disjecta membra* of prophetic eschatology, composed to present 1:2–2:27 as awaiting its true fulfillment not in the mundane realities of invasion by locusts or human armies but in the remote future of Jewish eschatological expectation. Prophecy to the whole community of postexilic Judah thus passes over into the concerns of a more sectlike group, treasuring up earlier oracles against their eventual fulfillment in God's good time. But it is entirely possible, especially if the prophet Joel lived a long time after the exile, that he himself was responsible for both processes. Such an understanding of Joel presents him as an example of what is sometimes called protoapocalyptic, anticipating the purely deterministic view of the coming end time that is found, say, in Daniel. Earlier divine "judgments" that have already broken in on the people in normal physical reality, bringing invasion or the destruction of crops through drought or insects, are

14. R. P. Carroll, "Eschatological Delay in the Prophetic Tradition," *ZAW* 94 (1982): 47–58.
15. H.-P. Müller, "Prophetie und Apokalyptik bei Joel," *Theologia Viatorum* 10 (1966): 231–52.

reinterpreted as representing the beginnings of God's final judgment in the end time.[16]

7. The current trend in the study of Joel is, however, to stress the unity of the book, not just in the sense that it had a single author, even if he reworked his own material, but in the stronger sense that the material in it coheres as a collection of elements contributing to a unified message. According to J. Bourke,[17] the book is an organic unity, all focused on the coming day of YHWH, of which the locust plague of chapters 1 and 2 is a microcosmic foretaste. Joel foresaw the end time as consisting of three stages: an immediate future in which a plague of locusts would ravish the land; an intermediate period of restoration that would provide a temporary lull in divine judgment; then the final day of YHWH in which the nations would be judged and Israel finally restored. On such a reading the book need not be seen as composite at all, and even the discrepancies that Duhm observed in chapter 1 among prophecies about locusts, armies, and drought do not matter very much: the eschatological scheme with which Joel was working may well have included all three.[18] Wolff has accepted a rather similar theory, arguing that 1:2–20 describes what may be called "local" manifestations of YHWH's judgment while 2:1–17 works out the same themes on a more universal scale. The reversal of Judah's fortunes in 2:18–27 then leads on to further and greater blessings in the remainder of the book. Like Müller, Wolff regards the book as a literary composition that rests on originally oral utterances, but he thinks in terms of a single author for the whole. He argues that there is a symmetrical structure to the whole book:

> When the book's entire message is taken into consideration, a decisive turning point... becomes apparent at the junction between 2:17 and 18. Here there is an abrupt transition, from the preceding cries of lament to the following oracles where divine response to the pleas is assured. *The portions of the book on either side of this midpoint form an almost perfect symmetry.* The lament over the current scarcity of provisions (1:4–20) is balanced by the promise that this calamity

---

16. The lengths to which a redactional theory about Joel can be taken may be seen in the theory of Danielle Ellul, summarized in P. L. Redditt, "The Book of Joel and Peripheral Prophecy," *CBQ* 48 (1986): 225–40, which postulates five stages in the growth of the book:

   1. 1:5–20 combined with 2:1–11 and 2:12–17
   2. 2:18–27 added to 1:5–2:17
   3. 1:1–4 added as an introduction
   4. 3:1–21 added, except for 3:4–8
   5. 2:28–32 added

In addition, the book has three separate redactional introductions: 1:1; 2:12; and 2:18–19a. Of such a theory it can be said that it is clearly possible, but it is hard to establish criteria by which to assess it. See D. Ellul, "Introduction au livre de Joël," *ETR* 54 (1979): 426–37.

17. J. Bourke, "Le Jour de Yahvé dans Joël," *RB* 66 (1959): 5–31 and 191–212.

18. Cf. the arguments of M. Treves, "The Date of Joel," *VT* 7 (1953): 149–56.

will be reversed (2:21–27). The announcement of the eschatological catastrophe imminent for Jerusalem (2:1–11) is balanced by the promise that Jerusalem's fortunes too will be reversed (4:1–3, 9–17 [3:1–3, 9–17]). The call to return to Yahweh as the necessity of the moment (2:12–17) is balanced by the pouring out of the spirit and the deliverance on Zion as the eschatological necessity (chap. 3 [2:28–32]).[19]

This may be tabulated thus:

1:4–20	2:21–27
2:1–11	3:1–3, 9–17
2:12–17	2:28–32

Joel 2:18–20 is here treated as a pivot around which the book turns (while 3:4–8 is seen as an insertion, a judgment with which most scholars agree). As is often the case with schemes of this sort, however, rather a lot seems to depend on how the sections are named: the notion of an "eschatological catastrophe" is conveniently vague, and it is not at all clear how or why the "pouring out of the spirit" answers the "call to return to YHWH" unless one stresses in each case the word *necessity,* which of course is Wolff's word, not Joel's. Furthermore, the "almost perfect symmetry" depends on actually *rearranging* the material so that 2:28–32 follows chapter 3![20]

8. One argument for disunity has sometimes been that there is a distinction between God's intervention through "nature," in such events as the locust plague, and his intervention in "history" through battles. Insofar as this distinction correlates with that between the two halves of the book, it could be thought to support the division. Or the unity of the book could be defended by insisting that, for example, the locust plague of chapters 1 and 2 is not intended literally but is purely a symbol of coming military encounters.[21] R. Simkins has argued strongly against this criterion, thereby supporting the general position represented by Wolff: "The natural catastrophe is not unrelated to the day of Yahweh, nor is it merely the harbinger of that day. Rather, the natural catastrophe is an integral aspect of Yahweh's activity on his day."[22] And again:

---

19. Wolff, *Joel and Amos,* p. 7 (my italics). A similar argument was mounted by Kapelrud in *Joel Studies,* while a literary case for the unity of the whole book has been proposed by D. Marcus, "Non-recurring Doublets in the Book of Joel," *CBQ* 56 (1994): 56–67, who points to a number of phrases that occur only in Joel but are distributed across the whole book, thus rendering the division between 1:2–2:27 and 2:28–3:21 insignificant from a stylistic point of view (see esp. pp. 66–67).

20. Ahlström, *Joel and the Temple Cult,* pp. 130–37, similarly thinks in terms of a reversal in the book's second half of what is prophesied in the first, again with 2:18 as the pivotal point, and for him even 3:4–8 is integral to the structure.

21. See the commentary on 1:2 below.

22. R. Simkins, "God, History, and the Natural World in the Book of Joel," *CBQ* 55 (1993): 435–52; the quotation is from p. 437.

In the book of Joel, then, the day of Yahweh is not a linear sequence of events on the plane of human history.... Joel has fused the human and natural dimensions, the historical and the cosmological dimensions, into one complex day of Yahweh that involves all creation: the invasion of the locust plague is the assault of the enemy from the north, the destruction of the locusts coalesces with Yahweh's judgment on the nations, and the deliverance of the people of Yahweh and the reestablishment of Jerusalem is fused with the regeneration of the land.[23]

Thus the day of Yahweh involves, indivisibly, both nature and history, and this distinction provides no basis on which to fragment the text. Simkins is prepared to call 1:2–2:27 "descriptive and prophetic" and 2:28–3:21 "apocalyptic or eschatological." But he is not prepared to conclude from this that the text is composite, since the distinction, though valid, should not lead us to postulate a false dichotomy within prophetic thought.

9. Apart from large-scale theories of single or composite authorship, many scholars have reckoned with the possibility that Joel, like the other prophetic books, may have been interpolated on a small scale in the course of its transmission.[24] There are no places where the manuscript or versional evidence suggests uncertainty about the inclusion of any of the material now in the book. But in general it has been thought likely that later editors have "improved" the text in some places.[25] Several commentators have suggested that the catastrophe in chapter 1 was originally drought rather than locust invasion (cf. Bergler, *Joel als Schriftprophet*, 31 and 335) and that the locusts have been added secondarily.

On one interpolation there is wide agreement: 3:4–8. This passage is usually thought to be in prose and may represent, as Müller puts it, an attempt to "anchor" the massive vagueness of 2:28–3:21 in some specific historical events (on which see the commentary below). The title in 1:1 is also, of course, redactional, identifying the prophecy as that of Joel ben Pethuel, who is not otherwise known to us.

10. Despite the persuasive arguments for a basic unity in the book of Joel, give or take a few interpolations, it seems to me the case constructed by Vernes

---

23. Ibid., p. 451.
24. A few have denied interpolation in general terms: thus W. Baumgartner, "Joel 1 and 2," in *Karl Budde zum 70. Geburtstag*, ed. K. Marti (BZAW 34), Berlin 1920, pp. 10–19, attacked theories that saw interpolations in chapters 1 and 2; and J. A. Thompson, "The Use of Repetition in the Prophecy of Joel," in *On Language, Culture, and Religion: In Honor of Eugene A. Nida*, ed. M. Black and W. A. Smalley, The Hague and Paris 1974, pp. 101–10, argues that repetitious material in Joel (for example, the duplication of material about locusts between 1:5–7 and 2:2–10) is proof of the sophistication of the prophet's style rather than of interpolation.
25. One case would be the proposal of O. Loretz, *Regenritual und Jahwetag im Joelbuch: Kaanäischer Hintergrund; Kolometrie, Aufbau und Symbolik eines Prophetenbuches* (Ugaritisch-biblische Literatur 4), Altenberge 1986, that 1:4–7 is a redactional addition, perhaps intended to suggest that the failing crops of chapter 1 are, like those of chapter 2, the result of a plague of locusts rather than of drought.

and Duhm still has considerable weight. As always in such matters, arguments are likely to be at least partly circular: reading the book in a certain way will lead to a conviction of its unity or disunity; a conviction of its unity or disunity will predispose one to read it in a certain way. It is certainly possible, as Simkins and Bourke (not to mention Wolff) have shown, to understand the scheme of judgment and salvation throughout the book as a unified whole, progressing from local problems (the locusts) to cosmic events. Nevertheless, it still seems to me that there is a real caesura after 2:27 that should be allowed its place in our interpretation.

The material in the book's first half gives every impression of being well ordered, and as Wolff and others have shown, this half falls in turn into two main sections, 1:2–20 and 2:1–17, with 2:18–27 providing YHWH's resolution of the terrible calamities that have called forth liturgies of lamentation and mourning. The same cannot be said, in my view, of the second half of the book. Here Müller's term *disjecta membra* seems to me altogether apt, as one image of postexilic Jewish eschatology follows another in no particular order. Merx was right, I believe, to describe these oracles as a muddle without "consistency or clarity" (*Consequenz und Klarheit*).[26] But he was mistaken to think that the muddle extended also to the first half of the book, which is polished and stylish by comparison with these essentially separate and isolated oracles. It is at 2:28 that the rot sets in, at precisely the point where we have the telltale formula "Then afterward," indicating here as elsewhere in the Old Testament that new material has been added to an old collection. It seems to me, accordingly, that Joel can best be seen[27] as essentially two separate collections of material, which should be discussed and dated independently of each other—always allowing, of course, that the process by which one came to be added to the other is also worthy of investigation.

11. Joel 1:2–2:27 is essentially a unified work dealing with the devastating effects of some physical disaster, which included at least locust plague and drought and may have also involved military invasion. Joel, a cultic prophet, calls his hearers to a solemn lament, assuring them that it is still possible for YHWH to relent. After this rite has been carried out, he is able to assure them that disaster will be replaced with prosperity. Either this complex of events was describable as "a day of YHWH" or 1:15a; 2:1c; and 2:11b are interpolated glosses, as Duhm thought. The "day" is eschatological in the sense that term sometimes has in scholarly discussion of prophecy, when it means something like "critical," "unique," or "more than a random event." But it is not eschatological in the sense of being concerned with a putative end time, which is not within the prophet's purview.

26. Merx, *Die Prophetie des Joel*, p. 21.
27. Following Vernes and Duhm.

All this changes from 2:28 onward, where we find the great themes of the expected new age that are reflected in much other late Old Testament prophecy and in the literature usually called apocalyptic: the overthrow of all the nations after they have been solemnly judged, miraculous regeneration for the land with water flowing out from the Temple, and the establishment of Judah in its own land in perpetuity. It seems to me that we have essentially two separate booklets here, and that they cannot really be regarded as forming an organic unity, only an imposed one. In the final section of this introduction, I examine how we might nevertheless choose to *read* Joel as a unity; but it seems clear that this is not a choice that the book itself forces on us, since it gives ample evidence of being a composite work.

To sum up: I would identify two parallel cycles of oracles about the dire state of the country in 1:2–20 and 2:1–17, each beginning with a call to take heed of the present situation and going on to proclaim the need for a public lamentation. There follows (2:18) a record that the laments were heard, as well as promises by YHWH of a restoration of the damage done by the locust plague and of a glorious future (2:18–27). This all seems to me well structured. The second half of the book is a rather miscellaneous collection of oracles, assembled in no particular order at all. Where the first half is concerned, there seems to be some correspondence between the two cycles of oracles about the locust plague, which might be tabulated as follows:

1:2–4	Details of disaster	2:1–11	Details of disaster
1:5–14	Call to lament	2:12–17a	Call to lament
1:15–20	The lament	2:17bc	The lament

Each of these units can naturally be broken down further, but at that point the symmetry is no longer apparent. It is possible that 1:2–3 might be regarded as an introduction to the whole of the words of Joel, rather than forming part of the description of the disaster, though I personally doubt this and think it probably an integral part of the first section.

In the commentary I follow this division, and for the second half of the book I simply treat each pericope separately, understanding the pericopes to be 2:28–29; 2:30–32; 3:1–3; 3:4–8; 3:9–13; 3:14–15; 3:16; 3:17; 3:18; and 3:19–21.

3. Historical Context

1. Probably because it is grouped with the preexilic prophets Amos, Hosea, and Micah in both the Hebrew and the Greek canon, Joel was assumed in ancient times to be a work from the same period as they. W. Vatke was among

Introduction 15

the first to propose a postexilic dating,[28] and the majority of modern commentators, whatever their views on the unity of the book, have tended to support this.[29] As we have already seen, all who treat 2:28–3:21 as a secondary addition to the words of Joel are likely to think that this passage, at least, is postexilic, though they may not go as far as Duhm in making it actually Maccabean—such very late dates have largely fallen out of favor. But that leaves the date of 1:2–2:27 more of an open question than if we treat the book as a unity, since many of the allegedly very late features appear in the second half. There are still scholars willing to defend a late preexilic dating, at least for the first half.[30] But a postexilic date has largely established itself as the preferred one.

In the nature of the case, it is impossible to discover an *exact* date for the events on which Joel seems to rest. If the disaster in chapters 1 and 2 is a plague of locusts (or several successive plagues), then such an event is inherently undatable by us. If, however, the locusts stand for a military invasion (see the commentary below), then in principle one might be able to discover which of all the threats to Judaean security this was; but in practice, there is extremely little to go on. Most commentators who subscribe to the majority dating give rather general arguments in its favor, which are summarized well by Wolff.

2. As far as a *terminus post quem* is concerned, it is said that 3:1–3 presuppose the exile, which is probably true (cf. 3:2, "because of my people and my heritage Israel, whom they have scattered among the nations"). There is no mention of a king, as there is in the books of the preexilic prophets, and the prominence of the priesthood in the book may argue for a setting at the earliest in the theocratic world of the Second Temple period. It is not at all certain, however, that the references to sacrifices in 1:13 and 2:14 necessarily imply that the institution of the *tāmîd*, the regular daily sacrifices in the Temple, was already in place; the references are vague and unfocused.[31]

---

28. W. Vatke, *Die biblische Theologie wissenschaftlich dargestellt: I. Die Religion des Alten Testaments*, Berlin 1835.

29. For continued defense of an eighth- or even ninth-century date, see, however, Kapelrud, *Joel Studies*, following J. Schmalohr, *Das Buch des Propheten Joel, übersetzt und erklärt* (ATA 7:4), Münster 1922; and see M. Bič, *Das Buch Joel*, Berlin 1960.

30. See esp. K. Koch, *Die Profeten*, Stuttgart 1978, 3d ed. 1995; English translation: *The Prophets*, 2 vols., London 1982–83; and Keller, *Joël*.

31. For this point, cf. R. Simkins, *Yahweh's Activity in History and Nature in the Book of Joel* (Ancient Near Eastern Texts and Studies 10), Lewiston, Queenston, and Lampeter 1991, against Wolff. Treves, "Date of Joel," presents a longer list with some more specific points: for example, the reference to the "holy mountain" in 2:1 must, he maintains, be post-Deuteronomic, while 2:7 and 2:9 imply that Jerusalem has a wall, which sets the book in the period after Nehemiah (though surely, *pace* also Wolff, the reference to "the wall" is far too vague to support such an argument: it is not as though Nehemiah found the walls of Jerusalem vanished without trace).

More generally, most readers are likely to gain an impression of a rather small community gathered around the Temple and ruled by priests and, perhaps, elders (if we take the *zĕqēnîm* of 1:14 thus, rather than simply as "old men"), and this seems to fit a time no earlier than the Second Temple period—say, the 400s at the earliest. Merx added the not insignificant point that the tone of Joel's prophecy is radically different from that of the preexilic prophets, with no denunciations of national sin and a great emphasis on the desirability of cultic rituals of lamentation. If, however, Joel was a cultic prophet, then for all we know he might even in preexilic times have spoken in such terms.

A comparatively late date becomes even easier to sustain with confidence once we take in material from the "second half" of the book, that is, from 2:28–3:21. Here, as Merx points out, we have stock themes from late postexilic prophecy: the outpouring of the Spirit (cf. Ezek. 39:29), signs and portents in the heavens (cf. Ezek. 32:7), the gathering of the nations for judgment (cf. Isa. 34:1). The reference to trade with Greeks in 3:6 implies contacts that were only in place well after the exile. (However, 3:4–8 may well represent an addition even to the second part of Joel, so its clearly postexilic reference does not necessarily show that the whole book is postexilic.) On the whole it seems fair, on the basis of a cumulative case, to see Joel as a postexilic composition in its present form; and there is a reasonable probability that even the earliest sections of 1:2–2:27 are already postexilic. There is also the evidence that the book quotes extensively from older texts, which we examine below; and this must imply that it is later than they.

3. Finding a *terminus ante quem* is harder. Ben Sira refers to "the twelve prophets" as an already finished collection (Sir. 49:10), and although we have no way of knowing that his book of the twelve contained precisely the present book of Joel, this probably makes Duhm's idea that 2:28–3:21 is Maccabean implausible. Wolff argues that 3:4–8 cannot be later than 343, when Tyre, mentioned as still an active city in Joel 3:4, was destroyed by Artaxerxes IV Ochus, while 3:6 implies that the Greeks were still seen as a distant people, not a hostile force in Palestine itself (contrast Zech. 9:13), and thus must precede the conquests of Alexander the Great. Since the whole passage is an addition to the book, the rest of the book must be earlier still. Wolff thus arrives at a date between 445 (when Nehemiah rebuilt the walls, which we have seen to be a shaky foundation for dating)[32] and 343.

Treves had tried to be even more precise in arguing for a still later date, the reign of Ptolemy Soter (325–285; cf. Josephus, *Antiquities* 12:7, 26, 29), who invaded Jerusalem—hence the prophecy that "strangers shall never again pass through it" (Joel 3:17) and the reference to Edom in 3:19, dormant until Ptolemy

---

32. Cf. J. M. Myers, "Some Considerations Bearing on the Date of Joel," *ZAW* 74 (1952): 177–95.

Soter's reign. But most commentators have regarded these references as too slight a basis for so late a dating: 3:17 and the mention of Edom may be referring back to the experiences of the early exilic age, when strangers certainly did pass through Jerusalem and Edom, according to Obadiah 11, assisted in the process.

Most precise of all are the datings proposed by F. R. Stephenson,[33] who thinks that 2:31 refers to an actual eclipse of the sun. According to Stephenson, only two such eclipses were visible from Jerusalem during the possible time span of the book of Joel: 29 February 357 and 4 July 336. Consequently, Joel must be dated in relation to one of these. But this is to assume that stereotyped language about heavenly portents is to be taken to refer to an actual event, a position for which there is no evidence.

4. In addition to references that can be correlated with external events, there is a certain amount of linguistic evidence that can be pressed into service. Wolff maintains that Joel shows traces of late Hebrew, the Hebrew we know from Chronicles and Qoheleth. He notes the following items of vocabulary that can be taken to indicate a late origin:

šelaḥ	2:8	weapon	2 Chron. 23:10; Neh. 4:17; Job 33:18; 36:12
sôp	2:20	rear	2 Chron. 20:16; Eccles. 3:11; 7:2; 12:13
ṣaḥănâ	2:20	stench	Sir. 11:12

He also notes a number of terms that are not attested elsewhere in the Old Testament but can be argued to be late formations: *'lh* (lament), 1:8; *'bš* (shrivel), *pĕrudôt* (seed grains), *megrĕpôt* (clods), and *mammĕgurôt* (granaries), all in 1:17; and *'bṭ* II (change course) in 2:7.

Crenshaw[34] adds a few other linguistic features: *'ănî*, the short form of the first-person singular pronoun *wĕ'im*, meaning "or"; *bêt* for the Temple; the expression "Judah and Jerusalem"; and *bĕnê ṣîyyôn* (children of Zion).

5. On the whole we may agree with Wolff that the mid-Persian period, somewhere in the 400s, is probably the likeliest date for Joel as we now have it, though the original core in 1:2–2:27 could be somewhat earlier but still probably postexilic. Joel thus falls into the same general period as Malachi and perhaps Jonah, with its later sections recalling Zechariah 9–14 in their protoapocalyptic themes. The author or authors are contemporaries of the Job poet but earlier than Qoheleth and probably belong in the period when the Pentateuch was making its way as the foundation document for Second Temple

---

33. F. R. Stephenson, "The Date of the Book of Joel," *VT* 19 (1969): 224–29.
34. Crenshaw, *Joel*, p. 26.

Judaism—what we may loosely call the age of Ezra and Nehemiah, prescinding here from discussion of the complicated questions of dating those two characters.

The book of Joel is thus an important source for a period of Israel's history on which the Old Testament throws relatively little light, the time of "the turmoil around the temple after the return of the exiles, the disappearance of Zerubbabel, and the rebuilding of the temple."[35] Although we must be vague as to an exact date, there seems no reason to agree with W. S. Prinsloo,[36] who argues that the evidence is so slender that we must content ourselves with reading the "final form" of the text with no notion as to its historical setting. It is simply not the case that all the proposed datings are purely "subjective": some are much more plausible than others, and there is no reason to give up in despair. We shall treat the book as coming from the Judaean community of the early Second Temple period, while being alert to the possibility that the second half may be substantially later than the first, since it represents a secondary addition to the words of Joel himself, whoever he may have been.

4. Joel as a Prophet

1. What is a prophet? There has been a tendency in Old Testament scholarship, at least since the work of J. Wellhausen, to regard the great preexilic prophets Amos, Hosea, Micah, Isaiah, and Jeremiah as setting the benchmark for assessing later books in the prophetic canon. On this basis, older critical scholars often regarded Joel as a somewhat degenerate prophet, if indeed he was properly to be seen as a prophet at all. Merx was particularly outspoken on this subject, seeing Joel as a far cry from the openness and coherence of the message of the "great" prophets. Observing the lack of order and organization in the oracles of 2:28–3:21, Merx wrote:

> In this arrangement I cannot see even complete consistency or clarity, let alone sublimity or any spiritual aspect, still less a deeply religious penetration leading to a perception of God's plan with his people. Here everything is external, a mere picturing of the situation, and in spirit it is fleshly, particularistic in a Jewish way, it is the expression of a man who is still deeply embroiled in the στοιχεια του κοσμου and has a narrow outlook.[37]

---

35. Redditt, "Book of Joel," p. 235.
36. W. S. Prinsloo, *The Theology of the Book of Joel* (BZAW 163), Berlin 1985.
37. "Ich vermag in dieser Stufenfolge nicht einmal völlige Consequenz und Klarheit, geschweige denn Grossartigkeit und geistvolles Anschauen, oder gar ein tiefreligiöses Durchdringen des Planes Gottes mit seinem Volk zu erblicken. Alles hier ist äusserlich, es ist Situationsmalerei und der Gesinnung nach ist es fleischlich, jüdisch-particularistisch, es ist das Sinnen eines Mannes, der noch tief in den στοιχεια του κοσμου befangen ist und engen Blick hat." Merx, *Die Prophetie des Joel*, p. 21.

Introduction

Such a quotation reminds us how deeply Wellhausen's denigration of postexilic Judaism as "particularistic" and "earthly" was rooted in common attitudes of the late nineteenth century. But even if we deplore the value judgments here, we may still ask if Merx had not correctly perceived a great difference between Joel and his preexilic prophetic predecessors. There is no denunciation of national sin, indeed no comment on "ethical" matters at all, but a conviction that the way to deal with national distress is to call a solemn fast. What would Isaiah have said (cf. Isa. 1:13b)?

From a modern perspective, it is usual to see a far less sharp rift between pre- and postexilic prophets and to stress that each prophet spoke the words that his contemporaries needed to hear. In times of national complacency this was a message of judgment, but in times of calamity and distress the prophets might well be called on to deliver oracles of hope and blessing, as we see classically in the work of Deutero-Isaiah. Joel belongs in the period when the prophetic task was no longer condemnation and denunciation but encouragement. Furthermore, it is not the case that he "merely" consoles. What he calls for is a cultic turning to YHWH, and this is to involve not simply the "outward" aspect that Merx so despised but also inner transformation: "rend your hearts and not your garments" (2:13; cf. Ps. 51:17). There is no reason to regard Joel as a "false" prophet, one who proclaimed "'Peace, peace,' when there is no peace" (cf. Jer. 6:14; 8:11).

2. It remains true that Joel presents a very different aspect from the preexilic prophets, and this is related in good measure to the style or manner of his prophecy. Merx had already pointed out the extent to which this is a *learned* prophecy, which draws on many quotations from older works and blends them into the new message the prophet has to deliver, rather than putting forward fresh formulations of his own (see below, p. 22–27). S. Bergler developed this into the theory that Joel was a *Schriftprophet*—both a "writing prophet" in a sense that was not true of Amos or Hosea, who delivered their oracles spontaneously, and a "scriptural prophet" in that he quoted extensively from existing scriptural collections of material, if not, indeed, from already formed biblical books.[38] Joel's purpose (and here Bergler harks back again to Merx) was to show that YHWH's promises in previous speech and writing had not failed but would truly come to fruition: "No word of the ancients has fallen by the wayside!"[39]

According to Bergler, Joel was a written text from the beginning, never an oral proclamation. Merx, indeed, had spoken of the beginnings of midrash in Joel and saw him as one who meditated on earlier scripture in formulating his own message. It is fair to point out that reminiscences of older texts are more

---

38. S. Bergler, *Joel als Schriftprophet* (BEATAJ 16), Frankfurt am Main 1988. Others have seen the quotations as resting on oral tradition; cf. Crenshaw, *Joel*, p. 192.

39. "Keines der Worte der Alten ist dahingefallen!" Bergler, *Joel als Schriftprophet*, p. 29.

common in the book's (possibly secondary) second half (2:28–3:21) than in what we are regarding as the words of Joel himself in 1:2–2:27, though even here there is the great quotation of Exod. 34:6-7 (or its source) in Joel 2:13. H. P. Müller argues that 2:28–3:21 is essentially a literary composition, designed to present the (as yet unfulfilled) hopes of 1:2–2:27 as about to be fulfilled in an apocalyptic frame of reference, that is, in the remote future—even if the author of this second half of the book is Joel himself, reflecting on the failure of his earlier prophecies (Müller, "Prophetie und Apokalyptik"). For all these scholars, Joel is essentially a written composition.[40]

3. Wolff helpfully sums up this debate by calling Joel a "learned prophecy," in which both terms bear equal weight: the book is unlike earlier prophecies in being learned, but it is also unlike other learned works (for example, the wisdom books) in being a prophecy. Wolff, indeed, does not concur in the view that Joel is pure "salvation prophecy," part of the "charge" against the book brought by scholars of any earlier period. He thinks that Joel faced a people who were complacent about their own status before God: "With its theocratic leadership and the canonized Torah to guide it, performing the daily sacrifices, and having purified itself from within of all that was foreign, the community's mood is one of confidence in its own salvation and in Jerusalem's election as the throne of Yahweh's kingdom."[41]

As far as I can see, however, the only evidence for the idea that people in Jerusalem were "complacent" is the fact that Joel calls on them to "rend" their "hearts" (2:13)—a narrow base on which to construct such a precise analysis of the psychological failings of the nation (see also below, on the theme of repentance). Joel's message is at least predominantly one of comfort, and our definition of "true" prophecy needs to be broad enough to encompass this.

4. There is a clear distinction from the preexilic prophets in Joel's "cult-friendly" stance. We hear none of the condemnations of the cult that meet us in the pages of Amos or Isaiah. This has led to the supposition that Joel, perhaps like Haggai and Zechariah, was a cultic prophet.[42] R. J. Coggins proposes that the prophets whose books we possess may be divided into two types. One was the prophet who composed oracles for delivery at any time that presented itself, oracles that were then collected (perhaps by disciples) into anthologies of the

---

40. F. E. Deist, "Parallels and Reinterpretation in the Book of Joel: A Theology of the Yom Yahweh?" in *Text and Context: Old Testament and Semitic Studies for F. C. Fensham* (JSOTSup 48), Sheffield 1988, pp. 63–79, perhaps goes furthest of all in regarding the book as essentially an anthology of eschatological themes: "The book was not intended to 'refer' to any concrete event in history, but was rather compiled to serve as a 'literary theology' of the concept 'The Day of the Lord'" (p. 63).

41. Wolff, *Joel and Amos*, pp. 5–6.

42. For this concept, see esp. A. R. Johnson, *The Cultic Prophet in Ancient Israel*, Cardiff 1944; and idem, *The Cultic Prophet and Israel's Psalmody*, Cardiff 1979.

Introduction

kind referred to (by Ivan Engnell) by the Arabic term *diwan*. The other type was the cult prophet, whose compositions grew out of, and were intended for use in, the public liturgy.[43] It is widely thought that it was such cult prophets who provided responses to prayers and intercessions, their (now unrecorded) utterances explaining the sudden and abrupt shift from prayer to expressions of confidence in psalms such as Psalm 20.

Coggins sees Joel as typical of this second group, as does Carroll: "It seems to be the case that the cult prophets were those prophets who were more confident about the future salvation of the nation, e.g. Joel, Second Isaiah and Haggai."[44] Indeed, it has become possible to refer to Joel as a "prophetic liturgy,"[45] a text written for cultic use and conditioned by cultic assumptions about the willingness of YHWH to intervene on his people's behalf when they call out to YHWH in lamentation. O. Loretz goes even further, specifying that Joel's cultic activity took the form of a rain-making ceremony[46]—which is how one might, of course, describe a cultic lamentation in which people prayed for rain, though it seems a tendentious way of describing such a thing, likening it to magic.

5. It seems to me, however, that Joel *draws on* liturgical forms rather than *being* itself a liturgy.[47] Wolff, similarly, speaks of originally cultic forms now detached from their cultic setting. What Joel offers is, in the manner of the pre-exilic prophets, a description of the current plight of the nation, following this with a call to take part in a liturgical act. But he does not provide the "text" for such an act, except in the very brief saying which he instructs the priests to utter: "Spare your people, YHWH, and do not make your heritage a reproach, a byword among the nations. Why should they say among the peoples, 'Where is their God?'" (2:17). Though not an exact quotation from any psalm known to us, this is very close in spirit to Psalm 44, and the line "Where is their God?" occurs at Ps. 115:2. One could not use Joel as an "order of service." One could read his prophecy during a service, as both Jews and Christians have done, but it does not seem to be designed for this purpose.

Joel's function seems to be to call on the people to react in certain appropriate ways to the judgment of YHWH as experienced through the locust plague,

43. See Coggins, "An Alternative Prophetic Tradition?"
44. Carroll, "Eschatological Delay," p. 49.
45. Müller, "Prophetie und Apokalyptik bei Joel."
46. Loretz, *Regenritual und Yahwetag*; cf. F. F. Hvidberg, *Weeping and Laughter in the Old Testament*, Leiden 1962.
47. A similar distinction is drawn by Ahlström, *Joel and the Temple Cult*; and by G. S. Ogden, "Joel 4 and Prophetic Responses to National Laments," *JSOT* 26 (1983): 97–106, who regards 2:28–3:21 as essentially the response to the prophet's prayers in the lament ritual implied in 1:2–2:27 but stresses that, in its present form, the book is a literary work inspired by the lament liturgy, not literally a liturgy itself.

specifically by convening liturgical assemblies in which the people can call on YHWH to save them. It may be that this was what cultic prophets were for, but it may also be that such was a normal function of the priests. Certainly, this is usually assumed by commentators on Amos, who point out that the prophet parodies a priestly *torah* in exhorting the people, "Come to Bethel—and transgress!" (Amos 4:4); the "straight" form would presumably have been something like "Come to Bethel and offer your sacrifices." So it may be that Joel, too, is adopting what was properly a priestly form of address in instructing the people to convene a solemn liturgical assembly.

Perhaps, then, Joel was in fact a priest; we cannot tell. (Wolff opposes the idea.) But perhaps he saw it as part of his prophetic calling to instruct even the priests themselves and to call on them to take an initiative in convening the assembly. At any rate, there seems no better designation to give him than that of a prophet, since he addresses the people of Judah, analyzes the plight they are in, and proposes by what religious route they can hope to improve matters, and these are classically prophetic tasks—however much the content of what is proposed (the calling of a cultic assembly) differs from what his preexilic predecessors might have demanded.

6. All this applies to what we are treating as the work of Joel himself, 1:2–2:27. Where the second half of the book is concerned, I am less confident that we are dealing with the words of a cult prophet or, indeed, of a prophet at all. The more we emphasize how much these chapters deal in stock themes of postexilic eschatological theology, the less necessary it is to ascribe them to a prophetic figure, and the more they might be seen as the work of a learned scribe, imbued with "scriptural" knowledge. Wolff indeed speaks of "sapiential-didactic" activity in Joel (*Joel and Amos,* p. 9), intending this as a description of the whole book, a "learned" prophecy; but whether or not it can be applied to the book's first half, it certainly seems reasonable as a description of the second. It will be seen that this conflicts with Plöger's notion of the second half as the work of protoapocalyptists, and it may seem strange to use "wisdom" vocabulary to describe material so obviously "eschatological" in orientation as 2:28–3:21. As we shall see later, however, this depends very much on what kind of eschatology we find in these oracles.

5. Quotations in Joel

One of the features of Joel that helps convince most modern commentators it is a relatively late book is the prevalence of what seem to be quotations from other parts of the Old Testament—though we cannot always be sure that the dependence is on Joel's part. Crenshaw[48] provides a useful list of these, which I repro-

---

48. Crenshaw, *Joel,* pp. 27–28.

Introduction

duce here, though changing the translations to conform with my own as used in the commentary:

1:15	Ezek. 30:2	Alas for the day!
1:15	Isa. 13:6; Ezek. 30:2; Obadiah 15; Zeph. 1:7	For the day of YHWH has drawn near
1:15	Isa. 13:6	as destruction from Shaddai it comes
2:2	Zeph. 1:14–15	a day of darkness and gloom, a day of clouds and thick darkness
2:3b	Isa. 51:3; Ezek. 36:35	[reversal of an image for paradise]
2:6	Nahum 2:10	all faces grow pale
2:13	Exod. 34:6; Jonah 4:2	he is gracious and merciful, slow to anger, and abounding in steadfast love
2:14	Jonah 3:9	Who knows? He may turn and relent.
2:17	Ps. 79:10	Why should they say among the nations, "Where is their God?"?
2:21	Ps. 126:3	YHWH has done great things
2:27	Isa. 45:5, 6, 18	I, YHWH, am your God and there is no other
2:28	Ezek. 39:29	I will pour out my spirit
2:31	Mal. 4:5	before the coming of the great and terrible day of YHWH
2:32	Obadiah 17	in Mount Zion and in Jerusalem there shall be those who escape
3:1	Jer. 33:15; 50:4, 20	in those days and at that time
3:2	Isa. 66:18; Zech. 14:2	I will gather together all the nations
3:4	Obadiah 15	I will turn your deeds back upon your own heads
3:8	Obadiah 18	for YHWH has spoken
3:10a	Isa. 2:4; Micah 4:3	[reversal of saying about beating swords into plowshares]
3:16	Amos 1:2	YHWH roars from Zion, and from Jerusalem he utters his voice
3:17	Ezek 36:11	So you shall know that I, YHWH your God ...
3:18	Amos 9:13	The mountains shall drip sweet wine

Not all these parallels are equally compelling. For example, it does not seem to me that we can be confident in speaking of a "quotation" in the case of a formula such as "for YHWH has spoken"; while the "reversal of an image for paradise" seems somewhat vague, and the alleged parallels are not at all close. Against Bergler[49] it seems reasonable to argue that some of the resemblances to other texts could come from oral memory, and that both Joel and his alleged "source" might be drawing on commonplaces, sayings at home in oral tradition, rather than one on the other. (This might be so, for example, of the "swords into plowshares" theme, where Joel may be reversing what is said in Isaiah and Micah but where equally it may be that all three prophetic books are drawing on a widespread saying.)[50] Furthermore, some of the parallels are with late postexilic texts where the possibility of a dependence on Joel may be quite high (see the commentary on Obadiah for the "quotations" from that book). All that being said, it seems to me there are several cases here where the likelihood of a use of older materials is high, perhaps justifying Bergler's and Merx's judgment that Joel is more an "epigonist" than an original prophet in the mold of Amos or Isaiah.

I single out especially the following examples of literary dependence in Joel:

> a. Alas for the day!
> For the day of YHWH has drawn near,
> and as destruction from Shaddai it comes.
> (1:15)

Here we seem to have a clear case of dependence on Isa. 13:6 and perhaps also on the "day of YHWH" in Zeph. 1:14–18. The difficulty is that we cannot be sure that Joel is therefore saying that the day of YHWH *predicted by Isaiah* is coming—that is, he may simply be drawing on congenial material, not necessarily referring the reader deliberately back to the older prophecy.[51] Interestingly, the day of YHWH is here not a day of national retribution through a battle but is linked to the locust plague, and YHWH's judgment is expressed through famine.

> b. a day of darkness and gloom,
> a day of clouds and thick darkness!
> (2:2)

Again Zephaniah's "day of YHWH" seems likely to be in the background, though once again (if my exegesis is correct) it is a day of famine caused by

---

49. Bergler, *Joel als Schriftprophet*.

50. There are useful warnings about too ready an assumption of literary dependence in M. V. Fox, "The Identification of Quotations in Biblical Literature," *ZAW* 92 (1980): 416-31.

51. It is assumed here that Isaiah 13 is an exilic prophecy of the fall of Babylon, but for later datings see O. Kaiser, *Isaiah 13—39* (OTL), London 1974 *ad loc.*

Introduction 25

locusts rather than a day of military defeat. It is possible that the passage in Zephaniah is a fuller development of this verse in Joel, and I do not see how this question can be resolved.

> c. for he is gracious and merciful,
> slow to anger, and abounding in steadfast love,
> and relents from punishing.
> (2:13)

The first two lines of this formula occur eight times in the Old Testament, at Exod. 34:6–7; Num. 14:18; Neh. 9:17; Ps. 86:15; 103:8; 145:8; Joel 2:13; and Jonah 4:2; additionally, Nahum 1:3 has "YHWH is slow to anger but great in power." The third line occurs otherwise only at Jonah 4:2. R. C. Dentan ("Literary Affinities of Exodus XXXIV 6f.") speculates that it was originally a liturgical formula, functioning as a confession of faith, and was first formulated in postexilic times; no quotation of it can be shown to be preexilic. There is no way of telling which of the other uses of the passage Joel is quoting, and of course, the possibility arises that it was a freely floating traditional formula that is not original to any of the passages where it now occurs: the three occurrences in the Psalms might support the idea that its roots lie in liturgy.

> d. Why should they say among the peoples,
> "Where is their God?"?
> (2:17)

This exact phrase occurs at Ps. 79:10 (cf. also Ps. 115:2). Again, we seem to be dealing here with a liturgical formula, at home in the lament tradition, in which YHWH is warned that the consequences of his allowing his people to suffer will be a loss of reputation among foreign nations (cf. also Ezek. 36:20). It would be hard to show that Joel is actually quoting from one or another of the psalms in which the expression occurs and easier to say simply that he is familiar with this piece of liturgical language.

> e. I, YHWH, am your God and there is no other.
> (2:27)

This formula has Deutero-Isaiah written all over it. (Cf. Isa. 40:25; 42:6, 8; 43:3, 11, 13, 15; 44:6, 24; 45:5, 21, 22; 48:12, 17; 51:15.) There seems a high probability that Joel was familiar with Isaiah 40–55.

> f. YHWH roars from Zion,
> and utters his voice from Jerusalem.
> (3:16)

It is obvious that there is some relationship with Amos 1:2. In support of the idea that the Amos reference is primary, we may note that Amos has other references to lions (3:4, 12; 5:19). The verse seems, however, unlikely to be an original piece of Amos's own prophecy, in view of its reference to Zion, and most commentators treat it as an editorial insertion.[52] In the complicated editorial history of the "Book of the Twelve," it is conceivable that it has been copied into Amos from Joel, but on the whole, the relationship seems more likely to be the other way; or it could, again, be a common liturgical formula at home in the Jerusalem cult. In this case we are dealing with a verse in what I have dubbed Deutero-Joel, the secondary material of 2:28–3:21.

Thus there is clear evidence that Joel depends on material that can be found elsewhere in the Old Testament, as well as perhaps sometimes being the source of quotations in later books. But in several cases the material quoted seems to have liturgical associations.[53] This may help confirm the idea of Joel as a cultic prophet, or at least as one familiar with cultic texts, as one would expect from the fact that he encouraged his hearers to engage in liturgical lamentation. On the whole, the idea of him as a learned prophet seems rather an exaggeration on this evidence; much of the material he quotes may have been orally mediated.

In addition to overt quotation from other sources, it is worth noting parallels in the thought of other Old Testament books. R. A. Mason points out the close resemblance in theme to Zechariah 9–14:

> There also we have the idea of God's bringing the nations against Judah and Jerusalem. In 12.1–13.6 he is said to bring them there in order to judge and destroy them; but in ch. 14 they are permitted to execute a more terrible judgment against his people and his city (vv. 2–3) before he comes as the divine warrior with all his "holy ones" to defeat and judge the nations and rule as universal king in Zion. There he re-establishes the natural order (vv. 6–8), brings the divine gift of rain for all who worship him (v. 17) and makes Jerusalem holy again (vv. 21–22). Indeed, Zechariah 9—14 is greatly concerned with the gift of rain (10.1) and attacks the false leaders of the people who turn elsewhere to secure it by magic and incantations. By contrast, God will send his spirit on all sections of the community so that they mourn for their sins and are then open to miraculous, divine cleansing (Zech. 12.10–13.1). Joel also is much concerned to call the priests to lead the people to lament and fast before Yahweh, and promises that, when they do so, Yahweh will give the gift of rain (2.23–27). In 2.28 (3.1) we also have the promise that God will "pour out" his spirit "on all flesh" (the same verb as in Zech. 12.10).[54]

I do not think we have to suppose any direct literary dependence, in either direction, between Joel and Zechariah 9–14; but these parallels do establish that

---

52. See Wolff, *Joel and Amos,* p. 121, who ascribes it to a Judaean redaction.
53. Cf. R. J. Coggins, "Interbiblical Quotations in Joel," in *After the Exile: Essays in Honour of Rex Mason,* ed. J. Barton and D. J. Reimer, Macon, Ga. 1996, pp. 75–84.
54. R. A. Mason, *Zephaniah, Habakkuk, Joel* (Old Testament Guides), Sheffield 1994, p. 120.

the two works come from a similar milieu and deal with similar themes, which we may suppose to have been preoccupations of the postexilic community.

The evidence discussed here helps confirm the idea, common since the great late-nineteenth-century commentators on the prophets such as Wellhausen and Duhm, that prophecy after the exile became more *derivative* than it had been while the First Temple stood and prophets addressed the kings of Israel and Judah. There was a prophetic tradition in which postexilic prophets were conscious of standing, and they drew on both the ideas and the words of earlier prophets in formulating their own message. Joel himself shows signs of this, but it is even more evident in the secondary additions to his book. One has the impression of a "pool" of free-floating prophetic oracles, either written or transmitted orally, that could be drawn on at will when a "new" prophecy was needed. The sense of originality that we get from the great preexilic prophets is lacking.

6. Theological Themes

Eschatology

In modern biblical studies the term *eschatology* often refers to a complex of events to do with a decisive change in the world—not involving an "otherworldly" perspective, which hardly occurs within the biblical canon, but certainly betokening a radical break with the ordinary progress of history. We call a prophetic hope or fear eschatological if it describes a situation in which things will never be the same again, and usually in works from the Second Temple period this means that Israel (or a chosen remnant of Israel) will enjoy previously unimaginable prosperity and divine blessing, and its opponents will be crushed or eliminated. Sometimes this includes a transformation even of the natural order, as in Joel 3:18: "On that day the mountains shall drip sweet wine, the hills shall run with milk, and all the watercourses of Judah shall flow with water; and a fountain shall come forth from the house of YHWH and water the Wadi Shittim." On this basis, it seems reasonable to call the second half of Joel eschatological, whereas the first half operates entirely within the limits of a particular situation, speaking of the devastation caused by the locust plague and its complete reversal by YHWH. At least, this is true until the very last words of the first part (2:26 and 27), where we read (twice), "And my people shall *never again* [*lĕʿôlām*] be put to shame," which might indicate that the reversal of fortune goes beyond this particular occasion. But until that point there is nothing to indicate that the promises are any more than those that arise in a limited time perspective.

With 2:28–3:21 we seem to be in essentially a different world. Here are a number of themes bearing on the end time, when God judges all the nations and inaugurates a new world order. Judah is blessed and all her enemies are put to rout. Whereas in 2:10 the darkening of sun and moon are an (hyperbolic) effect of the locust swarm, in 2:31 they are an independent event, along with blood and fire and columns of smoke on the earth, part of a series of heavenly portents preparing for the day of YHWH, here seen as a decisive change in human fortunes. Thus I would call 2:28–3:21 eschatological in a sense that does not apply to 1:2–2:27.

This contrast is made well by Müller, who stresses that, whereas 1:2–2:27 regards the future as open—YHWH can choose to respond to his people's prayer, and they in turn can choose whether or not to utter one—the theology of 2:28–3:21 is more deterministic in quality: these are the events that YHWH has planned and will carry out, whatever happens. The book thus moves, as Müller puts it, from the openness of real history to the determinism of those who "know" the secrets of the times. The author or authors of this section are like the later apocalyptists:

> The basic function of their word is ... not address but assertion, and the assertion now only happens to be dressed up as an address, in a literary way. Joel 1:5–2:27 understands reality as a possibility granted to the people of God in the present moment; Joel 1:2–4 and 2:28ff. by contrast presents reality as a universal fact which can be surveyed by the individual, and which is ultimately ordered, in spite of all dissonances, from the perspective of a future understood "futuristically."[55]

However, Müller stresses that even such an "apocalyptic" message can have an existential impact. Knowing the secret of the future that God is about to implement can challenge the hearers to radical obedience, in preparation for taking part in the glories of the age to come.

But this does not resolve a very important question about the second part of the book of Joel. Eschatological texts can be of two kinds.[56] To be convinced there will be an end time that will take a more or less dramatic form is not necessarily to believe that this time is imminent. In later rabbinic Judaism, for example, there is a highly developed eschatology involving predictions about the end of this age and the coming of the "age to come" (*hā'ôlām habbā'*), but this is normally combined with a sense that there is no great urgency about the

---

55. "Die Grundfunktion seines Wortes ist darum auch nicht die Anrede, sondern die Aussage, die nur noch literarisch gelegentlich das Gewand der Anrede trägt. Jo 1,5–2,27 erschließt Wirklichkeit als die dem Gottesvolk geschenkte Möglichkeit im gegenwärtigen Augenblick; Jo 1,2–4; 3f. dagegen stellt Wirklichkeit als ein vom einzelnen zu überblickendes Universum dar, das von einer 'futurisch' verstandenen Zukunft her trotz aller Dissonanzen letztlich geordnet ist." Müller, "Prophetie und Apokalyptik," pp. 250–51.

56. See J. Barton, *Oracles of God: Perceptions of Ancient Prophecy in Israel after the Exile*, London 1986; New York 1988.

Introduction 29

matter. It is good to know about God's ultimate plan for the world because this reassures one that God is in control and can be trusted, but it is quite compatible with being perfectly at home in the present world order and having no desire or expectation that circumstances should change in the immediate future. Where the prophets concentrated all their efforts on convincing their contemporaries that God was about to do something decisive and new—even though it might affect *only* the short-term future and have no long-term consequences— rabbinic writers were interested in the long-term outlook, but without any sense of urgency or existential force.

Now, it may well be that some of the predictions of the future in the Old Testament itself anticipate the rabbinic attitude. The fact that a writer speaks in vivid imagery of the end time does not necessarily mean that he supposes this end time to be about to break in. There is no necessary correlation between interest in eschatology and a belief that the end is about to come.

It therefore seems to me that the question of whether or not Joel 2:28–3:21 is eschatological—which I would answer affirmatively—is quite separate from the question of whether or not it contains expectations of *imminent* intervention. The first half of Joel certainly is about imminence: lamenting for the devastation wrought by the locusts can be expected to bring about a speedy reversal, a restoration of lost fertility. But there is no particular reason to think the author of the second half also believed in the imminence of his expectations. One reason for thinking he did not is that he does not present a coherent set of expectations, following any kind of ordered sequence—as Merx was quick to point out. One cannot form any exact impression from these oracles (if *oracles* is the right word) of just how events were expected to unfold, and indeed, in places the order seems positively awkward: first the spirit is poured out on "all flesh" (2:28–29), *then* there are signs and portents in heaven (2:30–32), *then* everyone who calls on YHWH is saved.

But that is not the end of the matter: next, the nations are gathered for judgment to the "valley of Jehoshaphat" (3:1–3). The next passage (3:4–8) is probably an interpolation, but it is followed by preparation for war against nations that appear already to have been judged (3:9–12). Then follows the reaping of the earth's harvest (3:13), then the announcement that the day of YHWH is near (3:14–15), accompanied by further portents. In 3:16, YHWH "roars from Zion" (probably quoting Amos 1:2), and in 3:17 YHWH sanctifies Jerusalem, so that it is saved from invasion by foreigners (who are supposed to have already been judged). Next comes the promise of miraculous fruitfulness for the land (3:18); but instead of marking the conclusion of the book, this leads into an oracle against Edom and Egypt (3:19)—where were they when the nations were being judged?—and thus to a further promise to Judah and Jerusalem that YHWH will avenge them (3:20–21).

It is hard to see any sequence here, and I would concur in P. D. Hanson's judgment that "the author simply employed a series of stereotyped apocalyptic phrases."[57] Taken individually, each of the oracles here could represent someone's concrete hopes for some immediate future. But once joined together, they do not amount to a set of expectations anyone could very well subscribe to; rather, they are incoherent. For this reason I believe we are not dealing here with real prophecy but with a scribal or learned compilation of prophetic fragments.

A number of scholars have said similar things to this. Thus Wolff distinguishes Joel from true "apocalyptic":

> Insofar as Joel distinguishes a preliminary divine response (2:19–26) from the ultimate time of salvation (3:1–5 [i.e. 2:28–32]) and sees the fate of Israel and the whole world of nations linked together in the events of the end-time (commenting here explicitly on older prophetic utterance [3:5 {i.e. 2:32}]), we see him once again standing at the threshold between prophetic eschatology and apocalypticism. But he has not crossed that threshold, since he does not establish a time sequence for the various events within the end-time.[58]

By "prophetic eschatology" I take Wolff to mean a kind of eschatology that is concerned with the events of the here and now, seen as under divine control as God brings about God's decisive purpose. We have seen that the first half of Joel is in *that* sense eschatological—a perfectly useful sense, though I have been using the term in a sense closer to what Wolff means by "apocalypticism," as referring to the end time. Wolff's point, then, is that the second half of Joel is not yet moving in the world of apocalyptic eschatology, that is, predicting in detail the events of the end that are about to break in on the world. Rather, the writer of the second half of Joel gathers together odds and ends of prophetic utterances and strings them together in no particular order. I think this means Wolff is correct to see the author of 2:28–3:21 as a learned, scribal figure, but I doubt very much whether he is to be identified with the prophet Joel.

Müller makes a similar point. The passage 2:28–3:21, he suggests, works with a fixed, universal scheme of salvation, a theoretical construct rather than a living address to the prophet's contemporaries. "The language no longer bears a prophetic summons, but tends to an eschatological dogma whose concern is in the end with theodicy."[59] This is quite a pregnant suggestion, since it seems to me, in general, that those who devise eschatological schemes without any anticipation that they are to be activated soon are indeed concerned with something we could call theodicy; that is, they want to demonstrate that God really

---

57. Cf. also Deist, "Parallels and Reinterpretation," p. 73.
58. Wolff, *Joel and Amos*, p. 14.
59. Müller, "Prophetie und Apokalyptik," p. 244.

Introduction 31

is in control of the world and has just purposes for it, in which the righteous will be vindicated and the wicked punished.[60]

This is quite distinct from the concern of the so-called apocalyptic type of seer, who thought that the end time would be breaking in at any moment. It is focused on the reliability of God, not on any expectation of imminent intervention. And this differentiates it from the kind of "sectarian" concern for the soon-to-be-revealed end time that was a feature, if Plöger and Hanson are correct, of the small antiestablishment groups that developed into "apocalyptic sects." It seems to me that the second half of Joel belongs more in the world of a concern for theodicy than of bated-breath expectations of imminent divine salvation for the righteous in Israel.

It is also possible that Carroll[61] is correct in seeing in these sections of Joel a concern to deal with a delay in the implementation of the prophetic oracles that lie at their base. These events, it is being stressed, really will occur—one day; there is no need for anxiety at the fact that they have not happened yet. "For in Mount Zion there shall be those who escape, *as YHWH has said,* and in Jerusalem survivors" (2:32; see the commentary for the emendation implied here). This could reflect the fact that the glorious future Joel had thought would so soon follow on the locust plague did not seem to have materialized. It reassures the reader that, as we read in Hab. 2:3, "there is still a vision for the appointed time; it speaks of the end, and does not lie. If it seems to tarry, wait for it; it will surely come, it will not delay." There is an element of whistling in the dark about such pseudoconfident utterances; they hide a profound anxiety.

Our discussion of "eschatology" in Joel has been wide-ranging, but I believe it is necessary to have some framework within which to discuss the right use of this difficult term. Since I regard 2:28–3:21 as a kind of Deutero-Joel, I do not think any discussion that treats the two parts of the book together is likely to come to any useful conclusions about its message for the future. Joel himself prophesied an imminent recovery from the ravages of the locusts, on the basis of a liturgical act of lamentation linked with an inward sense of brokenness. In a later generation, his prophecies were thought of as having a much wider scope than that and were seen as promises of an entirely new world order. The fact that this order had not arrived was a problem for some, who may well have wanted to reinforce what they saw as his message by emphasizing that it really would come true eventually. Others simply saw in Joel the makings of a promise that YHWH would ultimately be loyal to his people and would one day bring in a completely

---

60. Cf. Barton, *Oracles of God,* pp. 214–34, where I argue (p. 217) that "a knowledge of what God has in store for his people in the end helps to make sense of the present and encourages piety and faith."

61. Carroll, "Eschatological Delay."

fresh order of things. But the details of this coming change were vague and were fleshed out by simply collecting together various prophetic oracles (some of them maybe quite old) and stitching them together to make a kind of patchwork quilt.

The Mercy of God

Joel contains little that is new or surprising on the theological front, but it does provide classic formulations of some theological points. The first part, 1:2–2:27, represents a familiar pattern in the Old Testament: national disaster is seen as the action of YHWH against the people, but YHWH is ready to reverse the disaster and to grant new life in response to a wholehearted "turning" to God in prayer and lamentation. It is not actually asserted in Joel that the disaster is the result of national sin (see commentary on 2:13), and in this Joel differs sharply from the preexilic classical prophets, who always ground the suffering they either describe or foretell in the sins the people are reckoned to have committed. It is possible that the language of "rending the heart" (2:13) implies there is sin to be repented of, but if so, this is not spelled out in detail. But there is a great assurance that God is merciful.

This is brought out above all in the allusion to the attributes of God known from Exod. 34:6–7, which assures the reader that YHWH, God of Israel, is characterized by "steadfast love" (*ḥesed*) and does not enjoy inflicting suffering on the people. YHWH "relents" from punishment—this does not mean that he refrains from punishment but rather that he sets a term to his anger and will not carry on punishing to the point where the nation is wholly destroyed. R. C. Dentan[62] has interestingly shown that this contrasts with the Deuteronomistic idea of divine punishment, which knows no bounds and is not restrained by any mercy on God's part. For the Deuteronomistic school, God and Israel are bound by a solemn contract (the covenant), and God can be expected to punish any infringement to the full. In Exod. 34:6–7, and by implication in the other Old Testament passages where it is quoted, God is seen as merciful and forgiving, not allowing his wrath to get the better of his care for his people.

Dentan suggests that this reflection is more characteristic of wisdom, but I cannot see that there are any clear affinities: it seems rather to be a standard formula stressing an idea of God that was current in many streams of thought in Israel, among prophets as well as among the wise, which heavily mitigates the rigor of the full prophetic and Deuteronomistic emphasis on God's punishment of disobedient Israel. In effect, such an idea of God must have been current in the circles that wrote and used public lamentations, since the lament makes sense only on the assumption that God may take notice of it. Its use here can be paralleled in Lam. 3:19–33:

---

62. R. C. Dentan, "The Literary Affinities of Exodus XXXIV 6f.," *VT* 13 (1963): 34–51.

Introduction 33

> The thought of my affliction and my homelessness
> is wormwood and gall!
> My soul continually thinks of it
> and is bowed down within me.
> But this I call to mind,
> and therefore I have hope:
>
> The steadfast love of the LORD never ceases,
> his mercies never come to an end;
> they are new every morning;
> great is your faithfulness. . . .
>
> For the Lord will not
> reject forever.
> Although he causes grief, he will have compassion
> according to the abundance of his steadfast love;
> for he does not willingly afflict
> or grieve anyone.

On the whole, the presence of this way of thinking in Joel tends to underline his affinities with Israel's cultic traditions. One may also recall the words of another prophet who had associations with the cult: Ezekiel. (Cf. Ezek. 18:32, "For I have no pleasure in the death of anyone, says the Lord YHWH. Turn, then, and live.") The use of lament forms in Israel makes sense against the background of this kind of theological belief. YHWH is a God who is willing to respond to heartfelt prayer; he is not implacable.[63]

The Outpouring of the Spirit

Individually, the oracles in the second half of Joel manifest a number of important theological features. In 2:28–29 we meet the famous prophecy of the outpouring of God's spirit on "all flesh" (see the commentary). This speaks of the extension of spiritual endowment and empowerment in the end time from selected persons (such as the prophets) to all the people, young and old, men and women, free and slaves alike. This kind of democratization of the gift of the spirit is one of the most remarkable ideas in the book of Joel, whatever exactly endowment with the spirit is taken to mean. Its consequence is the knowledge that comes through dreams and visions, which in this period probably means knowledge of the future and perhaps also of the secrets of the divine realm.[64] There is no reserve here toward the idea of dreams, such as we find in Jer. 23:25–32, but they are treated as a normal expression of being filled with the spirit.

---

63. Cf. also the comments on theodicy, pp. 35–36 below.
64. Cf. Barton, *Oracles of God*, pp. 235–65.

Judgment on the Nations

Another great idea in the second part of Joel is that of divine judgment on foreign nations, which is characteristic of prophetic texts from the postexilic period. (Cf. the "oracles against the nations" in Isaiah 13–23, Jeremiah 46–51, and Ezekiel 25–39.) What is remarkable here is that the nations are all gathered together to a single place, the "valley of Jehoshaphat," or "valley of decision" (*ḥārûṣ*), where YHWH acts as their judge. We are clearly here no longer in the realms of even thinkable political reality but in a world where everyday things have been radically transformed. This is true also of the miraculous fruitfulness of the land in 3:18, which is reminiscent of Ezekiel's vision in Ezekiel 47. Whereas in Joel 1:2–2:27 it is almost touch-and-go whether YHWH will consent to spare the people and repair the damage caused by the locusts—though this is eventually promised—in this passage YHWH is unequivocally pro-Israel and opposed to foreign nations.

Older commentators, who saw the greatness of the classical prophets consisting in their message of universalism, generally saw this as a sad decline into "Jewish particularism." Thus Merx calls Joel "fleshly and Jewishly particularistic."[65] Modern writers do not hurl this kind of abuse at Judaism and are more aware that the development of Jewish monotheism could not have happened without the sense that YHWH was passionately attached to the people he had called: the election of Israel is not an optional extra in Old Testament religious thought, nor is it something that the great prophets rose "above." It remains true that the theology of Joel is extremely Israel centered, seeing foreigners as largely the enemies of Israel and hence of YHWH, and this is characteristic of prophecies in the Second Temple period—the more striking in a time when there was little outside threat to the peace and security of Judah as a small Persian province.

7. Reading the Book of Joel as a Whole

So far I have been discussing the theological ideas of the two parts of Joel separately, and this is in line with my argument that we are dealing with two originally distinct collections of oracles. Since, however, a majority of recent commentators regard the book as a unity, it makes sense to ask if any unifying theology can be seen as overarching the two sections.[66] One might find such a theology in the idea of the day of YHWH, seen as an event that has both small-scale manifestations (the locust plague, perhaps an invasion, perhaps a drought)

---

65. "fleischlich, jüdisch-particularistisch"; Merx, *Die Prophetie des Joel*, p. 21.

66. Prinsloo, *Theology of the Book of Joel*, regards this as the only correct task for a commentator on Joel.

Introduction 35

and large-scale implications—judgment on the entire world and the transformation of nature. If the book is to be read as a unified whole, this idea of YHWH's intervention to judge yet also to save Israel may form a useful pivot around which the message can be seen as turning. (See the commentary on 1:15.) T. B. Dozeman goes even further, arguing that we should read Joel in the context of the whole corpus of the "Book of the Twelve." In that context, the particularism we are right to see in Joel is mitigated by, for example, the book of Jonah: "When we read the texts in this direction (from Joel to Jonah), it is clear that the universal scope of Yahweh's compassion toward Nineveh in Jonah complements the exclusive focus of Joel."[67] The same might be true of a "canonical reading," in which the universal power and scope of YHWH's activity, as witnessed to by the second half of Joel, are seen as benign rather than vindictive in character, once such texts as Jonah are allowed to moderate the more uncompromisingly Israel-centered outlook of Joel taken alone.

A particularly interesting theological interpretation of the book of Joel as a whole is put forward by J. L. Crenshaw under the title "Who Knows What YHWH Will Do?"[68] Crenshaw sees the central concern of the book as theodicy. How, he asks, can Joel call God merciful, when the locust plague and other events of the "day of YHWH" bear clear witness to God's hostility? The answer, he thinks, is found in 2:14: "Who knows? He may turn and relent, and leave a blessing behind him." YHWH's unpredictability, which can be perceived as threatening, also contains the seeds of hope, for he may turn out, when he acts, to do so in love and mercy just as much as in hostility and anger. The question Joel addresses is that of the goodness and reliability of God. But the book does not resolve the problem in theory, though in practice it shows that the God who does visit the earth in judgment will in the end be found faithful to Israel. Like Job, Joel is not given a solution to the problem of discerning a good divine purpose in what happens on earth, but he is assured that the eventual outcome of all things will be good. God does not reveal his reasons for acting (and Crenshaw stresses, for example, that even God's judgment is not said in Joel to be the result of human sin), but the actions YHWH performs in the end turn out to be good for Israel.

Crenshaw's suggestion does raise the question of whether the book of Joel, in its finished form, should really be seen as prophecy at all, and not rather as a work about theodicy, like Job and perhaps also like Jonah. We recall Dentan's proposal that the passage that, in a sense, forms the book's heart, 2:12–14, is

---

67. T. B. Dozeman, "Inner-biblical Interpretation of Yahweh's Gracious and Compassionate Character," *JBL* 108 (1989): 207–23; the quotation is from p. 216.
68. J. L. Crenshaw, "Who Knows What Yahweh Will Do? The Character of God in the Book of Joel," in *Fortunate the Eyes That See: Essays in Honor of David Noel Freedman in Celebration of His Seventieth Birthday*, ed. A. B. Beek, A. H. Bartelt, and C. A. Franke, Grand Rapids 1995, pp. 185–96.

akin to wisdom in its spirit. Along such lines, one might argue that the redactor of Joel has taken a whole series of prophecies—perhaps from different periods—and blended them together to form a text whose main thrust is to assert the goodness and mercy of YHWH toward the people in all times of crisis, small or great, and the eventual vindication of YHWH's character in the events of the end time. This would be consistent with my own proposal that the book as it stands is not focused on a particular time of crisis but is meant to bring comfort and consolation by emphasizing that God is in control of all things and will carry out God's good purposes in God's own good time.[69]

---

69. Cf. R. E. Clements, "Patterns in the Prophetic Canon," in *Canon and Authority: Essays in Old Testament Religion and Theology,* Philadelphia 1977, pp. 42–55; also in idem, *Old Testament Prophecy: From Oracles to Canon,* Louisville 1996, pp. 191–202.

COMMENTARY ON JOEL

Superscription
Joel 1:1

1:1 The word of the LORD that came to Joel son of Pethuel.

Commentary

Nothing is known of Joel or his father (or ancestor) Pethuel beyond this verse. Unlike most other superscriptions in the books of the prophets, no information is given beyond this indication of the name of the prophet's father, and there is no attempt to contextualize the book in any particular period. This contrasts sharply with Amos, for example ("The words of Amos, who was among the shepherds of Tekoa, which he saw concerning Israel in the days of King Uzziah of Judah and in the days of King Jeroboam son of Joash of Israel, two years before the earthquake," Amos 1:1). A similar phenomenon can be found in Jonah 1:1, however ("Now the word of the LORD came to Jonah son of Amittai"), and in Malachi, which gives even less information ("An oracle. The word of the LORD to Israel by Malachi," Mal. 1:1). All the superscriptions must be regarded as redactional, and it is interesting that they have not been fully standardized.

The name Joel means "YHWH is God," virtually equivalent in meaning to Elijah, in which the same elements (YHWH and El) appear in the opposite order.[1] The name is common in the genealogies in Chronicles (1 Chron. 4:35; 5:4, 8, 12; 6:33, 36; 7:3; 11:38; 15:7, 11, 17; 23:8; 26:22; 27:20; 2 Chron. 29:12), Ezra (10:43), and Nehemiah (11:9). The only occurrence in a purportedly preexilic text is at 1 Sam. 8:2, where it is the name of one of Samuel's sons. If the genealogies were made up by the Chronicler, then we may regard the name as more important in the postexilic era, which would be consistent with a postexilic date for the book. But the genealogies may rest on much older material. Pethuel does not occur elsewhere in the Hebrew Bible, though the LXX has assimilated it to the name of Rebekah's father, Bethuel (Greek *Bathouēl*; see Gen. 22:22–23; 24:15, 24, 47, 50). The identity of Joel and Pethuel can only be guessed at: some have thought Joel was a priest (see the introduction) because of his evident involvement in the Jerusalem cult, but this must remain uncertain.

What is meant by saying that "the word of YHWH came" to Joel? Does it imply that the prophet heard a voice, as in the stories about Elijah (e.g., 1 Kings

---

1. Cf. Bewer, *Commentary on Obadiah and Joel*, p. 75.

19:13)? It is interesting to compare the superscriptions to the other prophetic books. The phrase "the word of YHWH came" occurs in Hos. 1:1; Jonah 1:1; Micah 1:1; Zeph. 1:1; Hag. 1:1; Zech. 1:1; Amos 1:1 has "the words of Amos"; Jer. 1:1 has "the words of Jeremiah"; Nahum 1:1 has "the oracle [*maśśā'*] of Nineveh"; and Mal. 1:1 has "An oracle [*maśśā'*]. The word of YHWH." But an alternative possibility is a reference to vision: thus Isa. 1:1, "The vision of Isaiah son of Amoz which he saw"; Ezek. 1:1, "I saw visions of God"; Obadiah 1, "The vision of Obadiah." Most interesting of all is Isa. 2:1, "The *word* that Isaiah son of Amoz *saw*." Sometimes "hearing" and "seeing" have been contrasted in discussions of the prophets, and it may be emphasized that the "classical" prophets relied on the *word* of God whereas their cultic predecessors and contemporaries trusted in visions. Such a contrast appears to be drawn explicitly in Jer. 23:28, where Jeremiah opposes false prophets who claim to have had "dreams" (admittedly not necessarily the same as visions) with the true prophet who has the word of YHWH: "Let the prophet who has a dream tell the dream, but let the one who has my word speak my word faithfully." Perhaps the preexilic classical prophets did, in general, draw such a distinction. But the redactional superscriptions of their books do not appear to regard the difference as significant, and the editors of Isaiah were certainly not trying to diminish the prophet by describing the content of his book as visions. The postexilic conception of a prophet is that he both hears and sees what God wants him to know, and there is no significant difference between the two states.[2]

Not all the contents of Joel consist of divine "words": there are also descriptions, especially of the locust plague, which are the prophet's own words (e.g., 1:6–7); laments uttered to rather than by God (e.g., 1:19); and exhortations by the prophet referring to God in the third person (e.g., 2:23). This is the usual pattern in prophetic books, which do not represent unbroken divine speech any more than they consist entirely of visions—in spite of the superscriptions which might lead us to expect this.

First Lament Cycle
Joel 1:2–20

1. The Disaster (1:2–4)

1:2   Hear this, old men,
          hearken, all inhabitants of the land!

---

2. Cf. Barton, *Oracles of God*, pp. 116–28.

First Lament Cycle 41

> Has this ever happened in your days,
> or in the days of your ancestors?
> 3 Tell your sons about it,
> and let your sons tell their sons,
> and their sons another generation.[a]
>
> 4 What was left by the cutting locust,
> the swarming locust has eaten.
> And what was left by the swarming locust,
> the hopping locust has eaten,
> and what was left by the hopping locust,
> the destroying locust has eaten.

a. *BHS* proposes that we should read 3b as referring to only two generations, treating "their children, and their children" as a dittograph—thus: "let your children tell another generation." But three generations are referred to in Ps. 78:3–6, and there seems no overwhelming reason to emend the text here.

Commentary

[1:2–3] The prophetic word begins with a call to "hear," which is a common way of beginning both prophetic oracles (cf. Isa. 1:2; Hos. 5:1; Micah 1:2; 3:9) and "wisdom" speeches (Ps. 49:1; 78:1). Wolff indeed maintains that the use of such a form of address shows the prophets' indebtedness to wisdom forms,[3] but this seems hard to demonstrate given the ubiquity of such imperatives, which already appear in the antique Song of Deborah (Judg. 5:3).

Is the call addressed to the old or to the "elders"? If the latter, then we might have here *zĕqēnîm*, "elders," as a technical term for the people who governed the postexilic state of Judah at least from the time of Ezra (Ezra 10:8), and thereby a confirmation of the postexilic dating of Joel.[4] Crenshaw, however, follows Wellhausen in thinking that the reference is simply to the old ("old-timers"): "Joel's interest lies in accumulated years, not in special rank and privilege. He appeals to those individuals in society who had the longest memory."[5] This seems reasonable in light of the way in which the address continues: "Has such a thing happened in your days, or in the days of your ancestors?" The truth is, however, that neither meaning provides a very good parallelism with "all inhabitants of the land," though in favor of the idea that the *zĕqēnîm* here are "ruling elders," one might recall Amos 1:5, 8, where "the inhabitants" of the

---

3. Wolff, *Joel and Amos*, pp. 25–26.
4. Thus Wolff, *Joel and Amos*, p. 25; cf. L. L. Grabbe, *Judaism from Cyrus to Hadrian*, London 1994, for details of the polity of the Second Temple period.
5. Crenshaw, *Joel*, p. 86.

land are parallel to "the one who holds the scepter." I am inclined to follow Crenshaw and note that the reference to the memory of two generations is balanced by the imperative to pass the message on to two further generations, or even three.

Are verses 2 and 3 part of the first lament cycle, or are they an introduction to the entire book, or at least to its first part (1:4–2:27)?[6] On the whole, I prefer to see them as part of the first cycle, paralleling the imperatives in 2:1. It can be argued that the prophet is foretelling a devastation so total that there will not be further generations, but on the view that he is talking simply about the immediate consequences of a locust plague, this problem does not arise; the disaster is unprecedented and will go down in history, but it is not a final destruction of Israel. There is no need, with Wolff, to think that the reference to several generations implies "the transition from prophecy to apocalypticism, with the end time events that have broken into the present."[7] Reference to events as unprecedented and incomparable seems to have been, as Crenshaw notes, a *topos* in the ancient world, as indeed it still is today. That in fact there was, and is, nothing in the least unprecedented about a plague of locusts is neither here nor there! The experience is so terrible that it seems at the time that no such thing can ever have happened before or will ever happen again.

[4] This verse has been the subject of very detailed investigation. It contains four different words for "locust": *gāzām, 'arbeh, yeleq,* and *ḥāsîl* (v. 4; cf. 2:25). It has long been a question what difference, if any, there is between the four terms, and in particular whether they refer to four different species of locust or to four stages in the development of the insect, as first suggested by K. A. Credner.[8] There is a full discussion of this topic in the commentaries: see the lengthy discussions in Wolff[9] and in Simkins.[10]

It seems to me that, whichever theory one follows, the practical effect of the fourfold naming of the locusts is primarily rhetorical, rather than being intended as an entomological description of the progress of a locust plague.[11] By heaping up names for the locusts, the prophet emphasizes the totality of the destruction they wreak.

But the description of the locusts in 1:1–7 and 2:2–11 raises difficult questions of interpretation. In both cases it is possible to argue either that the locusts are intended literally or that they symbolize a human army.[12] A metaphorical

---

6. Thus Rudolph.
7. Wolff, *Joel and Amos,* p. 26.
8. See K. A. Credner, *Der Prophet Joel übersetzt und erklärt,* Halle 1831.
9. Wolff, *Joel and Amos, ad loc.*
10. Simkins, *Yahweh's Activity in History and Nature,* pp. 101–20.
11. Thus already Merx, *Die Prophetie des Joel,* p. 14.
12. For the various options, see the discussion in P. R. Andiñach, "The Locusts in the Message of *Joel," VT* 42 (1992): 433–41.

First Lament Cycle

interpretation of both passages was normal in the precritical era and can already be found in the Targum, which renders "peoples, tongues, governments, and kingdoms" (*'mmy' wlisny' sltwny' wmlkwta*), and in the LXX(Q): *aiguptioi babulōnioi assurioi hellēnes*. The latter interpretation is already found in Jerome.[13] Modern commentators do not suppose there is an allegorical meaning here in terms of four world empires but sometimes do think the locusts stand for an invading army[14] and point out that ancient Near Eastern texts provide evidence that it was not uncommon to compare the march of an army to an invasion of locusts.

> Like the locusts that dwell on the steppe,
> Like grasshoppers on the border of the desert.—
> March a day and a second;
> A third, a fourth day;
> A fifth, a sixth day—
> Lo! at the sun on the seventh,
> Thou arrivest at Udum the Great,
> Even at Udum the Grand.
> Now do thou *attack* the villages,
> Harass the towns.
>   (CTA 14:103-11)

... my warriors swarmed like locusts out of the ships (and) on to the banks and brought about this defeat. (Sennacherib)[15]

The imagery occurs elsewhere in the Hebrew Bible. In Judg. 6:5 the Midianites and Amalekites used to come up against Israel "as thick as locusts" (cf. also 7:12), while Jer. 51:14 threatens Babylon that YHWH will "fill you with troops like a swarm of locusts." And Crenshaw cites a Sumerian text:

> Numerous like locusts
> they came striding,
> stretched out their arms in the desert for him
> like gazelle and wild ass snares,
> nothing escaped their arms,
> nobody did their arms leave.[16]

---

13. Cf. Y.-M. Duval, "Jérôme et les prophètes: histoire, prophétie, actualité et actualisation dans les commentaires de Nahum, Michée, Abdias et Joël," *Salamanca Conference Volume* ed. J. A. Emerton, (SVT 36), Leiden 1985, pp. 108–31.

14. Thus already E. Sellin, *Das Zwölfprophetenbuch* (KAT 12:1), 3d ed., Leipzig 1930; cf. G. S. Ogden and R. R. Deutsch, *A Promise of Hope: A Call to Obedience (Joel and Malachi)*, Grand Rapids 1987.

15. Both quotations are taken from Andiñach, "Locusts," pp. 438–39.

16. Crenshaw, *Joel*, p. 96, citing T. Jacobsen, *The Harps That Once...*, London and New Haven 1987, p. 379.

Perhaps we should, however, see some originality in Joel's reversal of the image, making locusts seem like an invading army. As so often in the prophets, a familiar trope is given new life, in this case by being reversed. I do not know of any other case inside or outside the Bible in which literal locusts become a metaphorical army.

Nevertheless, some have thought that a literal army *is* intended. If that is so, then its identity will depend on the date we assign to Joel. If the work is from the late preexilic period, then the Babylonians will be the prime candidates. But if it is postexilic, it becomes much harder to find a convincing identity for the army, since Judah was not seriously threatened by any hostile power during the Persian period, and we have seen reason to doubt whether Joel is as late as the wars of Alexander and his successors.

In favor of the military interpretation, it may be noted that the locusts are described as a "nation" (*gôy*) in 1:6. But, provided we think that the locusts have the same meaning in chapters 1 and 2, the description in chapter 2 seems to me difficult to reconcile with the idea that they stand for an army. For they are *compared* with an army in 2:4–9: "Their *appearance* is like the appearance of horses, and *like* war-horses they charge. Their sound is *like* the sound of chariots, they leap on the tops of the mountains, *like* the sound of a flame of fire devouring the stubble, *like* a powerful people drawn up for battle. . . . *Like* warriors they run, *like* soldiers they scale a wall." One can hardly describe an army as being like a plague of locusts while saying that the locusts in question are like an army, unless one is very incompetent in using metaphors, which the Old Testament prophets certainly were not. This passage seems best explained as referring to a real locust plague, which is vividly likened to an enemy invasion in its devastating consequences.[17]

V. A. Hurowitz has pointed to a striking parallel to the Joel text in an Akkadian hymn, Sargon II's *Hymn to Nanaya*. This mentions two kinds of locust, the *erebu* and the *zirziru,* and Hurowitz comments: "The mention of two types of locust indicating locusts of many types fulfils the same function as Joel's enumeration of four species of locusts at the beginning and end of his oracle (1:4; 2:25)."[18] The locusts "cut off the daily offerings of the gods and goddesses" (cf. Joel 1:9, 13), and they destroy grain and dry up orchards. They are described as follows:

> The evil locust which destroys the crop/grain,
> The wicked dwarf-locust which dries up the orchards,
> which cuts off the regular offerings of the gods and goddesses—

---

17. Thus J. A. Thompson, "Joel's Locusts in the Light of Near Eastern Parallels," *JNES* 14 (1955): 52–55.

18. V. A. Hurowitz, "Joel's Locust Plague in Light of Sargon II's Hymn to Nanaya," *JBL* 112 (1993): 597–603.

(Verily) Enlil listens to you, and Tutu is before you—
may by your command it be turned into nothing.

Nothing, of course, can be proved about Joel from this parallel, which is remote in time and place, but it may suggest that laments for the depredations caused by locusts could exist in cult hymns in the ancient Near East, and consequently that a literal interpretation of Joel's locusts is in order.

When we have said that the locusts are intended literally, in the sense that they are not simply a metaphor for an army, we have still not resolved all the questions about their interpretation. We shall see that some scholars think the real situation envisaged in chapters 1 and 2 is a drought,[19] and Bergler argues that the image of the consuming locust is merely a graphic way of talking about the drought.[20] It is sometimes said that drought and locust plague cannot occur together,[21] since locusts will obviously not invade an area where there is no vegetation, and hence that one or the other theme must be secondary: Bergler's interpretation avoids having to delete the locusts by turning them into a symbol for the drought. Though this might work for the first chapter of Joel (even here it seems to me implausible), it is hard to see how it can apply to chapter 2, where the locusts are the main point of interest.

More significant, it may be asked whether Joel is thinking of a real locust plague or is using the language of an invasion by locusts simply as a vivid way of talking about divine judgment—rather as Ezek. 14:21 refers to YHWH's four "deadly acts of judgment" as sword, famine, wild animals, and pestilence, or as Jer. 15:3 speaks of four kinds of destroyers: "the sword to kill, the dogs to drag away, and the birds of the air and the wild animals of the earth to devour and destroy." In the same way, we might think, Joel is talking about four kinds of locust but thinking more generally about an impending divine punishment. F. E. Deist speaks in this vein of a "*literary* world of calamities to serve as metaphors describing the character of the day of the Lord."[22] Brevard Childs similarly argues that there are a number of features that do not match a real locust plague, and that we should see the locusts as a vaguer symbol for the general destruction that will be wrought on the day of YHWH—part of a general return of chaos.[23] Especially if we think of the whole book of Joel as a unity, this more "eschatological" interpretation fits well with the oracles in 2:28–3:21 in which a new world order after widespread destruction seems to be envisaged.

Wolff tries to get the best of both worlds here by proposing that chapter 1 concerns a literal locust plague while in chapter 2 the locusts have turned into

---

19. See p. 54, below.
20. Bergler, *Joel als Schriftprophet*.
21. See Deist, "Parallels and Reinterpretation."
22. Ibid., p. 64.
23. B. S. Childs, "The Enemy from the North," *JBL* 68 (1959): 187–98.

semiapocalyptic agents of divine destruction. They are in a sense an army but not a literal, physical army, rather YHWH's eschatological army, which will carry out the divine judgment on the nations. Like the locusts in Rev. 9:3–6, they are mythological creatures that embody the destructive power of God, which will be manifested on the day of YHWH, understood as the moment when the end time begins. This has the advantage that it helps explain the escalation in terror from chapter 1 to chapter 2, as the more prosaically described insects of 1:4–7 turn into supernatural agents of destruction in 2:2–11.

If I am uncertain about Wolff's reading, it is because of the close parallelism between the scenarios of chapters 1 and 2. In both cases the locust plague (and perhaps also a drought) leads to a call to lament, and it is not until 2:18 that we meet with YHWH's response, which is not to enact an eschatological judgment but to restore the crops that the locusts have destroyed; eschatological themes do not clearly appear until the second half of the book, from 2:28 onward. It therefore seems probable that the references to locusts are literal throughout. By chapter 2 they are certainly described in exaggerated terms, but this is to convey the full terror of the plague, not to make them into eschatological beasts. Even the darkening of sun, moon, and stars (2:10) seems an acceptable hyperbole for the effect of a cloud of locusts covering the countryside, rather than a motif that needs to imply "eschatology." It was normal in any case in the ancient world to suppose that crucial events in the history of a nation might be accompanied by heavenly portents, and the locust plague here described certainly counts as a major national event, even if it happened in "nature" rather than in "history."[24]

Two points might be made here. The first is that Joel, unlike the preexilic prophets, is deeply concerned with the cult: his natural response to national disaster is to call for a fast and to get the priests to implore the favor of YHWH. Although the occasion seems to me overwhelmingly likely to have been a locust plague, the language of invitation to cultic lament is naturally somewhat stylized and may well include details not closely related to the specifics of what the locusts have done; hence, perhaps, the references to drought (1:17) and the pitiful lowing of cattle (1:18).

This is reminiscent of the psalms of lament, where we often find features that are, strictly speaking, incompatible at a literal level (e.g., Psalm 69, where the speaker is submerged in a flood but has a dry throat!) or a tendency to list afflictions from a stock range, even though they are not all appropriate to every user of the psalm. (Think of the psalmist in Psalm 22, who is surrounded by dogs, wild oxen, and bulls all at the same time, as well as suffering assaults by human enemies and the ravages of hunger.) Joel seems at home within this tradition of

---

24. Essentially I agree with Simkins, *Yahweh's Activity in History* and "God, History and the Natural World," that this dichotomy is a false one when discussing the prophets.

First Lament Cycle

prayer, and we should not press every detail of his description of the effects of the locust plague as if he were performing some kind of official enquiry into the state of the country.

Second, it is characteristic of the prophets to take some particular incident or object and to see in it a sign of the purposes of God. Amos's basket of summer fruit (Amos 8:1–3) or Jeremiah's almond branch (Jer. 1:11–12) are examples. In these cases, some casually seen object suggests, through wordplay, a deeper meaning and points to the coming of divine judgment. In the case of Joel it may well be that a locust plague triggered consideration of the reality of God's interventions in the affairs of Judah, leading him to describe what was at one level a local and temporary disaster in terms of a dramatic divine action in human history. This can account for the hyperbole of chapter 2 without the need to follow Wolff in calling this an eschatological prophecy—unless we are using the word *eschatological* merely to emphasize that the intervention is God's, not a "purely natural" catastrophe (but who in the ancient world believed that catastrophes were ever purely natural?). Chapter 2 is a superb literary description of a locust plague, using language that emphasizes the extremity of panic to which it reduces those who suffer from it. It need not be a description of some future eschatological event.

Some scholars have argued, with some plausibility, that Joel describes two *separate* locust invasions, one that has already happened (in chapter 1) and one that is still to come (in chapter 2). If we treat 2:1b, with its statement that the day of YHWH is "near" (*qārôb*), as an integral part of the text and not a gloss, then it does look as though the locust plague here is predicted rather than actual. This is, however, at variance with 2:18, which implies that YHWH has heard the people's prayer and is about to restore the prosperity of the land.

It is difficult in Joel to decide what is the moment of utterance, whether just before, during, or just after the invasion of the locusts, and this is made more difficult by the prophetic tendency to describe future events as though they have already happened. This is the phenomenon that scholars used to treat as if it were a special feature of the Hebrew language, the so-called prophetic perfect. Perhaps the entire description of the invasion by locusts in both chapters is a prediction of an imminent disaster rather than a description of it once it has happened. I do not see how we are to tell. The possibility that two separate locust plagues are meant could be implied in 2:25, "I will repay you for the *years* that the swarming locust has eaten" (though on "the years" [*haššānîm*] here, see the commentary below).

One problem for the literal interpretation of the locusts is the reference to the "northerner" (*haṣṣĕpônî*) in 2:20—note that NRSV's "northern *army*" represents an interpretation of the Hebrew. In an important article on the "foe from the 'north'" in Jeremiah, D. J. Reimer points out that the term *north* is generally nonspecific and is more likely to refer to *ṣpn*, the mountain of the gods, than to "the north" in a literal, geographical sense.[25] There is, geographically speaking, no "foe from the north" in the Old Testament.[26] The "northerner" in Joel 2:20 is thus likely to mean "the great enemy," not any specific enemy army that came literally from the north, and so there is no need to cast around for possible candidates such as the Babylonians. The question is whether *haṣṣĕpônî*, "the northerner," could have been used as the designation for an army of locusts. If not, then we should have to think again about our rejection of the "army" interpretation of the enemy, at least in chapter 2. But it seems to me there is no reason it could not have been so used, the more so as the locusts are explicitly compared to a human army throughout the description in 2:2–11, and this could be merely an extension of that imagery.

2. The Call to Lament (1:5–14)

5 Wake up, you drinkers, and weep;
    and wail, all you that drink wine,
because of the sweet wine,
    for it is cut off from your mouth.

6 For a nation has come up against my land;
    it is powerful and beyond counting;
its teeth are lions' teeth,
    and it has the fangs of a lioness.

7 It has turned my vines into a desolation,
    and my fig trees into splinters;
it has stripped off their bark and thrown it down;
    their branches have turned white.

8 Lament[a] like a virgin girded with sackcloth
    for the husband of her youth.

9 The grain offering and the drink offering are cut off
    from the house of YHWH.
The priests mourn[b]
    the ministers of YHWH.

10 The fields are devastated,
    the ground mourns;
for the grain is devastated,
    the wine dries up,
    the oil fails.

11 Be ashamed, you farm workers,
    wail, you vinedressers,

---

25. D. J. Reimer, "The 'Foe' and the 'North' in Jeremiah," *ZAW* 101 (1989): 223–32.
26. Though see W. H. Schmidt, "*safôn* Norden," *THAT* 2 (1976): 575–82.

First Lament Cycle 49

  over the wheat and the barley,
   for the crops of the field are ruined.
12 The vine is withered,
   the fig tree fails to yield.
  Pomegranate, palm, and apple—
   all the trees of the field are dried up;
  surely, joy withers away
   from humankind.

13 Put on sackcloth and lament, priests;
   wail, ministers of the altar.
  Come, pass the night in sackcloth,
   ministers of my God!c
  For grain offering and drink offering
   are withheld from the house of your God.

14 Sanctify a fast,
   call an assembly.
  Gather the elders
   and all the inhabitants of the land
  to the house of YHWH your God,
   and cry out to YHWH.

 a. "Lament," *'ĕlî*, is unique as a feminine singular imperative in this section of Joel, where otherwise masculine plurals are used. It is appropriate to the simile it introduces ("like a virgin"), but its oddness has led to some suggestions for reconstructing the text. The LXX has *pros me*, which presumably means the Greek translators read it as *'ēlay* but confirms that they had the same consonantal text as we have; but it adds *thrēnēson*, "lament to me." This could be explained as an addition that was necessary to provide an imperative once *'ĕlî* had been misconstrued as meaning "to me," but it could also suggest that the translators had a longer text that could have read *'ēlay hēlîlû*, "lament to me." This would then be perfectly parallel to the other imperatives of this section ("Wake up," v. 5; "Be dismayed," v. 11; and possibly—see below—"mourn," v. 9b). Wolff proposes this emendation, though noting that it "must remain tentative, especially since the simile in v 8 leads us rather to expect a feminine singular addressee."[27] He also suggests that v. 9b might be moved forward to precede v. 8 and repointed as an imperative: "Mourn [*'iblû*], O priests." The advantage of this reconstruction is that it produces three strophes of the same structure, 1:5-7; 1:9b, 8, 9a, 10; and 1:11-12, each beginning with an imperative. The second strophe will then run:

 Mourn, you priests,
  lament, you ministers of YHWH,

27. Wolff, *Joel and Amos*, p. 18.

>   like a virgin dressed in sackcloth
>   for the husband of her youth.
>   The grain offering and the drink offering are cut off
>   from the house of the LORD.
>   The fields are devastated,
>   the ground mourns;
>   for the grain is destroyed,
>   the wine dries up,
>   the oil fails.

This makes perfectly good sense and could be what the prophet wrote. The present state of the text can be defended, however. The LXX may, as we have seen, have been misled by the consonantal text and then have inserted an imperative itself; and there is no textual or versional support for Wolff's rearrangement of the text, which thus remains hypothetical, though attractive. The overall import of the passage is not in any case greatly affected, one way or the other.

b. It is possible that we should emend "they mourn" (*'ābĕlû*) to an imperative, "Mourn, O priests" (*'iblû*), though this is less appropriate if we keep the MT's arrangement than if we follow Wolff in placing v. 9b in front of v. 8. "The grain offering and the drink offering are cut off from the house of YHWH; the priests mourn" makes excellent sense.

c. "My God" is striking, implying that here at least the speaker is the prophet rather than YHWH. But the Greek version has simply "God" (*theō*[i]), which makes one wonder whether MT is a mistake (though followed by the Vulgate, *ministri dei mei*), pointing an original "*'ĕlōhî* or *'ĕlōah* as *'ĕlōhay* (Bewer, *Commentary on Obadiah and Joel*, 86), or simply losing the final *mem* of an original *'ĕlōhîm*. There is no reason, however, why the prophet should not have referred to YHWH here as "my God," even though in the next line he says "*your* God."

Commentary

[1:5] "Drunkards" (NRSV) may be unfair here for *šikkôrîm*, which from the parallel "you wine-drinkers" may simply be meant to convey "imbibers" (thus Crenshaw). This is not part of the prophetic tradition of condemning drunkenness, a tradition that goes back to Amos (6:6) and Isaiah (5:11–13; 28:1–8) and is also represented in wisdom teaching (Prov. 20:1, 23:29–35). Rather, it emphasizes the parlous state of the country, in which there is no wine to be had because of the stripping of the vines by the locusts (*'āsîs* is *fresh* wine). This is not a punishment for drunkenness but a deprivation of one of the pleasures of life: the loss of wine should alert the hearers to the scale of the disaster, if indeed they need any reminder.

The fact that the prophet seems to think it necessary to call on his hearers to "awake" seems to me to imply that this whole passage is to be taken as a prediction of a *coming* locust plague (couched in the "perfect" tense, as is so common in prophetic oracles), rather than as a description of something that is

First Lament Cycle 51

already apparent to all; compare Amos's "Fallen, no more to rise, is maiden Israel" (Amos 5:2), a funeral lament over someone the audience *does not yet realize* is about to die. If this is correct, then Joel, like the preexilic prophets, was concerned with foretelling the (immediate) future, perhaps when the signs of what was coming were as yet apparent to no one else. If this is felt to imply "supernatural" knowledge of the future and is objected to on rationalistic grounds, then it would be possible to say that the locust plague was already a fact but the wine-drinkers addressed in this verse had not yet realized its implications. But did anyone in the ancient world lack understanding of what a locust plague would mean? Crenshaw seems to imply that the drinkers were oblivious to what was happening around them: "Either the contentment resulting from drinking sweet wine under one's fig tree and vine or lethargy induced by constant consumption of intoxicating drink (cf. Hos. 4:11) furnishes an effective symbol for the national oblivion to divine action concealed in the locust hordes."[28] But if the invasion had already started, this is fairly implausible.

[6–7] These verses explicitly describe the onrush of the locust plague. The locusts are described as a *gôy,* "nation." (In 2:2, assuming this also refers to them, they are a *'am,* "people.") It should be noted that already in this chapter the locusts are described in more than realistic terms ("its teeth are lions' teeth, and it has the fangs of a lioness"); the contrast with chapter 2 is not so great as is implied by Wolff, who sees chapter 1 as concerning a literal locust invasion, chapter 2 as describing an eschatological foe. The "nation" of locusts is seen as similar to an invading army, an image for the locust also found in Prov. 30:27: "the locusts have no king, yet all of them march in rank." It aptly sums up the terrible efficiency of a plague of locusts, elaborated in 2:6–9. Duhm thought that vv. 6–7 referred to a literal army, practicing a "scorched earth" policy, but it seems far more likely that the prophet has the locusts in mind. The innumerability of locusts as well as their ruthless devastation of crops made a comparison with an invading army natural enough, and in the ancient Near East, armies were certainly compared to locusts.[29]

The fact that the locusts strip the vines explains why it is to the wine-drinkers that the prophet speaks first, but the association of vines with fig trees is proverbial in the Old Testament, the juxtaposition usually signifying peace and prosperity (e.g., Micah 4:4). Here the prophet trades on this association, presenting the destruction of vine and fig tree as a deliberate reversal of divine blessing. We do not have to see here "the special signs of the time of salvation,"[30] if that means the signs of *eschatological* blessing: sitting at peace under vine and fig

---

28. Crenshaw, *Joel,* p. 94.
29. See the examples cited in Simkins, *Yahweh's Activity in History,* pp. 126–27; and Thompson, "Joel's Locusts"; and cf. above, pp. 43–45.
30. Wolff, *Joel and Amos,* p. 29.

tree is also said of past or present blessedness in Old Testament narrative (e.g., 1 Kings 4:25; 2 Kings 18:31).

Interestingly, the vines and fig trees are described as "my" vines and "my" fig trees, just as the locusts have invaded "my" land. It is possible to see the speaker here as YHWH, and there is no reason why YHWH should not be the speaker throughout chapter 1, at least until v. 15 (and even there, YHWH could be dictating the words that the people are to speak). A second possibility is that vv. 6–7 are what the "drinkers" of v. 5 are being instructed to say as they weep and wail. In that case, "for" (*kî*) might instead be rendered "indeed" or "surely," as also in 1:12. Perhaps more likely, however, the prophet is identifying himself strongly with "his" people in their sufferings (cf. "my people" in Jer. 14:17), and we should see his own voice here.

[8–10] The exact reference of the simile "like a virgin dressed in sackcloth for the husband of her youth" has struck commentators as puzzling. The phrase "the husband of her youth," *ba'al nĕ'ûrêhā*, does not occur elsewhere in the Bible, though there is a close parallel in the expression "the wife of your youth," *'ēšet nĕ'ûrekā*, in Prov. 5:18; Isa. 54:6; Mal. 2:14–15. The most obvious sense would be the husband she had in her youth, that is, her first husband. But there seems to be a problem then with *bĕtûlâ* if we translate that "virgin," since a virgin in ancient Israel can hardly have had a husband.

One solution is to argue that *bĕtûlâ* does not mean a virgin but a woman of marriageable age, whether a virgin or not and whether in fact married or not.[31] In that case the problem disappears. The other explanation is that during a period of betrothal preceding a marriage the woman, though still a virgin, was already also regarded as a wife. Deuteronomy 22:23–24 probably supports this theory, since it treats intercourse with a betrothed virgin as adultery: engagement has for some purposes the same legal status as marriage.[32] In either case, I do not think the passage is obscure. The nation is called on to lament, with what in their culture would have been regarded as one particularly extreme form of grief: that of a woman, either engaged or not long married, whose husband had been killed. Wearing sackcloth (*śaq*), a garment of goat's hair, round the waist is a sign of grief, penitence, or fasting (cf. Judith 8:5; 9:1). The point of the simile is to emphasize the extreme distress in which the people will find themselves as a result of the invasion of locusts.

I do not see any reason to follow Kapelrud's argument that the analogy being drawn is with cultic lamentations by Anat over Baal in Canaanite ritual. The survival of such rituals into the postexilic period—even supposing they had been known in earlier times in Israel!—seems dubious, though Kapelrud himself thought that "the average arguments which are generally used to prove that

---

31. Thus G. Wenham, "*Betûlah*. 'A Girl of Marriageable Age,'" *VT* 22 (1972): 326–48; and J. Bergman, H. Ringgren, and M. Tzevat, "*betûlâ, betûlîm*," *TDOT* 2 (1975): 338–43.

32. Wolff has an extended excursus on the problem; see *Joel and Amos*, p. 30.

First Lament Cycle 53

Joel belongs to the postexilic period, are not worth a great deal."[33] The plausibility of such a theory depends on one's general appraisal of the likelihood that Canaanite "fertility" rites occurred in Israel. In any case, the passage can be explained without recourse to such theories.

The grain offering (*minḥâ*) and drink-offering (*nesek*) are said to be "cut off," just like the wine in 1:5. It is not certain that this is a reference to *daily* sacrifices (the so-called *tāmîd*), but it is noteworthy that the pairing of *minḥâ* and *nesek* occurs only in texts from the postexilic period, when the institution of the daily sacrifices in the Temple became customary (cf. Exod. 29:38–42; Lev. 23:13, 18; Num. 6:15; 15:24; 28:3–9; and 29:11, 16–39). In all these passages, *minḥâ* and *nesek* accompany the offerings of animals in sacrifice, and all are from the priestly material (P) in the Pentateuch. This is further evidence for seeing Joel as a prophet of the Second Temple period.

Since the priests both were responsible for the daily offerings and also benefited from them, in that they received their food from them, it makes good sense that the next verse speaks of the priests mourning—a further reason to doubt the wisdom of Wolff's rearrangement of the text (see textual notes above). Their mourning is both for themselves, like the wailing of the drinkers in 1:5, and also for the damage done to the cult of YHWH. This can no longer be "serviced" as it should because there are no wine or cereals from which to make offerings to YHWH, and hence divine displeasure can be expected. Grain, wine, and oil all fail (v. 10); consequently, no offerings can be made. The priests are devastated by this, since for them maintaining the proper cult is a way of life, indeed their whole *raison d'être*. This is a reminder that "cultic piety" was not necessarily insincere, whatever the preexilic prophets may have thought. Like the liturgical piety of some modern Jews or Christians, it may be a highly developed form of spirituality.

"The ground mourns": some commentators have suggested that we have here a second root *'bl* meaning not "mourn" but "be dry" (Driver, "Linguistic and Textual Problems"). This rendering is followed in the NEB and REB (cf. Wolff, "wilted"). In effect, this theory would imply a kind of pun between "mourn," already used of the priests, and "be dry," used of the land. But D. J. A. Clines has argued, I believe convincingly, that there is little evidence for *'bl* II. True, the Targum here renders *ḥrb* (be dry), but this may be an interpretative translation rather than resting on knowledge of a second Hebrew root. To say that the land "mourns" makes perfectly good sense, and Occam's razor would encourage us not to hypothesize additional senses for a root unless the text will not otherwise be intelligible. Inanimate objects mourn in Isa. 3:26; Jer. 12:10–11; and Lam. 1:4 and 2:8, and there is no reason why the land should not be presented as doing so here.[34]

---

33. Kapelrud, *Joel Studies*, p. 191.
34. See D. J. A. Clines, "Was There an *'bl* II 'be dry' in Classical Hebrew?" *VT* 42 (1992): 1–10.

More important, perhaps, than the exact vocabulary used is the fact that the land is presented as lacking in fruitfulness, and many commentators have seen this as implying that Joel is here speaking of a drought rather than a plague of locusts. Thus Crenshaw:

> One could stretch the imagery sufficiently to accommodate a single calamity, the locusts, in one of two ways: (1) by insisting that the loss of leaves to locusts brought such stress to plants during the dry season that they could not survive the heat until sufficient moisture came (J. D. W. Watts 1975:19–20), or (2) by understanding "grain, wine, and oil" as metonyms for the grain crop, the grape vine, and the olive tree, so that *'umlal* and *hôbîš* can bear the senses of withering and drying out (R. Simkins 1991:137). In any event, 1:20 removes all doubt, for here Joel explicitly mentions the effect of a drought that has left depleted water sources and an appearance of fire's ravages.[35]

It certainly does seem that Joel is concerned to predict drought as well as locust plague, though we need not deduce from this that the locusts have been added to the text secondarily: it is quite common for the prophets to speak of more than one kind of disaster, and Amos 7:1, 4, and 7 speaks of judgment by locusts, by fire, and by "plumb line" (if that is the correct rendering). If we treat Joel's words as predictive rather than as descriptive of the actual situation, there is no reason his imagination should not have encompassed both a locust plague and a drought (and fire, for that matter).

[11–12] Verse 11 begins with what certainly seems like a pun. "Be dismayed" is *hôbîšû*, from the root *bwš*, whereas *hôbîš* in v. 10 was from the root *ybš*: the farmers are to be distressed because the vines have withered and so wine has "dried up." The pun cannot be captured in English. (Verse 12 returns to the root *ybš*: "the vine *withers* . . . all the trees of the field *are dried up*.") "Dismayed" (NRSV) is thus, strictly speaking, "ashamed," as in the translation above, and may imply that the farmers are to blame (through their sins?) for the failure of the crops. But more likely it reflects the sense of shame that people feel at the failure of their efforts even when they are actually not to blame at all: "lack of a harvest is a disgrace for the peasant, just as childlessness is for parents (Ps 127:3–5), for it is evidence that the blessing has been withdrawn."[36] (Childlessness cannot strictly be a disgrace for *parents!*)

The "farmers" (NRSV) and "vinedressers" are, in Hebrew, *'ikkārîm* and *kōrĕmîm*. The first of these terms occurs also at Amos 5:16, and as a pair they can be found also at 2 Chron. 26:10 and Isa. 61:5, where they are employees (hence "farm workers" in my translation) rather than independent farmers. The

---

35. Crenshaw, *Joel*, p. 100. The reference to Watts is to J. D. W. Watts, *The Books of Joel, Obadiah, Jonah, Nahum, Habakkuk, and Zephaniah* (CBC), Cambridge 1975; that to Simkins is to his *Yahweh's Activity in History and Nature*.
36. Wolff, *Joel and Amos*, p. 32.

First Lament Cycle

crops they tend seem to form a list of all the most important produce of the soil: wheat, barley, vines, figs, pomegranates, palms, and apples (or perhaps apricots—the meaning of *tappûaḥ* is disputed). Joy itself shrivels or withers away (*ybš* again). This last line ("surely, joy withers away among the people") is introduced by *kî*, which regularly means "for" or "because" but can also introduce a strong asseveration: "surely, certainly" (see above on 1:6). T. Frankfort defends a causal reading, according to which the crops have failed because the farmers' *enthusiasm* for their work has ceased—but it is doubtful whether *sāsôn*, "joy," can really be interpreted as "enthusiasm."[37]

[13] In a fourth, shorter strophe the prophet urges the priests to engage in mourning rites. These comprise three elements: putting on sackcloth (the text says simply "gird" or "don," with the object—sackcloth—understood); lamenting (*spd*), which implies hitting or scratching the bare chest; and wailing. (Cf. 2 Sam. 3:31 and Jer. 4:8 for a similar combination.) The priests are also to spend the night (*lînû*) in sackcloth. This might mean that they are to spend the night in the Temple, like David fasting for his son (2 Sam. 12:16), but probably simply implies that they are not to change out of the sackcloth at the end of the day but to remain in a continuous state of mourning. In v. 9 the priests are described as "ministers of YHWH," here as "ministers of the altar" and "ministers of my God." Once again, it is the loss of the cereal and drink offerings that leads to the mourning by priests. "Withheld" could imply "withheld by the people"— who need the food and cannot spare it for sacrifice—but more likely it means "withheld by God" and so has the same force as "cut off" in v. 9.

[14] The fifth strophe of Joel's call to lamentation gives instructions for an official fast, involving an "assembly" of all the people. It is sometimes suggested that the community addressed by Joel must have been extremely small if they could all be assembled in the Temple (v. 14b), though it is fair to point out that they are to assemble "to the house" of YHWH (there is no preposition in the Hebrew at all, as is common after verbs of motion) rather than "into" it. "Assembly" (*'aṣārâ*) seems originally to have meant a day free from work[38] but by this time implied a religious event entailing a congregation of the people.

We know that fasts were often public events (cf. Zech. 7:3–5; 8:18–19) in postexilic times, and "assemblies" are referred to already by the preexilic prophets—see Isa. 1:13 and Amos 5:21. But whereas these prophets disapprove of such assemblies for worship, regarding them as no more than a religious smoke screen hiding social injustices, Joel clearly thinks they are an appropriate response to the announcement of judgment: as Wolff puts it, "We sense nothing in Joel of that critical disposition towards the cultus, and especially towards its customary fasting rituals, which we find in Jeremiah (14:12), Trito-Isaiah

---

37. See T. Frankfort, "Le כי de Joël I 12," *VT* 10 (1960): 445–49.
38. Thus E. Kutsch, "Die Wurzel 'ṣr im Hebräischen," *VT* 2 (1952): 57–69.

(58:1–14) and Zechariah (7:5–7)."[39] Wolff adds anxiously, "At the same time, though, the instructions regarding the cultus are by no means his real concern"—but that seems to me to be a Protestant conviction that a biblical prophet could not really be so concerned with cultic matters. In fact, the calling of a religious assembly appears to be very much Joel's "real concern"!

As in v. 2, we have the parallel "old men" or "elders" and "inhabitants of the land" and again may ask whether "elders" are a particular social group—the political leadership—or whether the word *zĕqēnîm* means simply "the old." Whereas in the earlier verse the term might refer to those with long memories, and hence "the old" may be the most appropriate translation, here a reference to the leadership seems more likely.[40] The prophet wants all the community, with its leaders, to come up to the Temple. (It is possible to read the terse Hebrew of v. 14b as "O elders, assemble all the inhabitants of the land," though I do not think this is the most probable interpretation.)

We do not know whether Joel was a priest or cultic prophet within whose remit it fell to summon assemblies of all the people for worship, or whether he is taking such a role on himself in virtue of his personal conviction of a prophetic call—Amos, we know, had used the probably priestly form of the summons to an assembly, though ironically, in Amos 4:4, "Come to Bethel—and transgress!" Verse 14 is surely in essence an instruction issued to the priests to "sanctify" the fast, that is, to inaugurate it solemnly. Fasting in Israel appears to have involved abstinence from food for a single day (cf. Judg. 20:26; 1 Sam. 14:24), as is still the case in Judaism with the fast of the Day of Atonement. It was not necessarily penitential in character but seems to have been primarily a way of expressing religious seriousness; here, no doubt, as Wolff puts it, "a sign of submission to the decreed calamity" (*Joel and Amos*, 33). The people are to "cry out" (*z'q*) to YHWH in lamentation, striving to move him to pity. In the following verses we are told, I believe, what they are to say in their lament.

Thus Joel's call to lamentation comprises five strophes, not identical in form but certainly well ordered. Each begins with an imperative, urging some section of the community or the whole of it to cry out to YHWH for a reversal of its plight, which is described as a locust invasion and as a drought, causing the loss of all significant agricultural produce and thus threatening the people with starvation, and an accompanying inability to offer YHWH the prescribed sacrifices. Joel begins by addressing the people immediately affected by the destruction of the vines (1:5) but moves on to the priests and farmers. He then instructs the priests to assemble the people at large for a great ceremony of communal fasting and lamentation, in an attempt to persuade YHWH to reverse their fortunes and restore the lost crops.

---

39. Wolff, *Joel and Amos*, p. 33.
40. Against Crenshaw, *Joel*, p. 104.

First Lament Cycle

Joel is wholly lacking in two features that are commonplace in earlier prophets: (1) opposition to an organized cult and (2) the conviction that it is now too late to expect any remission of the disaster that afflicts the nation. He regards cultic activity as a matter of course and plainly thinks there is a point in lamenting and calling on God to restore the nation's fortunes. Underlying this is what was clearly the "standard" theology of the temple cultus, the belief in a God who can punish—sometimes for reasons human beings can understand but sometimes inscrutably—yet who remains merciful and can be moved by entreaty. Judaism has not developed the idea found in some Christian theology, that God never changes his mind; it has traditionally had a more straightforward approach to pleading, even arguing, with God when God is perceived as acting in a hostile way.

3. The Lament (1:15–20)

15 "Alas for the day![a]
     For a day of YHWH has drawn near,
         and as destruction from Shaddai it is coming.
16   Is not the food cut off
         before our eyes,
     joy and gladness,
         from the house of our God?

17   The seed shrivels under the clods,
         the storehouses are desolate;[b]
     the granaries[c] are ruined
         because the grain has failed.
18   How the animals groan!
         The herds of cattle wander about
     because there is no pasture for them;
         even the flocks of sheep are stunned.[d]

19   To you, YHWH, I cry.
     For fire has devoured
         the pastures of the wilderness,
     and flames have burned up
         all the trees of the field.
20   Even wild animals cry out to you
         because the watercourses are dried up,
     and fire has devoured
         the pastures of the wilderness.

a. *'āhâ*, "alas," is rendered *oimmoi oimmoi oimmoi* in Greek and *a a a* in Latin, but there is no reason to suppose this reduplication was ever present in the Hebrew; this is a matter of mourning conventions in the other languages.

b. Verse 17 is the most difficult verse in the book from a linguistic point of view, since all the words in v. 17a except *taḥat*, "under," are *hapax legomena* and the meaning can only be guessed at. Since the second half of the verse refers to the withering of the grain and consequent emptying of the granaries, it is reasonable to think that it has something to do with this theme, and the subject, *pĕrudôt*, is generally taken to mean "seeds," following Syriac and Aramaic cognates, though the word would normally in BH be a passive participle meaning "separated things." 4Q78 reads "heifers" (*pārôt*), however, as does LXX (*damaleis*). LXX then makes them "leap" (*eskirtēsan*) in their stalls rather than "shriveling," the usual rendering of MT *'ābĕšû*, based on an Arabic cognate *abisa* (meaning "to frown"). 4Q78 has instead *'āpĕšû*, "they rot"; cf. Latin *computruerunt*. The fourth word in the verse is *megrĕpōtêhem*, which is rendered "their shovels" (whose?) by some, following postbiblical Hebrew *megrapâ* and Aramaic *magrôpîtā'*, a "shovel" or "trowel"; rabbinic commentators take the word as coming from *grp*, "sweep away"— hence "their brooms." *BHS* proposes emending to *ḥattû gārĕnōtêhem*, "their threshing-floors are dismayed." It is pretty clear that we are never going to know what this verse means and that there is no realistic prospect of restoring the original Hebrew or, if MT is correct, of deciphering it.

c. In v. 17b there is one problem word, *mammĕgurôt* where we should expect *mĕgurôt*, "granaries"; *BHS* explains the additional *mem* as a dittograph. The point is that the storage systems for grain are now in ruin, perhaps abandoned by those who looked after them because there was no longer anything in them.

d. The verb here in MT is *ne'šāmû*, normally "bear guilt," but we should probably emend with *BHS* to *nāšammû* (cf. LXX *ephanisthēsan*) and interpret as "are destroyed, demolished."

Commentary

[1:15–16] The approach adopted here is that in these verses we have the words of the lamentation that the priests and people are exhorted to make in vv. 13 and 14. Like other laments in the Old Testament, it contains a further description of the people's plight (cf. Jer. 14:17–22). But at least in v. 16 this is in the first-person plural, suggesting that the speaker is now the congregation (or its chosen representative) at prayer. It is perfectly possible to defend the view that we have here further words of the prophet himself, but it seems to me that the whole of chapter 1 makes more coherent sense on the supposition that the prophet first exhorts the people to lament and then provides the "text," as it were, for their lamentation. The same can then be said of chapter 2, though there the actual lament is very short (2:17bc).

The lament begins "Alas for the day," or perhaps "for today"—*hayyôm* commonly has this sense in the Bible. There seems to be a connection here with Ezek. 30:2 (on which see the discussions on p. 24, above, and p. 59, below). In what follows, it becomes clear that "this day"—the present occasion—is being interpreted as "a day of YHWH," or perhaps "*the* day of YHWH." Amos is our earliest evidence of the expectation of a special time called *yôm YHWH*, on which (we can deduce from his reference in 5:18) YHWH was expected to bless the people either with material prosperity or by overcoming their enemies. Amos rejects this interpretation, saying that there will indeed be a "day of YHWH" but that it will confound the people's confident expectations by being the very day on which their enemies will triumph over them. After Amos, the "day of YHWH" seems to have passed into prophetic tradition with the new sense he had given it—a day of destruction and disaster for Israel—and it is this conception we meet, for example, in Zeph. 1:14–18. When the ultimate disaster struck in the early sixth century and Jerusalem was overwhelmed by the Babylonian army, this was interpreted by the author of Lamentations as the implementation of YHWH's "day" (cf. Lam. 1:12, "the day of his fierce anger"; also 2:1 and 21). In Joel 3:14, which we have argued comes from a later hand, the day of YHWH is the day of his judgment on foreign nations, but here it is clearly the day of YHWH's punishment of Judah.

The phrase "the day of YHWH" (*yôm yhwh*) occurs five times in Joel: here at 1:15 and also at 2:1, 11, 31; and 3:14. There is a vast secondary literature on this term as it occurs in the prophetic corpus, where it is found sixteen times in all in predictions of the future (Isa. 13:6, 9; Ezek. 13:5, Joel 1:15; 2:1, 11, 31; 3:14; Amos 5:8 [twice], 20; Obad. 15; Zeph. 1:4, 14 [twice]; and Mal. 3:23; *yôm layhwh* occurs additionally at Isa. 2:12; Ezek. 30:3; and Zech. 14:1).[41] Scholars have divided into two main camps as to the origins of the phrase. Some, like von Rad, have seen it as referring to YHWH's day of battle against the enemies of Israel;[42] others have regarded it as in origin a cultic term meaning a feast day of YHWH,[43] which the prophets, beginning with Amos, adopted as a term for the day when YHWH would intervene in history. They probably did this because feast days were regarded as points at which YHWH's involvement with his people was especially salient (Mowinckel's hypothesized Enthronement Festival being the chief such feast day). As Carroll puts it, "This day was a day in the cultic life of Israel associated with the divine theophany."[44]

Whatever the origins of the "day of YHWH," most scholars would agree that in the Prophets it became a technical term for a great day on which YHWH would intervene in a unique way to judge either Israel or foreign nations. When

---

41. See K. Cathcart, "Day of Yahweh," *ABD* 2 (1992): 84–85 for a general survey.
42. G. von Rad, *Holy War in Ancient Israel,* Grand Rapids 1991; English translation of *Der heilige Krieg im alten Israel,* 3d ed., Göttingen 1958.
43. S. Mowinckel, *He That Cometh,* Oxford 1958; English translation of *Han som kommer,* Copenhagen 1951; cf. K. Jeppesen, "The Day of Yahweh in Mowinckel's Conception Renewed," *SJOT* 2 (1988): 42–55.
44. Carroll, "Eschatological Delay," p. 53.

Amos says, "Alas for you who desire the day of the LORD! Why do you want the day of the LORD? It is darkness, not light" (Amos 5:18), he presupposes a popular expectation centered on this "day" that saw it as a time of good fortune for Israel, whether in a military or some other sense. He then reverses this expectation, indicating that the day will instead be a day of terror: "as if someone fled from a lion, and was met by a bear" (Amos 5:19). In later prophecy the day comes to be the occasion for divine judgment in general, and prophets differ as to whether this will primarily be judgment on Israel itself (as in Isa. 2:12) or on its enemies (as in Obad. 15).

What is meant by the day of YHWH in Joel? A certain amount depends on the disputed questions of the authorship and unity of the book. Three of the references occur in the first half, two in the second; and those in the first half, as we have seen, are regarded by some commentators as additions, possibly by the author of the second half!

What are we to make of Joel's references to the day of YHWH if, with a majority of recent commentators, we see the book as essentially a unity? Probably then Wolff's interpretation will be the correct one. The references to the day of YHWH in chapter 2 are meant to show that the locust plague of chapter 1 was only the precursor of the invading army of chapter 2, and that army is no mere "random" disaster for Judah but the implementation of the great "day of YHWH" foretold in earlier prophecy: it has, that is to say, eschatological overtones as portending the decisive judgment of God's people. (The locust plague is to the day of YHWH as microcosm is to macrocosm, as Bourke puts it.)[45] But if they return to YHWH he will forgive and restore, and in that case the day of YHWH will turn out to be what it had been in popular expectation from before the time of Amos: the day on which YHWH will shower blessings on the chosen people, pouring out the spirit and blessing all those who "call on the name of YHWH."

Even if the book is essentially a unity, however, other explanations of the day of YHWH are possible. In an important article, J. Everson argues that there is no single "day of YHWH" concept in the Old Testament. He points out that, in addition to the predictive uses of the term listed, a "day" of or from YHWH is also mentioned five times in contexts where reference is to the past: Isa. 22:1–14; Jer. 46:2–12; Ezek. 13:1–9; and Lamentations 1 and 2. As he remarks:

> In striking contrast to the thesis that the Day of Yahweh is always set forth as a single event in the future, these texts demonstrate that it is not only appropriate but extremely helpful to speak of a sequence of historical days of Yahweh when speaking of the prophetic interpretation of history.[46]

---

45. Bourke, "Le Jour de Yahvé."
46. J. Everson, "The Days of Yahweh," *JBL* 93 (1974): 329–37; the quotation is from p. 331.

First Lament Cycle 61

In other words, YHWH does not have a single "day" in an eschatological sense but rather a number of "days," that is, occasions on which he is especially present in destruction or blessing:

> The texts demonstrate that the Day of Yahweh was not viewed in the preexilic and exilic eras of Israel's history as a singular, universal, or exclusively future event of world judgment. Rather, the Day of Yahweh was a powerful concept available to the prophets for their use in interpreting various momentous events—past, future or imminent.[47]

Thus we might translate *yôm yhwh* as "*a* day of YHWH" rather than "*the* day of YHWH." Even Joel 2:31 means "the great and terrible day of YHWH in question at present" rather than referring to some supposed ultimate eschatological event.

I am not wholly persuaded by this argument, but parts of it are illuminating. Joel contains other terms besides "the day of YHWH" that appear to refer to a decisive divine event. For example, 2:28 contains the expression "Then afterward" (*wĕhāyāh aḥărê kēn*), which many would regard as a marker of eschatology, and in 3:18 we have "In that day" (*bayyôm hahû'*), which is also widely treated as a technical term for prophetic expectations of the end time. I think Everson's interpretation is sustainable in the first half of the book, so that we might take 1:15; 2:1; and 2:11 as referring to the specific plight of the people caused by the locust plague or drought or invasion (whichever we think it is). But in the second part I would lean toward a fully eschatological interpretation, while seeing the passages in question as coming from another hand than Joel's.

On this basis we would not need to delete the "day of YHWH" references in the first half but could interpret them in Everson's manner; but the two references in 2:28–3:21 might still have a more large-scale meaning. There is nothing unusual in additions to a biblical book taking up terms from the existing text and using them in a different sense; and this would imply, in effect, that the author of 2:28–3:21 construed Joel in the way that many commentators since have done, as referring to a more eschatological event than Joel had, in fact, had in mind when using the phrase "day of YHWH" himself.

The whole issue is clearly very uncertain, and we cannot pretend to any confidence in interpreting it. But my preference is for reading the day of YHWH in 1:2–2:27 rather as in Amos, as referring to some quite concrete "day" (i.e., occasion) within the experience of his hearers: in this case, the occasion on which the country was ravaged by locusts (since I continue to think that this, rather than military invasion, is intended in the first two chapters). This was a "great and terrible day of YHWH." The later writer, who contributed 2:28–3:21, construed Joel as referring to what, by his time, the "day of YHWH" had come to

---

47. Ibid., p. 335.

mean, that is, the moment at which human history would reach a decisive turning point and Judah's fortunes would be restored beyond imagination, in a new world order.

So there is no need to read the term in 1:15 as having an "eschatological" sense, if by that we mean it is regarded as the end of this world order: it is simply a day of YHWH's decisive intervention in Israel's affairs. Accordingly, I would take *qārôb yôm yhwh,* which NRSV renders "the day of the LORD is near," to mean "a day of YHWH has drawn near," that is, "is upon us." This would mean rejecting the suggestion by both Wolff and Crenshaw that "the context suggests that he [Joel] understands the locust invasion as a sign of the nearness of an even more destructive force."[48] On the contrary, the prophet sees in the devastation of the country evidence that the day of YHWH is already upon the people, and that it is in the destruction all around that the implementation of YHWH's "day" is to be seen. (Incidentally, the locusts seem no longer to be in focus at all; references seem to be to drought [vv. 17–18] and perhaps destruction of the crops by fire [vv. 19–20], unless "fire" is some kind of symbol for the devastation brought by the locusts.)

The day of YHWH here comes as "destruction from Shaddai." This ancient name for God is traditionally rendered "the Almighty," following the Greek *pantokratōr* and Latin *omnipotens.* This follows rabbinic etymological speculation that the name comes from *še day,* "the one who is sufficient." In fact, it is widely taken by modern scholars to come from a word for "mountains," insofar as its etymology can be established at all. It is the preferred term in P for the name of God in the patriarchal period (see Exod. 6:3) and is also common in Job. But it is used here to good effect because of the term for "destruction," which is *šōd.* Crenshaw imitates this in his English rendering, "like devastation from the Devastator";[49] and compare Wolff, "like might from the Mighty One,"[50] following M. Buber and F. Rosenzweig, "wie Gewalt vom Gewaltigen."[51] (LXX *hōs talaipōria ek talaipōrias* does not treat *šadday* as a divine name at all but does preserve the pun.)

Once again Joel refers to food as "cut off" (*nikrat*) "before our eyes," emphasizing the direct evidence of the people's senses and, as before, that this means not only starvation for them but also the cessation of sacrifices in the Temple ("joy and gladness from the house of our God"). If these are indeed the words of the people's lament, as I am supposing, then we have here a familiar feature in the lament literature of the Old Testament, the thinly veiled appeal to God's own self-interest: by allowing the famine, YHWH deprives himself of the offerings he would otherwise receive.

---

48. Crenshaw, *Joel,* p. 106.
49. Ibid., p. 106.
50. Wolff, *Joel and Amos,* p. 19.
51. M. Buber and F. Rosenzweig, *Bücher der Kundung,* Cologne 1958, p. 622.

First Lament Cycle

Of course, this is misery for the people, too, since they can no longer share in the joy of worship at the Temple, but they naturally think it worth reminding YHWH that while the famine lasts he shares it with them: YHWH thus has an interest in bringing about a restoration of material prosperity. (Cf. Isa. 38:18–19, where YHWH is reminded that he cannot be praised by the dead and hence should restore his worshiper to fullness of life!) This kind of approach is part of that frankness in speaking to God that much of Christian tradition finds it hard to cope with but that has continued to exist in Judaism.

[17–18] Not only were people starving, but animals too naturally suffered from the lack of food, and v. 18 emphasizes their plight; even sheep, which require much less lush pasture than cattle, "are stunned."

[19–20] In keeping with our interpretation of this whole passage as the people's lament, we should see the speaker here ("To you, YHWH, I cry") not as the prophet but as the lament speaker, like the individual who stands for the community in the book of Lamentations (e.g., Lam. 3:1). (Of course, we cannot rule out the possibility that it might be the prophet himself who would have assumed this role.) The reason for the cry is now stated as being the destruction by fire of the trees of the field (cf. v. 12) and even of the "pastures of the wilderness," which means, as Crenshaw points out, the uncultivated areas on the edge of the desert that would normally provide grazing for small animals even in times of poor fertility. The "watercourses" (*'ăpîqê māyim*) are streams that dry up in summer; here they are dry at a time when animals would have expected to find them full of water (cf. Ps. 42:1).

The emphasis here is on the totality of the destruction. The locusts are not mentioned, but it sounds as if the locust plague is to be followed by a drought and perhaps literally by fires in open country. We cannot rule out the possibility that this is to some extent a stylized account of natural disasters, which may not reflect precisely what happened in Joel's day; this is all the more likely if I am correct to interpret the whole of Joel's prophecy as predictive rather than reactive. What he foresaw was a total destruction of all natural resources through locusts, drought, and fire: to imitate his own way of presenting the matter in 1:4, what the locusts left the drought devoured, and what the drought left fire devoured. This theme, "Just when you thought the worst was over, a new catastrophe struck," is already to be found in Amos 5:19:

> as if someone fled from a lion,
> and was met by a bear;
> or went into the house and rested a hand against the wall,
> and was bitten by a snake.

The sense of cumulative disaster makes for an extremely vivid presentation, and it, too, is present in Amos—in 4:6–11, where some of the afflictions mentioned by Joel are already to be found (famine, drought, blight, locusts, plague, and fire). It may be noted, too, that such calamities are predicted in the "futility curses" at the end of Deuteronomy (28:20–44), which most scholars think derive from the language of Assyrian treaties:

> The sky over your head shall be bronze, and the earth under you iron. The LORD will change the rain of your land into powder, and only dust shall come down upon you from the sky until you are destroyed.... You shall carry much seed into the field but shall gather little in, for the locust shall consume it. You shall plant vineyards and dress them, but you shall neither drink the wine nor gather the grapes.... You shall have olive trees throughout all your territory, but you shall not anoint yourself with the oil, for your olives shall drop off.... All your trees and the fruit of your ground the cicada shall take over. (Deut. 28:23–24, 38–42)

We do not need to press the details of the prophetic vision too literally; what Joel is seeking to do is to show that an overwhelming destruction is coming and to prepare his hearers to utter a lament that will appropriately cover whatever befalls them. He probably draws on a literary tradition of describing disaster just as much as on observation of what has actually befallen the people in his own day.

The first chapter of Joel presents a unified and consistent picture. The prophet announces an unprecedented disaster, which will go down in history as incomparable. It involves, first and foremost, an invasion of locusts, but then also a drought and, perhaps, raging fires. The overall effect is to produce starvation and hardship that affects humans and animals alike. Because his perspective is a cultic one, the prophet emphasizes above all the effect on the Temple service: there can no longer be offerings to YHWH. He urges the people, and especially the priests, to utter an appropriate lament, in which they are to bewail the coming of a great "day" of YHWH, that is, a visitation of general disaster, and to pray that the fortunes of Judah may be restored.

The theology underlying this chapter is a simple one. It is taken for granted that the will of God lies behind natural disaster and that God is free to inflict it or to reverse it. Unlike the preexilic prophets, Joel does not have much to say about any supposed causes of divine judgment that might lie in the sins of the people, nor does he call for repentance—only for fasting and general self-abasement. God is thought to be willing to hear the laments of the people, who are not above reminding YHWH that by bringing agricultural dearth, he deprives himself of their offerings and sacrifices. YHWH is believed to be merciful, and (despite bringing pain and desolation) can also be expected to hear humble lamentations—there is some *point* in lamenting. But there are as yet no predictions that God will indeed hear the prayers: that waits until the next chapter. This first cycle of lamentation thus ends with an open question: Will God take heed, or remain implacable? The question of why God brings disaster is not raised in these verses; there is probably an assumption that God is

First Lament Cycle 65

inscrutable in his judgments. This contrasts with some of what is said later in the book, where, as we shall see, a concern for theodicy is more prominent.

This interpretation of Joel 1 differs considerably from that of Wolff. He sees far more eschatological overtones, even already in this chapter, and holds that the prophet is giving "heed to the unfulfilled eschatological prophetic word about the Day of Yahweh."[52] He thinks Joel is reverting to Amos's use of this "day" as an occasion when YHWH will judge Israel (Judah) itself, against the intervening use of the term to refer to a judgment on foreign nations in Ezekiel 30 and Isaiah 13, and that in using the term, Joel is expressing "an extremely critical word . . . in veiled manner against the cultic community of Jerusalem which has constituted itself theocratically."

I see no evidence that Joel is critical of the Jerusalem community at all in this chapter, and certainly not that he is opposed to its "theocratic" constitution—indeed, if the *zĕqēnîm* are "elders" in 1:14, then the constitution is not in the usual sense "theocratic" at all. Wolff seems to have a great desire to find criticism of the cultic establishment in Joel, where it seems to me that, on the contrary, the prophet regards the cultus, at least insofar as it provides the opportunity for "solemn assemblies," as a very good thing, while the cessation of sacrifice because of the famine is regarded as an unmitigated disaster. Nor is there any sign that Joel looks "beyond" the sacrificial system to some greater consummation of events. Wolff's statement "The history of salvation has not already reached its fulfilment in the cultus to which Joel so matter-of-factly assents. A final convulsive event is still to come"[53] seems to me pure wishful thinking.

An element of Protestant reserve toward all things cultic or theocratic seems apparent here, and it prevents Wolff from seeing that Joel is really rather well disposed to the cult, whose temporary interruption he mourns. A theology that incorporates insights from Joel will have to be much more hospitable than Wolff is to including a *liturgical* perspective. It is perfectly possible to do this without selling out to a kind of *ex opere operato* attitude in which liturgy is simply a matter of "correct" performance. Consider the wise comments of Alexander Schmemann:

> To some—the "liturgically minded"—of all the activities of the Church, liturgy is the most important, if not the only one. To others, liturgy is esthetic and spiritual deviation from the real task of the Church. There exist today "liturgical" and "non-liturgical" churches and Christians. But this controversy is unnecessary for it has its roots in one basic misunderstanding—the "liturgical" understanding of the liturgy. This is the reduction of the liturgy to "cultic" categories, its definition as a sacred act of worship, different as such not only from the "profane" area of

52. See Wolff, *Joel and Amos*, p. 36.
53. Ibid.

life, but even from all other activities of the Church itself. But this is not the original meaning of the Greek word *leitourgia* [or, we may add, of Hebrew *'ăbôdâ*]. It meant an action by which a group of people became something corporately which they had not been as a mere collection of individuals—a whole greater than the sum of its parts. It meant also a function or "ministry" of a man or a group on behalf of and in the interest of the whole community. Thus the *leitourgia* of ancient Israel was the corporate work of a chosen few to prepare the world for the coming of the Messiah.[54]

In such an understanding of liturgy, it is not a mere "rite" but the expression of an entire attitude to God and to human life that shapes the people of God. Some such attitude we may take to lie at the root of Joel's anguish that "the cult" has been suspended.

Second Lament Cycle
Joel 2:1–17

1. The Disaster (2:1–11)

2:1 Blow the trumpet in Zion;
sound the alarm on my holy mountain!
Let all the inhabitants of the land tremble,
for a day of YHWH has come, it has drawn near—
2 a day of darkness and gloom,
a day of clouds and thick darkness!
Like blackness[a] spread upon the mountains
a populous and powerful people is coming;
nothing like them has ever existed from ancient times,
nor will it again after them
in the years of all the generations still to come.

3 Fire devours before them,
and behind them a flame burns.
The land is like the garden of Eden before them,
but after them a desolate wilderness,
and nothing escapes them.

4 Their appearance is like the appearance of horses,
and like warhorses they charge.

---

54. A. Schmemann, *The World as Sacrament*, New York 1963.

Second Lament Cycle

5   Their sound[b] is like the sound of chariots,
       they leap on the tops of the mountains,
    like the sound of a flame of fire
       devouring the stubble,
    like a powerful people
       drawn up for battle.

6   Before them peoples are in anguish,
       all faces grow pale.[c]
7   Like warriors they run,
       like soldiers they scale a wall.
    Each keeps to its own course,
       they do not swerve from their paths.[d]
8   And none jostles another,
       each one keeps to its own track;
    and they burst through the weapons[e]
       and cannot be stopped.
9   They leap upon the city,
       they run upon the walls;
    they climb up into the houses,
       they enter through the windows like a thief.

10   Before them the earth quakes,
       the heavens tremble.
    The sun and the moon are darkened,
       and the stars withdraw their shining.
11   YHWH utters his voice
       at the head of his army;
    Truly, his host is vast;
       Truly, those who obey his command are mighty.
    Truly the day of YHWH is great;
       very terrible—who can endure it?

     a. Reading *šĕḥōr*, "darkness," for *šaḥar*, "dawn," in 2:2, with *BHS* and Duhm.
     b. Inserting *qôlām* with *BHS* to read "their sound is like the sound of chariots," a better parallel with "their appearance is like the appearance of horses."
     c. "All faces grow pale" is a crux. The Hebrew *qibbĕṣû pā'rûr* has been variously translated "gather redness" and "gather fear." *pārûr* (without the *aleph*) is a cooking pot, and both the Greek and Latin versions seem to have taken this to be the word here: *pan prosōpon hōs proskauma chutras, omnes vultus rediguntur in ollam*, "all faces are like/ become a (scorched) pot." The Masorah notes that the *aleph* is not read, presumably implying the same identification. The hypothesis would then be that it is the redness of the pot that the prophet has in mind, and he is referring to the faces of everyone becoming

red with fear, "bright red with the rushing of blood to this area under extreme excitement."[1] But it is also possible to take *qibbĕṣû* to mean that this redness is "gathered up," that is, dispersed: hence the rendering "grow pale." The truth is that we do not know what *pā'rûr* means, and the identification with *pārûr* is no more than a guess, albeit an old one. It has been explained from the root *p'r,* "glorify," and the root *pwr,* "boil," but neither gives a satisfactory sense here. "All faces grow pale" makes perfect sense in the context, but there is no way of knowing that it is correct.

d. "They do not swerve from their paths" implies an emendation to the Hebrew text, which has *lō' yĕ'abbĕṭûn,* "they do not make a pledge." One plausible emendation is J. Wellhausen's[2] to *yĕ'awwĕṭûn,* changing only one letter, with the sense "they do not make their ways bent" (from root *'wt*). An alternative approach appeals to comparative philology and takes the verb to be a different root, *'bt,* cognate with Akkadian *ebetu,* "to bend," or with Arabic *'bt,* "to spoil."[3] The parallel line "each keeps to his own course" establishes what the meaning must be, even though there can be no certainty about the original Hebrew or its precise sense, and the LXX *ekklinōsin* represents an intelligent guess.

e. "They burst through the weapons" translates Hebrew *bĕ'ad haššelaḥ yippōlû.* The obvious meaning of this is "they fall down the aqueduct"; cf. Isa. 8:6, *mê haššilōaḥ,* perhaps implying that the enemy enter Jerusalem through the underground watercourses. But *šelaḥ* means a weapon in Neh. 4:17 and 23, and LXX renders *en tois belesin autōn,* "on their spears." (*belis* is also used at Neh. 4:23.) Wolff's rendering "through the midst of missiles they attack"[4] reflects this understanding of the line. The locusts cannot be stopped with weapons (2:8) or prevented from jumping onto the wall (2:9—root *šqq* is used of locusts jumping also at Isa. 33:4) as soldiers could be.

Commentary

The major debate among commentators about this passage concerns its relationship with chapter 1. A decision about this both depends on and itself influences what is taken to be the reference of the lengthy description of the invading hordes. One possibility is that, whereas chapter 1 is about a locust plague, this chapter concerns military invasion; another is that the locusts of chapter 1 are seen as the precursors for something on a larger scale, the invasion of an "apocalyptic army," as Wolff calls it. Some commentators, as we have seen, believe both chapters are about an enemy army, under the figure of locusts. It is possible to think that they concern two successive incursions of locusts, and we might point in support of this to 2:25, with its reference to the "years" (plural) that the swarming locust has eaten (but see the commentary on this verse).

1. Crenshaw, *Joel,* p. 123.
2. J. Wellhausen, *Die Kleinen Propheten übersetzt und erklärt* (Skizzen und Vorarbeiten 5), 3d ed., Berlin 1898; reprint 1963.
3. G. R. Driver, "Studies in the Vocabulary of the Old Testament," *JTS* 34 (1938): 400–402.
4. Wolff, *Joel and Amos,* p. 38.

Second Lament Cycle 69

Wolff argues that "it is out of the question that the same calamity should underlie both chapters,"[5] and adduces three reasons for this:

1. Chapter 1 deals with a locust plague that has already arrived—hence the verbs are in the perfect (*qatal*) form, whereas in chapter 2 the invasion is described in the imperfect (*yiqtol*), which indicates that it is now happening or about to happen.
2. "The introduction to the call to repentance, with its connecting 'but even now' (וגם־עתה 2:12), shows that the occasion for returning, which exists 'now,' is distinguished from the earlier occasion for lamentation in chap. 1."[6]
3. Both the call to repentance and the sense that the disaster is intensified in chapter 2 show that this is a separate occasion.

He goes on to argue that the problem envisaged in chapter 2 is not a locust plague but an enemy army, and not just any army but an "apocalyptic army."

I argued above (p. 44) that, on the contrary, the invading force in chapter 2 must be locusts, since they are *compared* to an army and so cannot *be* one. But I do not find Wolff's reasons for contrasting chapters 1 and 2 to be decisive in any case:

1. The distinction in the tense forms used is not a very powerful argument, given the way in which the two nonconsecutive forms (*qatal* and *yiqtol*) oscillate in Hebrew verse, and especially in the Prophets. As we have seen, chapter 1 may in any case be a prediction, not a description of a past state of affairs, despite the use of perfect forms. Even if it does describe a past event, the same could well be true of chapter 2, despite its use of the imperfect—2:18 suggests that the people's penitent response lies in the past, and 2:23 also speaks of YHWH as *having given* the early rains. Verses 10 and 11 of chapter 2 are already in the perfect, not the imperfect. Nothing can really be said about the time references in Joel on the basis of the verb forms used.
2. Nothing that I can see would prevent the exhortation in 2:12 from being parallel to the call to fasting and mourning in chapter 1; it does not seem to imply that an earlier response failed (if that is indeed what Wolff implies—I find his argument here obscure).
3. The fact that the disaster is described in heightened terms in chapter 2 need not mean it is a different disaster. As we have noted, even the locusts of chapter 1 are spoken of in much more than literal terms and are already associated with a "day of YHWH."

5. Ibid., pp. 41–42.
6. Ibid., p. 42.

As argued in the introduction, my own hypothesis is that chapter 2 represents a second description of the same calamity as related in chapter 1, namely, the locust invasion. I see no difficulty in the idea that the prophet might have formulated a response to the same event in two different ways. I believe that the enemy of chapter 2 are still locusts and that there is no more of an "apocalyptic" element here than in chapter 1. What is predicted is a perfectly literal locust invasion, described with magnificent poetic hyperbole, rather than some event that breaks the mold of human history; and I would distinguish this from the language and imagery of 2:28–3:21, where we are in a different world and can genuinely begin to use the term *apocalyptic*.

The "day of YHWH" predicted in chapter 2, just like that in chapter 1, is an occasion when YHWH judges the people decisively; but beyond it lies the possibility of a restoration of the normal conditions of life, with sacrifices restored to the Temple (2:14), the locust plague removed (2:20), and the effects of the devastation made good in the future. This is not an apocalyptic hope for some drastic overturning of the ordinary conditions of life but rather a real (though perhaps not very realistic) hope for their return: a hope that the devastated land will have a normal future.

[2:1–2] Since we read "*my* holy mountain," the speaker here is presumably YHWH himself, giving instructions through the prophet that a warning signal is to be given. The addressees are the watchmen on the city walls, looking out for the approach of any enemy; the watchers are to sound an alarm by blowing the ram's horn, or *šôpār*. Whereas chapter 1 seems to deal mainly with the assault of the locusts on the countryside around Jerusalem, here the city itself is in focus, as we see further in vv. 6–9. It is clear that the passage is not continuous with chapter 1, since the instruction to the watchmen begins a new section in which news of the locust invasion has not yet arrived. Clearly, the blowing of the ram's horn is not a cultic act, since here it does not initiate the fast, as it does in 2:15, but rather constitutes an alarm that causes all the population to "tremble." This justifies us in treating this *šôpār* essentially as the watchman's trumpet.

The idea of Zion as YHWH's "holy mountain" has ancient roots in preexilic Judaean tradition and ultimately goes back to a common ancient Near Eastern notion of the mountain of the gods (Saphon in the Ugaritic texts from Ras Shamra), which passes into classical tradition in the form of Mount Olympus.[7] Associated with this idea in the Old Testament is the conviction that the mountain of God is impregnable: we find this asserted in Ps. 48:1–2, 4–8:

> Great is the LORD and greatly to be praised
> in the city of our God.

---

7. Cf. R. J. Clifford, *The Cosmic Mountain in Canaan and the Old Testament* (Harvard Semitic Monographs 4), Cambridge, Mass. 1972.

> His holy mountain, beautiful in elevation,
>   is the joy of all the earth,
> Mount Zion, in the far north [ṣāpôn],
>   the city of the great King. . . .
>
> Then the kings assembled,
>   they came on together.
> As soon as they saw it, they were astounded;
>   they were in panic, they took to flight;
> trembling took hold of them there,
>   pains as of a woman in labor,
> as when an east wind shatters
>   the ships of Tarshish.
>
> As we have heard, so have we seen
>   in the city of the LORD of hosts,
> in the city of our God,
>   which God establishes for ever.

The same idea underlies some of the oracles in the book of Isaiah, though the prophet Isaiah himself may well have been skeptical about it or even have rejected it: see Isa. 29:1-4.[8] But the experience of the destruction of Jerusalem by the Babylonians at the beginning of the sixth century meant the demise of this doctrine. Though Lamentations agonizes over how such a fate could befall YHWH's own city, the prophets had prepared the way for understanding God's commitment to Zion as conditional on the nation's response. This idea is central to the work of the Deuteronomistic school, who added conditions to YHWH's recorded promises to the city, as well as to its ruling dynasty (see, e.g., 1 Kings 9:1-9). Nevertheless, the restored postexilic city still saw itself as inheritor of the ancient promises. So, for Joel, Zion is still God's "holy mountain" but no longer understood as an impregnable fortress.

"A day of YHWH has come, it has drawn near." There is a question about *bā'*, translated "is coming" in NRSV, because it could equally well be a finite verb (participle and perfect tense of *bā'* have the same form in the masculine singular). It might thus mean "has come," in which case "it is near" (*qārôb*) would have to mean "has drawn near," as in my translation. Crenshaw rules out the finite translation, but it seems to me just as possible and to make little difference to the sense, since it is clear in any case that it is the invasion of YHWH's "army" in the remaining verses of the section that constitutes the coming of YHWH's "day"—it is not merely a precursor of the day. It is possible that "for it is near" is a gloss by a later scribe, since it seems to fall outside the metrical

---

8. See the discussion in R. E. Clements, *Isaiah and the Deliverance of Jerusalem: A Study in the Interpretation of Prophecy in the Old Testament* (JSOTSup 13), Sheffield 1980.

structure of the passage. In that case, it might be an attempt to interpret the passage as referring to the scribe's own day, in the same way as the New Testament and the biblical commentaries from Qumran often indicate that particular texts are being fulfilled in their own time.

Zephaniah 1:14–16 is the closest parallel to this passage in the prophetic literature and may well have served Joel as a model. There can be little doubt that here the prophet is using the old concept of the day of YHWH, which goes back to Amos. Indeed, it must have have preceded Amos, since he refers to it as something that people are looking forward to (Amos 5:18; see the comments above, p. 60). Images of clouds and thick darkness are common in descriptions of YHWH's day (Zeph. 1:15) and probably derive from the old theophany tradition (cf. Exod. 19:16; Deut. 4:11); but here there is a specific reference to the way in which the locust army spreads across the mountainsides, like a dense black cloud.

Verse 2 picks up from 1:2 the idea of the incomparability of the disaster YHWH is bringing on his people. Wolff attempts to contrast it with the locust plague of chapter 1, arguing that "the enemy announced in chap. 2 has not only never appeared in recent generations (1:2b) but never before at all, nor afterwards will he ever appear again (2:2b). The locust disaster was *unusual*, but the new distress to be brought on by the enemy will be *unique*."[9] But this is to press the difference between the two formulations much too hard; the point in both places is that what is about to happen has no precedent. This does not move the invasion of chapter 2 on to a new, "eschatological" or "apocalyptic" plane; the idea is simply a literary *topos* designed to emphasize just how amazing and unexpected the coming disaster will be, and how vast will be its scale.

[3] It is not clear whether the flame and fire before and after the invading force are to be understood literally or metaphorically. One could more easily understand the idea of a fire following the locusts, in the sense that the land after their depredations might look as though it had been scorched, but the preceding flame is harder to interpret. It is noteworthy that chapter 1 already associates fire with the locust plague (1:19, 20). It may well be that this element, like the darkness and cloud, comes from the theophany tradition, as in Ps. 97:2–5:

> Clouds and thick darkness are all around him;
> > righteousness and justice are the foundation of his throne.
> Fire goes before him,
> > and consumes his adversaries on every side.
> His lightnings light up the world;
> > the earth sees and trembles.
> The mountains melt like wax before YHWH,
> > before the Lord of all the earth.

---

9. Wolff, *Joel and Amos*, p. 42.

Second Lament Cycle 73

In that case, Joel sees the coming of the locust plague as accompanied by portents that mark it out as a divine visitation, which is precisely what, in his view, it is.

No greater contrast between the countryside before and after the locusts have passed can be drawn than by comparing its initial state to the garden of Eden. We know little about how this garden was envisaged in Hebrew tradition. Apart from the description of the garden in Genesis 2 and 3, there is an extended treatment of another myth about it in Ezekiel 28, where the king of Tyre is likened to the first man "in Eden, the garden of God" (28:13), adorned with precious jewels. Interestingly, Eden is there identified as "the holy mountain of God" (28:14), and the first man is guarded (rather than kept out, as in Gen. 3:24) by a cherub. There is probably an extensive mythology behind these casual references, but it is uncertain how far we can now reconstruct it.[10] The contrast between the garden of Eden and a desert was probably, by Joel's day, another literary *topos* (cf. Isa. 51:3 and Ezek. 36:35).

[4–5] The comparison of a locust to a horse is apparently a cross-cultural phenomenon (German has a term for locust, *Heupferd,* "hay horse"),[11] and it appears also in Rev. 9:7: "In appearance the locusts were like horses equipped for battle." Verse 4 compares their appearance with that of warhorses charging into battle, while v. 5 describes the sound they make as like the rumbling of chariots (see the textual notes above). With horses and chariots an army advanced more quickly than anything else in the ancient world could move, and the comparison of the locusts to this massive onslaught captures well the sense of terror Joel is trying to instill in his hearers/readers. This time the locusts are not said to be accompanied by fire; rather, the sound of their advance is compared to the sound of flames devouring stubble. Few Old Testament passages have the vividness of this, but a close parallel (describing a literal army, however) can be found in Nahum 3:1–3.

[6–9] That "peoples" (*'ammîm*) writhe before the incoming army leads some commentators to see them as threatening more than simply Judah,[12] and this may be an element borrowed from the tradition of YHWH's theophany (cf. Ps. 97:6, where "all peoples" see the glory of YHWH as he appears in splendor). The locust plague is clearly envisaged in larger-than-life terms, however, and Joel may envisage it as covering surrounding countries as well as Judah itself. The locusts march in perfect formation (cf. Prov. 30:27) and scale the wall of the city far more easily than an invading army would be able to manage.

This passage conveys a sense of complete hopelessness in the face of this

---

10. Cf. M. Barker, *The Older Testament: The Survival of Themes from the Ancient Royal Cult in Sectarian Judaism and Early Christianity,* London 1987; idem, *The Gate of Heaven: The History and Symbolism of the Temple in Jerusalem,* London 1991.
11. See Crenshaw, *Joel,* pp. 91 and 121.
12. See Wolff, *Joel and Amos,* p. 46.

small but deadly enemy. Worst of all, locusts steal into people's houses through the windows "like a thief." This recalls the famous passage in Jer. 9:21: "Death has come up into our windows." The prospect of finding one's own house full of locusts bent on eating everything in sight is a horrible one that the prophet makes all too vivid.

[10–11] The earth quakes "before him" or "before it" (*lĕpānāyw* in the Hebrew), but "before them" is justified if we think that the army of locusts is being identified as a single entity. In contrast, the reference could be to YHWH, who is leading the locusts (v. 11), and in these two verses the emphasis is no longer on the devastation brought by the locusts but on the meteorological changes that attend YHWH's visitation of the earth. (See below for a further possibility.) The closest parallel is Isa. 13:10 (cf. also Jer. 4:23–28; Ezek. 32:7–8):

> For the stars of the heavens and their constellations
>   will not give their light;
> the sun will be dark at its rising,
>   and the moon will not shed its light.

This does not necessarily imply, however, that there is here a "transformation from history to a realm beyond history."[13] It was normal in the ancient world to think that the heavenly world acted in sympathy with great events on earth. In Isaiah 13, the "cash value" of the transformation of sun, moon, and stars is the overthrow of Babylon, just as in Isa. 34:4 "the host of heaven shall rot away, and the skies roll up like a scroll," and yet this is not the end of the world but simply a portent of YHWH's judgment on the Edomites (34:9–15). Similarly, in Ezekiel 32 the context is divine judgment on the Egyptian pharaoh and his country. We must be careful not to read back into the texts our own knowledge that changes to sun and moon could occur only as part of a cosmic catastrophe; for the ancient writers, the heavenly bodies were at God's disposal and could undergo dramatic changes without that spelling an end to life on earth or even to the historical process. It was, of course, a miracle when "the sun stopped in midheaven, and did not hurry to set for about a whole day" (Josh. 10:13), but not such a miracle as it would seem to us, who know what this would imply about the earth's rotation!

Joel is thus drawing here on an already well established tradition about the things that happen in the universe when God appears in judgment, but he is not necessarily saying that all history—still less the whole of human life—is coming to an end. He is, rather, emphasizing the vast scale of the disaster, which is so significant that it is accompanied by heavenly portents.

---

13. Crenshaw, *Joel*, p. 126.

Second Lament Cycle

In v. 11 we hear for the first time explicitly that YHWH is himself leading the huge army of locusts, so that the invasion does indeed constitute a "day of YHWH." NRSV is probably correct to ignore the first two occurrences of *kî* (literally, "*for* vast is his host; *for* numberless are those who obey his command") and to render the third as "truly" (rather than "for the day of YHWH is great"); these are all examples of *kî* as an intensifier rather than as introducing an explanation or reason. For the sake of mirroring the Hebrew more closely, I have included all three cases in my translation.

It should be noted that the verbs in vv. 10 and 11 are in the perfect tense (*qatal*), whereas up to this point the imperfect (*yiqtol*) has been used. This could indicate that the prophet is talking about events that preceded the locust invasion, in other words, that the heavenly luminaries *had been* darkened and YHWH *had* uttered his voice before the locusts set off on their march. Then *lĕpānāyw* in v. 10 could mean "before this." But little is known about the use of the Hebrew tenses in such verse passages as this, and with our present knowledge we cannot be sure that the change is significant.

It could reasonably be said, however, that the tenses in vv. 10 and 11 suggest there is no sequence of actions from v. 9 to v. 10, as though the earthquake and darkening of the sun *followed* the locusts' incursion into the city; more probably, the cosmic signs are an accompaniment of the journey of the locusts. The argument that chapter 2 uses imperfect tenses whereas chapter 1 uses the perfect, and that therefore chapter 1 refers to an event that is already past whereas chapter 2 looks forward to a further disaster, comes to grief on the variation in tenses at this critical juncture. As we have seen, it is probable that both chapters are to be understood as predictive and, indeed, as referring to the same events.[14]

2. The Call to Lament (2:12–17a)

12   Yet even now, says YHWH,
       return to me with all your heart,
     with fasting, with weeping, and with mourning;
       rend your hearts and not your garments.
13   And return to YHWH your God,
       for he is gracious and merciful,

---

14. Wolff, *Joel and Amos*, pp. 46–47, comments rather obscurely: "There is a final transition now from the imperfects used thus far (which described events whose meaning is clarified in connection with vv 1b–3 and 10–11) to forms in the perfect, which substantiate the acts as weighty in their own right." This seems to imply that the difference between *qatal* and *yiqtol* is aspectual rather than a matter of tense, which is probably not the case (see T. Goldfajn, *Word Order and Time in Biblical Hebrew Narrative*, Oxford 1998, for the most recent detailed discussion of this vexed issue).

slow to anger, and abounding in steadfast love,
  and relents from doing harm.
14 Who knows? He may turn and relent,
  and leave a blessing behind him,
 a grain offering and a drink offering
  for YHWH, your God.

15 Blow the trumpet in Zion;
  sanctify a fast;
 call an assembly;
16 gather the people.
 Sanctify the congregation;
  assemble the aged;
 gather the children,
  even babies sucking at the breast.
 Let the bridegroom leave his room,
  and the bride her canopy.

17a Between the vestibule and the altar
  let the priests, the ministers of the LORD, weep.

Commentary

Here is one of the two passages in Joel that are widely known (the other is 2:28–31), this one because of its use in Christian liturgies for the beginning of Lent. This use has generalized a call to lament, uttered in the hope of averting the destruction brought by the locusts, into a divine imperative to repent of all one's sins in the hope of divine forgiveness. Or did the call preexist the crisis in which Joel used it? We cannot rule out the possibility that this call to lament was a stock part of the liturgy in Joel's day in any case and was deployed by him because it seemed appropriate in the context of his predictions of the locust invasion. If it did have an origin outside the prophet's own work, it would have been for use in time of drought, in view of v. 14, which speaks of the possibility that YHWH may "leave . . . a grain offering and a drink offering," that is, may restore fruitfulness to the land (cf. Jer. 14:17–22). It remains, however, entirely possible that it was composed especially for the occasion by the prophet, since already in chapter 1 we read of the cutting off of grain offerings and drink offerings (1:9, 13), which may have been Joel's characteristic way of describing the famine.

It is possible to argue for a difference between this call to lamentation and that in 1:5–14 on the basis that chapter 1 is concerned with a calamity that has already happened and to which mourning and lamentation are an appropriate

Second Lament Cycle

response—but with no hope that it can be averted—whereas in chapter 2 the disaster is threatened but there is hope that lamentation and fasting may be in time to prevent it from happening.[15] If any reliance *could* be placed on the change of tenses—which we have already seen to be unlikely—we should have to say that the day of YHWH has already come in the darkening of the skies and roaring of YHWH at the head of his army in 2:10–11. But my own interpretation is that both chapters deal in prediction rather than in description of what has already happened, and that in both there is held out a hope that timely lamentation and fasting can improve the people's lot. Either they may actually avert the locust plague, or they may persuade YHWH to intervene and eliminate—perhaps miraculously—its worst effects, restoring fruitfulness before there is time for the destructive results of the locusts and the drought to bring total ruin. So I do not see any great contrast between the two chapters on this point and continue to believe that both deal with essentially the same foreseen events.

[2:12] "Yet even now" implies that the final moment for judgment has even yet not quite arrived: there is still a chance of averting the disaster. And, as in Amos (Amos 5:14–15), it remains worthwhile to turn back to YHWH, even though the prophet has been predicting the disaster that will befall in what seem to be unconditional terms. The fact that the offer of salvation comes from God himself, not just from the prophet, is underscored by the expression "says the LORD" (*nĕ'um yhwh*), common in the Prophets at the conclusion of oracles, which occurs nowhere else in the book of Joel.[16]

"Return (to YHWH)" is also an expression at home in prophetic oracles, and again Amos provides copious examples: consider Amos 4:6–11, where a whole series of disasters that are similar in many cases to what is prophesied by Joel have failed to cause Israel to "return" to YHWH. There was, no doubt, a shared cultural assumption, by no means restricted to the prophets, that a time of national crisis would produce a "turning" to the national God in the hope that YHWH would save the people. Such an assumption was normal throughout the ancient world. It should make us wary of translating *šûb*, "return," as "repent." What is being spoken of here is not necessarily national lamentation for any sins supposed to have caused God's dramatic intervention but simply a "turn" to God in supplication. This turning would naturally be accompanied by the traditional signs of mourning and lament: fasting, weeping, and mourning and the tearing of clothes. Wolff notes that in Deuteronomistic vocabulary, *return* often refers not to repentance but to a willingness to hear the word of YHWH (cf. Deut. 30:2, 10; 2 Kings 23:25), and this gives an appropriate sense here too.[17]

---

15. Thus Crenshaw, *Joel*, p. 129: "Corresponding to the tenses, chapter one invites the people to lament their awful plight, whereas chapter two insists that timely and genuine repentance may actually avert imminent disaster."
16. Cf. F. Baumgärtel, "Die Formel *ne'um jahwe*," *ZAW* 73 (1961): 277–90.
17. See Wolff, *Joel and Amos*, p. 49.

An alternative explanation of "turn" is provided by G. Ahlström,[18] who thinks the emphasis falls on "to me": "turn to me, not to other gods" (this is of a piece with his generally cultic interpretation of Joel). Jeremiah 4:1–2 might tend to support this, since there it is clear that turning to YHWH means turning from other deities:

> If you return, O Israel, says YHWH,
>   if you return to me,
> if you remove your abominations from my presence,
>   and do not waver,
> and if you swear, "As YHWH lives!"
>   in truth, in justice, and in uprightness,
> then nations shall be blessed by him,
>   and by him they shall boast.

But there are no real indications in Joel that the people are worshiping gods other than YHWH, and we should remember that the prophecy, unlike that of Jeremiah, comes from a postexilic period in which syncretism seems to have been far less to the fore. It is better to interpret Joel to mean simply that the people should turn in appeal to YHWH, asking God to save them from the threatened disaster or, if we think that it has already begun, to restore their fortunes after it has passed by.

In support of this perhaps surprising conclusion, we may recall that one of the differences between Joel and the preexilic classical prophets is that Joel contains little or nothing that could be described as denunciation of sin. He does not take the people to task or suggest that the locust plague has come about because of any specifiable misdemeanor on the part of his hearers. When he outlines what the priests are to say during their liturgical observances, he highlights the danger that Judah's sufferings will cause them to become a "byword" among other nations and that YHWH's heritage will become a reproach, leading people to ask, "Where is their God?" This is an appeal to a kind of enlightened self-interest on YHWH's part and is part of the stock-in-trade of biblical laments (cf. Psalm 44, which actively denies that the people have done anything to deserve the suffering they are undergoing). It is related also to the theme of YHWH's vindication of his name, that is, YHWH's reputation, found in Ezekiel (Ezek. 36:21 and often). By implication, it rules out the idea that the people have done anything to deserve their plight.

This question is obviously bound up with what we make of 2:12–13. Does "return" not speak automatically of "repentance"?[19] G. S. Ogden denies this: "The call to turn to YHWH in 2:12–14 does not call for a repentant attitude, but

---

18. Ahlström, *Joel and the Temple Cult*, p. 26.
19. Cf. J. A. Soggin, "*šûb* zurückkehren," *THAT* 2 (1976): 886–88.

Second Lament Cycle

for a total turning, as expressed by means of the lament ritual, to God as the only source of aid in a crisis."[20] In support of this, it might be noted that Joel nowhere speaks of the people being *forgiven*, only restored to prosperity.

In a detailed study of fasting in the Old Testament and in postbiblical Judaism, H. A. Brongers points out that fasting is hardly required at all by law in biblical times: with the exception of Lev. 16:29, the ritual of the Day of Atonement, the law does not mention fasting. Rather, it is to be seen as a pious custom and often, as in Joel, is "a potent auxiliary of an intercession-prayer."[21] Certainly it *could* be undertaken out of a sense of sin, but the idea of repentance is not inherent in it.

Crenshaw in particular argues that the reason for Joel's insistence that the community engage in a communal fast and a liturgy of lamentation was that he could not see any good reason why YHWH should have been punishing them. Turning from sin is impossible if you do not know what sin you have committed, but turning to God in prayer and asking for mercy might still have its point. Simkins argues that Joel may be akin to Deutero-Isaiah, who also promises deliverance but does not mention any current sins: "In both texts . . . 'return to Yahweh' does not mean 'repent of your sins.' Second Isaiah is clearly not saying, 'Repent from your sins so that Yahweh will redeem you.' Yahweh's forgiveness of sins and redemption are never in doubt."[22]

Most commentators, however, think that "return" in Joel does imply penitence, and much energy has been exerted in trying to decide what is the sin of which the people are being encouraged to repent. As Crenshaw points out, in the absence of any specification of the sin in the text itself, one can only argue as to what is likely or plausible:

> (1) Joel's formulation of the invitation, "return to me," implies that the people were currently following after another deity; (2) the internalization of sorrow suggested by "rend your hearts" indicates pride that has not brought a genuine remorse; (3) the same expression in juxtaposition with ritualistic acts belies confidence in the efficacy of external behaviour; (4) the necessity of commanding priests to mourn and intercede points to a failed leadership; (5) the calamity that has struck the covenant community demonstrates guilt, for the ancient treaty promised prosperity for faithfulness and adversity for breaking the conditions laid down at its ratification; (6) mockery of the Judeans by foreigners issued in shame, which may even have driven YHWH's inheritance to another deity.[23]

---

20. Ogden, "Joel 4," p. 105; cf. also Ogden and Deutsch, *Promise of Hope*, ad loc.
21. H. A. Brongers, "Fasting in Israel in Biblical and Post-Biblical Times," in *Instruction and Interpretation*, ed. A. S. van der Woude (OTS 20), Leiden 1977, pp. 1–21; the quotation is from p. 10.
22. Simkins, *Yahweh's Activity in History*, p. 190.
23. Crenshaw, *Joel*, p. 189.

The problem with trying to work out *a priori* what is likely to have been the sin for which repentance is needed is that one can easily read into the text one's own "favorite" sin, and it is perhaps suspicious when Protestant commentators explain that what Joel found fault with was the people's reliance on ritual[24] or their complacency about their keeping of the *torah* and failure to heed the prophetic word.[25] Wolff thinks the enemy of chapter 2, which he identifies as YHWH's eschatological army, is coming on Judah to punish these sins, and only repentance can avert such a disaster.[26] The truth is that we do not know the answer to this question.

For my part, I doubt Joel was attributing the disaster to any specific sin at all, despite the language of "turning" (*šûb*) in 2:12. The logic of fasting and lamenting is to bewail the present adversity in the presence of God and to ask God to restore. This normally, in the ancient Near East, implied an acknowledgment that one might have sinned, that some misdemeanor (perhaps an unrecognized one) might be causing divine anger. But the lamentation was not necessarily, in and of itself, an act of repentance but rather a way of imploring God to be faithful. A heart that is "rent" (2:13) is not necessarily a repentant heart but one that acknowledges its own desolation. But even if repentance is a theme in Joel, the attempt to discover the sin to which it is an appropriate response seems to me a hopeless quest.

[13] Commentators are generally agreed that the prophet means "tear your hearts as well as your clothes"; "do not simply engage in external ritual but also lament inwardly." This is not part of an "anticultic" prophecy, like the preexilic prophets' polemic against cultic ritual (cf. Isa. 1:11–15; Amos 5:21–24) or even Trito-Isaiah's protest about fasting as a cover for social injustice (Isa. 58:1–9). It is clear that Joel intends his hearers to engage in the normal rituals of communal fasting and lamentation, which would have included rending the garments. There is no protest in Joel at "empty ritual" (*pace* Crenshaw) but rather a desire that what is done externally also be internalized. The "heart" is not so much the seat of feeling and emotion as of thought and reflection in the Old Testament, so that the prophet's intention is not so much that people should feel bad (they already do) as that they should subject their minds to YHWH in obedience and faith.

The God to whom the people are to return is identified as "gracious and merciful, slow to anger, and abounding in steadfast love, and [who] relents from punishing." As discussed in the introduction (see p. 25, above), this formula occurs several times in the Old Testament in various forms and has some claim

---

24. See G. Wanke, "Prophecy and Psalms in the Persian Period," in *The Cambridge History of Judaism*, ed. W. D. Davies and L. Finkelstein, Cambridge 1984, vol. 1, pp. 174–77.

25. Thus Wolff; see above, p. 65.

26. Redditt, "Book of Joel," thinks similarly that the people's sin is reliance on the cultic establishment (presupposing something like Plöger's model of the parties in postexilic Judaism).

to have functioned as a kind of creed identifying the most salient characteristics of YHWH. It occurs in various forms at Exod. 34:6; Num. 14:18; Neh. 9:17; Ps. 86:15; 103:8; 145:8; Nahum 1:3; and Jonah 4:2, only the last of which includes the formula "and relents from punishing" at the end. The attempt to discover which of these is the "origin" of the formula seems doomed to failure, and we must be content merely to note that people in Israel seem to have thought it desirable to have a list of the divine attributes—something to remember when it is said that the Old Testament does not contain any "theology." The meaning of the various attributes is well summed up by Crenshaw:

> Together, they characterize YHWH as a superior who looks with favor on an inferior within a prescribed relationship (*ḥannûn*), one who turns toward another with solicitous concern akin to that of parents (*wĕraḥûm*), taking a long breath and counting to ten instead of having a short fuse when offended (*'erek 'appayim*) so as to demonstrate constant kindness (*wĕrab-ḥesed*), and even reconsidering intended punishment when circumstances warrant such action (*wĕniḥām 'al-hārā'â*).[27]

It is worth noting that none of the attributes refers to anything specific that God has done in the past—there is no reference to "saving history," even though parts of it no doubt could be cited as evidence of various attributes of God. The list of the divine attributes stands as a kind of timeless expression of the character of YHWH, which justifies the people in turning to God in confidence in their time of trouble.

[14] "Who knows? He may turn . . ." means "Perhaps he will turn"; it does not express perplexity but tentative confidence.[28] Interestingly, the effect of the people's turning may be that YHWH "turns" in response—turns from the destructive course of action and toward mercy. The parallel with Jonah, which we have just seen in the list of the divine attributes, continues with this sentence, which occurs almost verbatim at Jonah 3:9 in the mouth of the king of Nineveh: "Who knows? God may relent and change his mind; he may turn from his fierce anger, so that we do not perish." The parallel slightly supports the position that the disaster is threatened rather than having already occurred—the formula is concerned with the possibility that it may yet be averted rather than with some kind of restoration to follow.

This is also borne out by the possibility that YHWH may leave behind him "a blessing," spelled out as "a grain offering and a drink offering," that is, the agricultural produce that will cease to exist if the locust plague, drought, and fire are allowed to take their toll. The hope is that the threatened disaster may not happen after all. If we insist that the disaster is already occurring, then we shall have to think that the hope is for a future restoration of fertility, so that

---

27. Crenshaw, *Joel*, p. 136.
28. J. L. Crenshaw, "The Expression *mî yōdea'* in the Hebrew Bible," *VT* 36 (1986): 274–88.

next season there may again be cereal and drink offerings to present before YHWH; but it seems to me this would be a much weaker point. This verse supports our argument that in chapter 2, as in chapter 1, the locust plague is foretold, not yet experienced.

[15–16] This time the trumpet call is not the sign of the watchman but a cultic blowing of the *šōpār* to inaugurate a solemn liturgy. The imperatives that follow seem to be stylized and are more or less the same as at 1:14: "sanctify a fast, call an assembly, gather the people." The "aged" to be assembled here do seem to be "the old" rather than "the elders," since they are in parallel with "the children" and "babies sucking at the breast" (cf. Ps. 148:12). The extremity of the need is seen, perhaps, in the inclusion even of babies in the cultic assembly, which they would presumably not normally have attended. It is further stressed by the call to bridegroom and bride to leave their rooms and attend in the Temple. As Crenshaw points out, three things are implied by the "sanctification" of the fast—abstention from food, work, and sexual activity—and all three could not normally apply to a newly married couple.[29] But here even they have to abandon their honeymoon to come to the Temple and lament. The suspension of marriage as a sign of extreme disaster seems to be a *topos* in the Old Testament (cf. Ps. 78:63; Jer. 7:34; 16:9; 25:10). The "room" of the bridegroom (*ḥeder*) is the normal term for an inner or private room (cf. Song of Songs 1:4), whereas the bride's "canopy" (*ḥuppâ*) occurs only here and at Ps. 19:5.

[17a] The priests are called on to assemble between the entrance hall (*'ûlām*) to the Temple and the altar of burnt offerings. The entrance hall measured ten by twenty cubits, according to 1 Kings 6:3; it succeeded in accommodating the twenty-five men whom Ezekiel saw worshiping the sun with their backs to the altar (Ezek. 8:16). The priests are to lead the people's lamentations.

3. The Lament (2:17b)

Let them say, "Spare your people, YHWH,
  and do not make your heritage a mockery,
  a byword among the nations.[a]
Why should they say among the peoples,
  'Where is their God?'"

  a. The versions LXX and Vulgate take *lmšl bm gym,* which NRSV renders "a byword among the nations," as meaning "that the nations should rule over them" (LXX *tou katarxai autōn ethnē*), deriving *mšl* from the verb *to rule* rather than as being the noun *māšāl*. This clearly would not fit the context in Joel, where nothing is said about foreign domination over Judah but only about natural disaster—unless we take the view that chapter 2 is about the invasion of a foreign army, which we have already seen reason to

29. Crenshaw, *Joel*, pp. 140–41.

reject. Wolff defends the rendering "that the nations should rule over them," since he does think chapter 2 is about an invading army. It would also be possible to think that Joel is simply quoting from an all-purpose lament that included a reference to foreign domination, even though it was not particularly appropriate in the context. On the whole, it seems to me better to see *māšāl* as in parallel with *ḥerpâ,* "mockery," and to avoid any implication of military defeat in these verses (cf. Jer. 24:9, "a disgrace, a byword," *lĕḥerpâ ûlĕmāšāl*).

Commentary

Whereas chapter 1 includes a lengthy lament, here we have only the bare essentials of one, and it is probably not to be imagined that this was the whole content of the lamentation the prophet expected the priests to utter. Form-critically the text is certainly a standard lament, paralleled in many of the psalms of lament in the Psalter. What is interesting is the content of the prayer. There is no mention of the people's sin: the text is not a confession. Rather, it concentrates on the damaging implications *for YHWH* of allowing the people to suffer such devastation—it will result in YHWH's "heritage" (*naḥălâ,* a favorite word in Deuteronomistic texts)[30] becoming a "byword" (*māšāl*). In other words, foreign nations will come to see the Judaean community as a parade example of desolation and will draw the inevitable conclusion that their God abandoned them. This line of argument is found also in Ps. 44:9–16, where it is coupled with a confident assertion that the nation has *not* done anything to deserve its suffering:

> If we had forgotten the name of our God,
>   or spread out our hands to a strange god,
> would not God discover this?
>   For he knows the secrets of the heart.
> Because of *you* we are being killed all day long.
>   (Ps. 44:20–22)

Here disaster is God's fault, not the people's. Joel does not go that far, but he is clear that it is in God's own interest to reverse the people's misfortune, so that divine honor is no longer impugned by their degradation. All this creates a strong impression that the reputation of YHWH is bound up closely with that of his people, a theme developed in detail in Ezekiel (cf. Ezek. 36:20).

The theology of the second lament cycle in Joel hardly differs from that of the first. It assumes that YHWH can inflict disaster on Israel by using the

---

30. See F. Horst, "Zwei Begriffe für Eigentum (Besitz): *naḥălâ* and *aḥuzzâ*," in *Verbannung und Heimkehr: Beiträge zur Geschichte und Theologie Israels im 6. Und 5. Jahrhundert vor Chr. (Festschrift für Wilhelm Rudolph,* ed. A. Kuschke, Tübingen 1961, pp. 135–56; and G. Wanke, "*naḥălâ* Besitzanteil," *THAT* 2 (1979): 55–59.

natural world against them and does not speculate on the reasons why YHWH may do so, as earlier prophets did: there is no attempt to identify particular sins that led to the people's downfall. The appropriate reaction to disasters on this scale is for the people to engage in ritualized lamentation, which is meant to have both an outward aspect (fasting, weeping, tearing the clothes) and an inner one ("rending the heart"). The urgency of the need to lament outweighs all normal restrictions on worship: young children and even the newly married are expected to take part. YHWH himself gives the instruction to engage in these rituals of self-abasement and misery and at least half-promises that they will be effective.

YHWH's merciful character is well known from existing theological formulas that stress God's unwillingness to punish the people and his steadfast love for them, which has the power to avert the threatened disaster even at the last hour. Oddly, the lament the priests are to utter on the people's behalf does not refer to the list of YHWH's attributes but appeals simply to God's known commitment to Judah. On that basis, it is argued that YHWH cannot afford to let his own special possession among the nations become a byword for ill treatment by its God.

The Divine Response
Joel 2:18–27

2:18 Then YHWH became jealous for his land,
    and he had pity on his people;
19 and YHWH answered, and said to his people:
"Behold, I am sending you
    grain, wine, and oil,
    and you will be satisfied with it;
and I will no more make you
    a reproach among the nations.

20 "I will remove the 'northerner' far from you,
    and drive him into a parched and desolate land,
his front into the eastern sea,
    and his rear into the western sea;
its stench and foul smell[a] will rise up.
    (For he has done great things!)[b]

21 "Do not fear, O soil;
    be glad and rejoice,
    for YHWH has done great things!

The Divine Response

22 Do not fear, you wild animals,
      for the pastures of the wilderness have become green;
   for the tree bears its fruit,
      the fig tree and vine give their full yield.

23 "O children of Zion, be glad
      and rejoice in YHWH your God;
   for he has given you the early rain[c] for your vindication,
      he has poured down showers for you,
      the early and later rain, as before.[d]
24 The threshing floors will be full of grain,
      and the vats will overflow with wine and oil.

25 (I will repay you for the years
      that the swarming locust has eaten,
   the hopper, the destroyer, and the cutter,
      my great army, which I sent against you.)

26 "And you shall eat and eat, and be satisfied,
      and praise the name of YHWH your God,
      who has acted so surprisingly for you.
   And my people shall never again be shamed.[e]
27 You shall know that I am in the midst of Israel,
      and that I, YHWH, am your God, and there is no other.
   And my people shall never again be shamed."

a. "Foul smell" (ṣaḥănâ) occurs only here in the Hebrew Bible, but its sense is dictated by the parallelism with bā'š, "stench."

b. The verse ends with "Surely [or 'For'] he has done great things," which looks very much like a dittograph of v. 21c, where it is YHWH who is the subject. If the line is correctly placed here, the subject would have to be the "northerner," and we could follow Crenshaw in interpreting the "great things" pejoratively as "a great outrage" ("for he has acted reprehensibly" is Crenshaw's own rendering).[1] But the line is undoubtedly awkward and should perhaps be deleted.

c. In v. 23, 'et-hammôreh is here rendered "the early rain," which makes good sense in the context of language about renewed fruitfulness; liṣĕdāqâ—literally "for righteousness"—then has to be taken as "in moderation" or perhaps, as NRSV, "for your vindication," whatever exactly that means. yôreh is the normal word for early rain, though the form môreh does occur at Ps. 84:6. The LXX, however, reads ta brōmata, "food," which avoids the excessive repetition of words for rain in the verse, though "food for/according to righteousness" is still not exactly lucid; it might rest on a reading

1. Crenshaw, *Joel*, p. 152.

hamma'kāl as suggested by Wolff (*Joel and Amos,* 55), though it is not clear how that would have been corrupted to *hammôreh*. Wolff argues that "food according to righteousness" would be food appropriate to the relationship between YHWH and Israel; Crenshaw thinks of *ṣĕdāqâ* as implying an idea of cosmic order, so that it would mean "food in its due season" or "in appropriate measure."

But the Vulgate translates *doctorem justitiae,* "a teacher of righteousness," and this of course invites comparison with the important concept of the Teacher of Righteousness, *mwrh hṣdq,* at Qumran. But the resemblance is probably coincidence,[2] since the Qumran texts never appeal to this verse in reference to their Teacher of Righteousness. (Unfortunately the verse is not extant in any Qumran manuscripts of the prophets.) Isaiah 30:20 seems to enshrine the idea of a (eschatological?) figure who can be called "your teacher" (*môrêkā*), and it may well be that MT is to be interpreted in the light of such hopes. But an original reference to a "teacher" would be of very doubtful relevance in these verses, which are otherwise all about renewed fertility. So it seems preferable to follow NRSV in thinking that *môreh* here meant, for Joel, "early rain," even if later readers saw it as a reference to a "teacher." The "early" and "late" rains are, respectively, the showers in autumn and spring.

d. NRSV follows a common emendation of *bāri'šôn,* "in the first (month?)," to *kāri'šôn,* "as originally," "as formerly" (cf. LXX *kathōs emprosthen*)—though perhaps *bāri'šôn* could mean this anyway.

e. BHS proposes deleting this line as a dittograph of 27c, though it looks equally superfluous there; either occurrence could be a dittograph of the other!

Commentary

It is widely held that laments or pleas for help uttered in the Temple cultus were customarily followed by an oracle declaring that God had heard the lament, and that this explains the sudden transition from lament to assurance in some of the psalms. Thus, in Psalm 20, a prayer for the king to be blessed by YHWH in vv. 1–5 is followed in vv. 6–8 by a thanksgiving that YHWH will certainly do so: "Now I know that the LORD will help his anointed." It is plausible to think that after the first part of the psalm a cultic official (priest or prophet) arose and uttered a favorable oracle in response to the intercession. Similarly, in Psalm 60 a lament about military defeat (vv. 1–5) is followed by a declaration that God will favor the people and give them dominion over their enemies. It seems likely that this pattern, lament followed by oracle of blessing, was well established in the Temple cult even in preexilic times.

At first sight, it would appear something similar is happening at Joel 2:18, with a transition from the prayers of lament that conclude the two cycles of chapters 1 and 2 to oracles of blessing from YHWH. What is odd here, however, is that verses 17 and 18 are introduced by verbs in the "waw consecutive"

---

2. Despite C. Roth, "The Teacher of Righteousness and the Prophecy of Joel," *VT* 13 (1963): 91–95.

The Divine Response

(*wayyiqtol*) form. There has been no reference to actual events in the real world, as opposed to those within the prophet's vision of the future, up to this point, unless we count 1:4 with its programmatic description of the locust plague. It looks as if we have to supply some transitional material to the effect that the people did as the prophet urged them to do and indeed uttered the lamentations he had called on them to offer. There is only one parallel in the prophetic literature to a narrative implying that what the prophet commanded has been carried out, without a specific narrative framework that says so, and that is Mal. 3:16. After a long series of oracles but no narrative, we read:

> Then those who revered YHWH spoke with one another. YHWH took note and listened, and a book of remembrance was written before him of those who revered YHWH and thought on his name. They shall be mine, says YHWH, my special possession on the day when I act. (Mal. 3:16-17)

The effect created is slightly surreal and the reader feels disoriented. The same is true, I believe, of Joel 2:18. "Then the LORD became jealous for his land"—when? When the people did as the prophet told them? Or when the prophet had delivered his message? Or even *within* the prophetic vision—so that the narrative account is simply another part of what the prophet is predicting? The last possibility cannot be ruled out; everything in the book, including the narrative about YHWH's having pity on the people, could be taking place within the prophetic vision and might not refer to events that actually occurred in the external world.

The transition from 2:17 to 2:18 is so rough that it is not surprising some commentators have felt that it was intolerable. Merx, for example, insisted that the waw consecutives (*wayyiqtol*) should be repointed as jussives (*weyiqtol*), and that everything from 2:18 to the end of the book was part of the prayer that the priests are urged to utter: "Then may the LORD become jealous for his land ... and may he say: 'I am sending you grain ...,'" and so on. For him, the narrative verbs of MT are "ernsthaft undenkbar," "seriously unthinkable."[3] But the very oddity of the tenses probably makes it unlikely that we should emend the Masoretic pointing.

However we look at it, 2:18 represents a definite turning point in the book, from lamentation to divine response, even if it is not a record of such response but only a promise of it, recorded (in familiar prophetic style) as though it had already happened. For the later generations that preserved and transmitted the words of Joel, it did not matter whether the restoration/salvation from impending disaster was recorded as having happened in reality or as being an inevitable consequence of the laments. In either case, the value of the prophet's words consisted in their implications for later generations, who could feel reassured that

---

3. Merx, *Die Prophetie des Joel*, p. 16.

in any similar calamity they could count on divine help. Little notice was taken of the tenses in prophetic books, since it was assumed that everything, even narrative, had also a future reference.

[2:18–19] YHWH's "jealousy" has a dual aspect in the Old Testament. On the one hand, it means YHWH's intolerance of any rivals, as in the Ten Commandments: "You shall have no other gods before me. You shall not make for yourself an idol. . . . You shall not bow down to them or worship them; for I YHWH your God am a jealous God" (Exod. 20:3–5). In the Deuteronomistic History, jealousy is one of the most obvious divine attributes, as YHWH insists that he will not stand for any other gods being worshiped in his land or by his people. On the other hand, God's "jealousy" can be his passionate commitment to his people, his refusal to let any rival wrest them from his control, and hence his insistence on saving and protecting them. In contexts where this is the meaning, English versions often use the word *zeal* (cf. Isa. 9:7, "The zeal of YHWH of hosts will do this").

The two senses are linked by the concept of YHWH's unique relationship with Israel, which makes him incensed if Israel ever abandons YHWH for a rival and yet keeps him always in deadly earnest about their well-being and willing to smash anyone who gets in the way of it. Once the people have lamented to YHWH and turned to him in sincerity, his "jealousy" is triggered, and he begins to have pity on them and to "answer" them—literally, in the sense of uttering an oracle of blessing. It may be doubted whether any distinction is to be drawn between "land" and "people" in 2:18: YHWH is committed to both, and they occur in synonymous parallelism.

The oracle in v. 19 picks up elements of both cycles of lamentation: "grain, wine, and oil" are the great theme of chapter 1, while the fact that Israel (Judah) has become a "reproach" is the central point of the lament in 2:17. Thus YHWH's promise offers an immediate reversal of the disaster. God restores the fruitfulness of the ground and also removes at a stroke the derision the nation felt it had attracted from its neighbors when its God was apparently unable to keep it in a fitting state by guaranteeing fertility. Once again, it is difficult to tell whether the prophet is speaking about a reversal of a disaster that has already overtaken the people or about its being averted in the nick of time.

[20] On the identification of the "northerner" ("army" is supplied by NRSV, where the Hebrew says simply "the northerner"), see above, pp. 47–48. If we take the Hebrew *ṣĕpônî* to refer to any mighty enemy, rather than to have a strict geographical reference, then there seems no reason why the locust horde could not be meant. Nevertheless, the term otherwise always refers to a human enemy in the Old Testament, so Joel would be using it here in an original way; but then, as we have seen, his comparison of the locusts to a human army in 2:4–9 is very detailed and circumstantial.

The Divine Response

The "northerner," whatever it is, is certainly of enormous size, since it stretches from the "eastern sea" (the Dead Sea) to the "western sea" (the Mediterranean)—in other words, across the whole width of the southern Judaean desert, which is the "parched and desolate land" the prophet refers to. One may reasonably say that the enemy called the northerner, whether it is the locusts or not, is being "mythologized," identified with a Satanlike figure, though this does not necessarily mean it is an apocalyptic entity. This is rather like the situation in Ezekiel 29 where the Egyptian pharaoh is identified with the great crocodile or dragon of the chaos myth, or like Isaiah calling Egypt "Rahab who sits still" (Isa. 30:7). The "stench" from the decaying army could equally refer to dead men or dead locusts.

[21–24] Oracles beginning "do not fear" are commonly at home in the world of the so-called *Königsansprache,* or address to a king in time of war (cf. Isa. 7:4). Here, however, the address is successively to the ground, the animals that graze on it, and the "children of Zion," and they are told of YHWH's reversal of his curse on the land, which will result in a revival of fertility. All the destruction that was foretold in the preceding material now goes into reverse: the pastures grow green again; the fig trees and vines yield fruit; and there is rain once more. Things are restored to the way they were before the various natural disasters struck, or else the predicted disasters are averted so that harvests follow their normal pattern—which of these is meant depends on our general decision about how far Joel is describing what happened and how far he is predicting what will happen unless steps are taken (by lamentation) to avoid it. It is clear that, of the various plagues mentioned in chapters 1 and 2, it is primarily the drought that is in focus here, with no explicit reference to the locust invasion.

"Children of Zion" occurs also at Ps. 149:2, again in a context of rejoicing, and serves as a reminder of how Jerusalem-centered Joel's prophecy is. When he says "Israel" he in practice means Judah and perhaps specifically Jerusalem and its immediate environs, where the community he is addressing lives.

"For YHWH has done great things" in v. 21 recalls Ps. 126:2–3.

[25] In this verse YHWH promises to "make good" (*wĕšillamtî*) the years in which the locusts had destroyed. There is something odd about this. First, there is no evidence in what precedes that the locust plague lasted more than one year, unless we take the two cycles in chapters 1 and 2:1–17 respectively as referring to the parallel events of successive years; and, indeed, there is some difficulty in thinking that in the year after the disasters sketched in chapter 1 there would have been anything for a fresh plague of locusts to eat! (Some commentators have suggested an emendation from *šānîm,* "years," to *šĕnîm,* "double," implying not a locust plague of more than one year's duration but a double restitution.) Second, there is a clear reference back to the four designations for locusts of 1:4, which have played no role in the intervening material. I wonder if this

verse might be a later insertion, deliberately recalling 1:4 and making a neat *inclusio* with it; as it stands, it seems to interrupt the natural progression from the full granaries of v. 24 to the eating in plenty of v. 26. Accordingly, I have placed it in parentheses in the translation.

[26–27] These verses, then, continue the theme of v. 24: YHWH's restoration of the people's fortunes means full stomachs and consequent praise for the God who has dealt "wondrously" (*lĕhaplî'*) with his people—perhaps rather "surprisingly" or "remarkably" (cf. Judg. 13:19). "And my people shall never again be put to shame" occurs as a kind of refrain at the end of both verses. It is a finely balanced question whether this is rhetorical repetition for effect or, more prosaically, dittography. In effect it can be both: the repetition could be accidental, a scribal slip, yet have produced a worthwhile poetic effect that we may well wish to retain.

It is worth noticing the covenantal language in these verses. Israel is called "my people," and YHWH impresses on them that he is to be their God "and there is no other"—reminiscences here of Deutero-Isaiah. Compare Isa. 45:5:

> I am YHWH, and there is no other;
> besides me there is no god.

And 45:17:

> Israel is saved by YHWH
> with everlasting salvation;
> you shall not be put to shame or confounded
>   to all eternity.

The implication seems to be that the disasters with which YHWH had threatened his people implied a temporary cessation of his special relationship with them, but this is now restored, and the covenant is reenacted. "There is no other" in context may not mean any more than that there is no other god for Israel, but (following Deutero-Isaiah) it may also have implications of monotheism: that there is no other god at all. This makes a fitting climax to what we take to have been the original prophecy of Joel. The threat of natural disaster is at an end, and with it the threat that YHWH had lost interest in or had turned against Israel.

Wolff, by contrast, argues that the covenant formula here is not the conclusion of Joel's prophecy but quite deliberately points forward to the next oracle in the book, 2:28 (Hebrew 3:1), on the outpouring of YHWH's spirit:

> The recognition formula does not constitute a conclusion. For the aim of the previously announced response of Yahweh is that he be recognized not only as the God of Israel and the only God, but also as the God who continues to act. . . . V. 27b clearly points to the future. The temporary reversal in the calamity is to lead

The Divine Response

to the recognition that Yahweh's people ultimately will not be destroyed. This sentence points to the continuation in chaps. 3 and 4.[4]

Crenshaw also comments on the similarity with Ezek. 39:28-29, where also the recognition that YHWH is the God of Israel is followed by a pouring out of the spirit:

> Then they shall *know that I am YHWH their God* because I sent them into exile among the nations, and then gathered them into their own land. I will leave none of them behind; and I will never again hide my face from them, when I *pour out my spirit* upon the house of Israel, says the Lord YHWH.[5]

This does not seem to me, however, to have enough force to overrule the impression of a fresh beginning in 2:28, introduced by the telltale "Then afterward" (literally, "And it shall be after this"), which to my mind clearly points to 2:28 as the start of a new section. I do not know where Wolff gets the idea that v. 27 speaks of a "temporary reversal in the calamity": it seems to promise a permanent end to it, and to be quite self-contained. The conclusion that "my people shall never again be put to shame" is surely final enough. Wolff seems to think that "I, YHWH, am your God and there is no other" has some kind of static quality, and that one would not know this God "continues to act" if there were not some further specification of what he will do next; but this is all quite unnecessary: the reimposition of the covenant formula and the announcement of YHWH as the only God say all that is necessary on this subject. (Wolff seems to feel that Joel had to rule out an interpretation of the nature of God that would surely never have occurred to anyone in ancient Israel, namely, that YHWH was the God of Israel and yet somehow no longer active in its affairs. On the contrary, to say that YHWH is the God of Israel and that there is no other is to say all that needs to be said, as Deutero-Isaiah well illustrates.)

With these concluding oracles of Joel we are in a world far removed from that of the preexilic prophets, with their certainty that YHWH's judgment was about to fall on Israel and could no longer be averted. For Joel, as for Deutero-Isaiah, it was certain that YHWH was a God of judgment, but Joel was equally certain that YHWH would hear heartfelt pleas for mercy, so that his last word was bound to be one of salvation. This does not deserve the old jibe of "cheap grace" leveled at the postexilic prophets, because Joel makes it clear that the call to engage in a liturgy of lamentation and self-abasement must be taken with the utmost seriousness. But, provided that it was, YHWH could be relied on to "repent" of the evil he had planned to bring on his people and to restore his covenant bond with them. Judgment by locust, drought, and fire was a seriously meant threat, but it did not represent the full extent of what YHWH had to say

---

4. Wolff, *Joel and Amos*, p. 65.
5. Crenshaw, *Joel*, p. 160.

to the people. God's full message must always include the element of salvation, precisely because of what is known of YHWH's character from the formula quoted in 2:13: that YHWH is a God "gracious and merciful, slow to anger, and abounding in steadfast love, [who] relents from punishing."

Oracles of Salvation
Joel 2:28–3:21

In 2:28 (Hebrew 3:1) there begins a collection of miscellaneous oracles concerning the judgment of the nations and the future salvation of Israel. As argued in the Introduction, it seems likely that the collection is later than the work of the prophet Joel himself and that most of the individual oracles are also inauthentic. They are virtually impossible to date. It is possible that some of them refer to events expected by their author to take place soon, but it is more likely that they represent a selection from a pool of oracles about the more remote future: things that will happen one day but are not expected as imminent and on which no present decisions depend. In other words, they constitute what may be called eschatological predictions, whose fulfillment lies in a distant or at least undatable future and which give hope more by their assurance that God is ultimately in control of the world's fate than by any immediate prospect of fulfillment. They do not amount to a coherent set of expectations, such that we could draw up a temporal scheme in which we might expect them to be fulfilled in any particular order; they are individual shafts of light in an obscure future. They are, as Wolff puts it, "prophetic promises for a more distant time."[1]

We know very little about the context in postexilic Judaism in which such oracles were manufactured. Unlike the oracles in Joel 1:2–2:27, they do not seem to have been called forth by any particular crisis (3:4–8 is probably the exception here, though its background remains desperately obscure) but are "all-purpose" oracles, relevant (or irrelevant) at any given moment.

If we define Old Testament prophecy in terms of its response to pressing crises in the nation's life, then such oracles are not in any normal sense "prophetic." They are literary works, perhaps produced by a scribal class rather than by ecstatics. It is in this section of Joel that one can most easily feel the force of the suggestion that the author was (to use Bergler's expression) a *Schriftprophet*, a writing prophet in the literal sense of that term. As we have seen, such a description fails when applied to Joel himself, the author of the dual lamentation cycle and the promises of 2:18–27, who—like his preexilic and postexilic predecessors—is genuinely engaged with a concrete historical

---

1. Wolff, *Joel and Amos*, p. 65.

Oracles of Salvation 93

situation, in which he has a "word" of YHWH that he feels constrained to deliver. But it is appropriate as a description of the author(s) of the second part of the book. This collection of oracles concerns not a specific crisis in the life of the postexilic Jerusalem community but the "age to come"—not yet the otherworldly age of later Jewish and Christian expectation but certainly a time removed from direct contact with the exigencies of the existing world order and projected into the more remote future. Kimchi said that Joel was concerned with the "Messianic Age,"[2] and this is a fair assessment of the book's second part; even though there is no expectation of a messiah as such, this part of the book is interested in the time of salvation that lies in the future.

If we insist on reading the work as a unity, then the presence of this future-orientated material will be bound to influence how we read 1:2–2:27 too, for *taken as a whole* Joel is a book about the end time, of which the locust invasion and its resolution are harbingers. A historical-critical reading, however, is entitled to distinguish between the two parts of the book and to identify quite different contexts for each.

The oracle collection in 2:28–3:21 comprises a number of individual themes of Jewish eschatology, and there will be no attempt to see them as forming an ordered sequence: each will be discussed in its own right.

1. The Outpouring of God's Spirit (2:28–29)

2:28 Then after all this it will happen that:

I will pour out my spirit on all flesh;
    your sons and your daughters shall prophesy,
your old men shall dream dreams,
    and your young men shall see visions;
29   And even on the male and female slaves,
    in those days, I will pour out my spirit.

Commentary

Additions to the oracles of the prophets commonly begin with a connective phrase indicating "after all this." I have deliberately translated it rather cumbersomely and set it on its own in my translation, since in my view it introduces the whole of the rest of the book.

wĕhāyāh 'aḥărê kēn is not found very often in the Old Testament, but there are many similar phrases that introduce "afterthoughts," implying that a prophetic

---

2. "The days of the Messiah"; see Merx, *Die Prophetie des Joel*, p. 45.

prediction will one day have come true and then other events—not foreseen by the original prophet—will follow. Examples (not exhaustive) are:

in days to come	bĕ'aḥărît hayyāmîm	Isa. 2:2; Micah 4:1
on that day	bayyôm hahû'	Isa. 3:18; 4:2; 10:20; 11:10, 11; 17:7, 9; 19:16, 18, 19, 23, 24; 22:20; 26:1; 27:1, 2, 12; Jer. 4:9; Hos. 2:16, 21; Amos 9:11; Zeph. 3:11; Hag. 2:23; Zech. 13:1, 2, 4; 14:6, 8, 13, 20
at that time	bā'ēt hahî'	Isa. 18:7; Jer. 4:11; 31:1
days are coming	yāmîm bā'îm	Jer. 23:5, 7; 31:27, 31, 38; 48:12; Amos 9:13
in those days and at that time	bayyamîm hahēmmâ ûbā'ēt hahî'	Jer. 33:15; 50:4, 20; Joel 3:1

It is rarely possible to prove that oracles introduced with such formulas are secondary to the material they follow, but such has been the general judgment of most commentators. In the case of Joel 2:28, it appears that the formula has been added after a prophecy that is complete in itself, and that the new material opens up a completely new set of ideas. No longer do we hear of the end of natural disaster and the restoration of fertility and fruitfulness, but instead we find a prediction of the coming transformation of human nature by the outpouring of YHWH's spirit, not on the land but on people. That the spirit could be associated with renewed fruitfulness may be seen from Isa. 32:15:

> until a spirit from on high is poured out on us,
> and the wilderness becomes a fruitful field,
> and the fruitful field is deemed a forest.

But in Joel no such association is made. So I believe it is safe to conclude here that the oracle is an addition to an already completed work.

The outpouring of God's spirit is the idea for which Joel is best known, certainly in Christian circles, because of Peter's quotation of this prophecy on the day of Pentecost according to Acts 2:16–21. It is important, however, to ask what we can make of it in its original context.

The spirit (rûaḥ) of YHWH is, in the first place, that in YHWH which corresponds to the spirit or vital force in human beings—the principle of YHWH's own life, the breath in YHWH's own nostrils, to speak anthropomorphically (see Albertz and Westermann, "rûaḥ Geist"). But this spirit can be communicated to human beings if YHWH chooses to "breathe into their nostrils the breath of life" (Gen. 2:7).

Oracles of Salvation

This may have one of two effects. First, it may be seen as the means by which dead flesh is transformed into living beings: this is the sense in Genesis and also in Ezekiel's vision of the valley of dry bones in Ezekiel 37. There, YHWH's "spirit" turns the corpses that are the "house of Israel" back into living people. But the second effect—and this is closer to what the author of Joel 2:28–29 has in mind—is to communicate the *power* of YHWH. This can be seen when, in the book of Judges, the "spirit of YHWH" rushes into people (e.g., Judg. 11:29; 14:19), empowering them to do great deeds, often of a violent kind. But it can also be seen in the empowerment of prophets. Thus Saul "prophesies" once the spirit of God has come upon him (1 Sam 10:10), and the seventy elders of Israel in Numbers 11 also prophesy when YHWH has placed on them a portion of the spirit he has given to Moses (Num. 11:25).

It is this spiritual gift of prophecy with which Joel 2:28–29 is concerned. Indeed, it reads almost as a fulfillment of Moses' hope expressed in Num. 11:29: "Would that all YHWH's people were prophets, and that YHWH would put his spirit on them!"[3]

The prophetic inspiration that the spirit of YHWH brings is seen, interestingly, as expressing itself in dreams. This is a normal mode of divine communication in the Pentateuch and especially in E material (cf. Gen. 20:3 and the story of Joseph in Genesis 37–48). But Jeremiah, at least, expresses severe reservations about dreams in Jer. 23:25–32:

> I have heard what the prophets have said who prophesy lies in my name, saying, "I have dreamed, I have dreamed!" How long? Will the hearts of the prophets ever turn back—those who prophesy lies, and who prophesy the deceit of their own heart? They plan to make my people forget my name by their dreams that they tell one another, just as their ancestors forgot my name for Baal. Let the prophet who has a dream tell the dream, but let the one who has my word speak my word faithfully. What has straw in common with wheat? says YHWH. Is not my word like fire, says YHWH, and like a hammer that breaks a rock in pieces? See, therefore, I am against the prophets, says YHWH, who steal my words from one another. See, I am against the prophets, says YHWH, who use their own tongues and say, "Says YHWH." See, I am against those who prophesy lying dreams, says YHWH, and who tell them, and who lead my people astray by their lies and their recklessness, when I did not send them or appoint them; so they do not profit this people at all, says YHWH.

The implied contrast here between the divine word and the false dreams appears to find no echo at all in the Joel text, for which "seeing visions" and "dreaming dreams" are highly desirable activities. It is possible that we have

---

3. *Pace* Wolff, *Joel and Amos*, p. 66, there is no reason whatever to think that in his enthusiasm for the renewal of prophecy, the Joel writer was opposing the canonization and establishment of the Torah as the basis for life in Judah.

here evidence of a change in the self-understanding of prophecy in the post-exilic age, when it came to be thought that dreams were indeed the normal vehicle through which divine inspiration was imparted.[4]

The divine spirit is said to be poured out on "all flesh." The general consensus of commentators has been that "all flesh" here does not mean "all humankind" but "all Israel" (in practice, "all Judah")—hence "*your* sons and *your* daughters shall prophesy."[5] This, however, as A. R. Hulst has shown, would put this reference at odds with all other uses of the phrase "all flesh" (*kol bāśār*) in the Old Testament.[6] There are forty or so occurrences of the phrase, and the main difference in meaning from one to another is between "all human beings" (e.g., Jer. 45:5) and "all living beings" (e.g., Gen. 7:16). There seem to be no other places where the meaning is clearly "all Israelites." Yet it is difficult to see just what would be implied by an extension of the outpouring of YHWH's spirit beyond the bounds of Judah, which would make this prophecy one of the most "universalistic" in the Old Testament, alongside oracles such as Isa. 19:19–25. It would presumably mean that knowledge of YHWH would be available to all humankind without exception, an idea almost unparalleled in the Old Testament.

No doubt part of the resistance to this idea is linked with the assumption that the oracle is by Joel. When a prophet is so narrowly concerned with the affairs of the Judaean community centered on Jerusalem, as Joel evidently is, it becomes very difficult to imagine that he could have harbored such universalistic ideas as are implied in 2:28, taken at face value. This difficulty is removed if we regard the verse as secondary to Joel's authentic oracles. The pouring out of the spirit on all human beings—including both foreigners and, as is made explicit, slaves—might then belong to the "signs of the end" as part of the "gathering in of the Gentiles," which is a theme in rabbinic eschatology. It should be noted that the next oracle also includes a promise of salvation for "*everyone who calls on the name of YHWH*" (2:32), though the exact implication of this is also disputed (see below). And the "male and female slaves" might well have included non-Judaeans.

The matter seems to me to be finely balanced. Perhaps the restriction to "*your* sons . . ." does swing the argument in favor of restricting the oracle to Judaeans, but the universalist note should certainly not be ignored. The additions to Joel are much more concerned with the fate of non-Israelites than was the prophet himself, and the Christian use of this text to refer to the quasi-prophetic inspiration of non-Jews, even if it developed it beyond its original intention, took up a hint that is clearly present in the text.

---

4. See Barton, *Oracles of God,* pp. 117–21, 127–28, 289.

5. See Wolff, *Joel and Amos,* p. 67; Crenshaw, *Joel,* p. 16; Weiser, *Das Buch der zwölf kleinen Propheten,* p. 103.

6. See A. R. Hulst, "*Kol basar* in der priesterlichen Fluterzählung," in *Studies on the Book of Genesis* (OTS 12), Leiden 1958, pp. 28–66.

2. The Day of YHWH (2:30-32)

30 I will show portents in the heavens and on the earth,
   blood and fire and columns of smoke.
31 The sun shall be turned to darkness, and the moon to blood,
   before the coming of the great and terrible day of YHWH.
32 Then everyone who calls on the name of YHWH shall escape;
   for in Mount Zion there shall be those who escape
   (as YHWH has said)
   and in Jerusalem survivors whom YHWH shall call.[a]

   a. NRSV prints this passage as prose, but *BHS* treats it as verse, successfully as it seems to me (cf. also Crenshaw). There is no obvious change in style or meter at this point, and by following *BHS*'s suggested transposition of "in Jerusalem," the last verse can be made to run in synonymous parallelism, as in my translation.

Commentary

It does not seem probable that the "portents" (*môpĕtîm*) here are meant to *follow* the outpouring of the spirit in 2:28-29—nor to precede them, for that matter. We simply have another fragmentary prophecy of the end time, which cannot be arranged with others into a chronological sequence. The outpouring of the spirit produces a new "inspired" community, which is an end in itself. Here the signs in heaven and earth portend a much more apocalyptic future, in which the arrival of the day of YHWH is presaged by changes in the whole of nature and results in a transformation of the community in Judah and Jerusalem so as to include all who "call on the name of YHWH"—possibly including foreigners but more likely, I think, comprising those Judaeans and Jerusalemites who escape physical disaster on the day of YHWH and who turn back to their God.[7]

A *môpēt* is an event or object that points beyond itself to some remarkable divine intervention. Thus Isaiah and his prophetically named children are described as *môpĕtîm* in Isa. 8:18, and Isaiah himself is a *môpēt* when he walks around Jerusalem naked and barefoot in Isa. 20:3, prefiguring the suffering of its people. The plagues of Egypt are also *môpĕtîm* in Pss. 78:43; 105:5, 27; and 135:9, perhaps because they are forerunners of the great divine act in the exodus. The English word *portent* in fact is a very adequate rendering. The portents in these verses, however, are "cosmic" events, or at any rate meteorological ones. The sun turning to darkness is plainly an image taken from a solar eclipse, which produces an eerie darkness when it is total and a cold twilight when it is partial. The moon turning to blood might be drawn from the experience of lunar eclipses, when the moon appears reddish, though obviously the two kinds of eclipse cannot occur together.

   7. Cf. Wolff, *Joel and Amos*, pp. 68-69.

There is a long prophetic tradition identifying the darkening of the sky as a portent of disaster in the human world (cf. Isa. 13:10; 34:4; Jer. 4:23; Ezek. 32:7–8; Amos 8:9). The blood, fire, and columns of smoke suggest either natural disaster (perhaps earthquake or volcanic eruption) or invasion and war. At all events, the coming of YHWH's day is announced beforehand by unmistakable signs, according to the normal ancient perception that "coming events cast their shadows before." It should be noted (cf. also above, on 2:10) that all these disturbances in the cosmos do not imply that the day of YHWH brings cosmic catastrophe, for it leaves Judah and Jerusalem intact with survivors (probably from war) still there, waiting to turn back to YHWH.

"As YHWH has said" (*ka'ăšer 'āmar yhwh*) is interesting. It could mean simply "as YHWH says," that is, it could function in the same way as *nĕ'um yhwh* in 2:12, authenticating the oracle as a word of YHWH. But it could also, as the English translation suggests, refer to some earlier word of YHWH that will be fulfilled when there are "those who escape": "a conscious proclamation of transmitted material, and not perchance a new oracle of Yahweh."[8] If so, however, it is not possible to identify the oracle with any certainty in any prophetic words that have come down to us in the Old Testament. I wonder, however, whether Isa. 4:2–6 might be a candidate—if, indeed, it is older than Joel! It, too, refers to "those who escape" in Israel, using the same word as Joel 2:32 (*pĕlêṭâ*), and similarly speaks of "whoever is left in Zion and remains in Jerusalem"; Jerusalem is described as "bloodstained," and there are cloud, smoke, and fire, though admittedly these seem to refer to the traditions of the exodus (the pillars of cloud and fire) rather than to cosmic disturbances. Note also that Obadiah 17 says that "on Mount Zion there shall be those who escape," but it is quite unclear which of the two texts, in Obadiah and Joel, is quoting the other, or whether both depend on some earlier text or, indeed, coincide accidentally in a not particularly surprising choice of words.

The pairing of *pĕlêṭâ* with *sĕrîdîm*, "survivors," occurs elsewhere: see Josh. 8:22; Jer. 42:17; 44:14. If the author of Joel 2:32 is indeed referring to some earlier text (even if now lost), this underscores the extent to which this section comes from a "learned" prophet, harking back to older oracles rather than speaking quite freely, as the independent prophets in ancient Israel seem to have done. (It is possible that the words are a later gloss by an editor who noticed some of the parallels we have picked up, too, and with that possibility in mind, I have placed the line in parentheses in my translation.)

3. Judgment on the Nations (3:1–3)

3:1 For behold, in those days and at that time, when I restore the fortunes of Judah and Jerusalem, 2 I will gather all the nations and bring them down

---

8. Ibid., p. 68.

Oracles of Salvation

to the valley of Jehoshaphat,[a] and I will enter into judgment with them there, because of my people and my heritage Israel, whom they have scattered among the nations, and divided my land. 3 They have cast lots for my people, and traded boys for prostitutes, and sold girls for wine, and drunk it.

a. The "valley of Jehoshaphat" is not known to any geographers, ancient or modern, though from the time of Eusebius, at least, it was identified with the Wadi Kidron.[9] But what is meant by an *'ēmeq* is a plain broad enough to assemble a great multitude of people, not a narrow wadi. Theodotion and the Vulgate correctly decipher the name Jehoshaphat as "YHWH judges," giving *eis tēn chōran tēs kriseōs* and *domini judicium*.

Commentary

Here is another theme common in later Jewish speculation about the end time: the judgment of the nations. There is little point in asking "Which nations?" for the *gôyîm* are a vague category including all non-Jews but not further specified. What is foreseen here is a time when YHWH will intervene to judge them for all their offenses and thereby to vindicate his own people ("Judah and Jerusalem," as in the previous oracle). Once again, it makes little sense to ask how this act of judgment fits in with the outpouring of the spirit or the portents of 2:30–32; it is simply another eschatological theme only loosely connected to anything else.

The theme of the nations being gathered for judgment occurs in other postexilic texts; consider Isa. 66:18, "I am coming to gather all nations and tongues," and, more closely similar to Joel 3:2, Zeph. 3:8:

> Therefore wait for me, says YHWH,
>   for the day when I arise as a witness.
> For my decision is to gather nations,
>   to assemble kingdoms,
> to pour out upon them my indignation,
>   all the heat of my anger;
> for in the fire of my passion
>   all the earth shall be consumed.

The basis for YHWH's judgment on the nations is how they have behaved toward Israel, scattering it among the nations, dividing the land and enslaving its people. This had been part of prophetic polemic against foreign nations as long ago as the time of Amos (cf. Amos 2:6, 9). "Casting lots" over the people is a sign of contempt—their fate is decided by a mere throw of the dice. (Cf. Obad. 11, where the Babylonians are said to have cast lots over Jerusalem,

---

9. Ibid., p. 76.

and Nahum 3:10, where a similar fate befell even the dignitaries of the Egyptians.)

What is more surprising is the very exact specification of the nations' offense in Joel 3:3. The sale of captives into slavery was normal in the ancient world, but it is interesting that the particular detail of selling boys and girls into slavery, perhaps for trivial sums (the price of a prostitute or of a bottle of wine; cf. Amos's complaint that people trade the needy for "a pair of sandals," at Amos 2:6), is singled out for comment. One cannot but wonder if the author had some specific incident in mind; but wondering is as far as we can go, since there is nothing to help us locate the occasion in question. (This passage is printed as prose here, as in NRSV—though, as the last sentence shows, it does contain significant elements of parallelism that could justify *BHS* in treating it as verse.) It may be that the passage continues in 3:9–13, being interrupted by 3:4–8, widely regarded as an insertion by a later hand.

4. Judgment on Tyre, Sidon, and Philistia (3:4–8)

4 And also:
What are you to me, O Tyre and Sidon, and all the regions of Philistia? Are you paying me back for something? If you are paying me back, I will swiftly and speedily turn your deeds back upon your own heads. 5 For you have taken my silver and my gold, and my rich treasures you have carried into your palaces. 6 You have sold the children of Judah and the children of Jerusalem to the children of Greece, so as to remove them far from their own border. 7 Behold, I am rousing them from the places to which you have sold them, and I will turn your deeds back upon your own heads. 8 I will sell your sons and your daughters into the hand of the children of Judah, and they will sell them to the Sabeans, to a nation far away; for YHWH has spoken.

Commentary

This passage is widely recognized to interrupt the oracle about judgment on the nations that begins in 3:1–3 and continues in 3:9. Most scholars regard it as prose (despite *BHS*). Even nowadays, when it has become usual to defend the essential unity of authorship of the book of Joel, commentators are willing to see it as an interpolation. It may have been placed here on a catchword principle, because like 3:3 it deals with the sale of people as slaves. The passage begins *wĕgam*, "and also," "furthermore" (not represented in NRSV), possibly a connecting device to stitch it onto the foregoing oracle. It deals with the relations between Judah and the inhabitants of the Palestinian coast, the Phoenician cities of Tyre and Sidon in the north and the Philistine area in the south. Both

Phoenicians and Philistines are accused of having plundered silver and gold from Jerusalem and of having sold Judaeans to the Greeks (*yĕwānîm*; cf. "Ionians").

Commentators have been exercised to discover a possible historical context for joint action by Phoenicians and Philistines against Judah (cf. Jer. 47:4) and have generally concluded that this can only have been during the late Persian period, in the mid–fourth century (see Elliger, "Ein Zeugnis"; Wolff, *Joel and Amos*, 77–78). Tyre and Gaza were still allies in 332 B.C.E. when they were conquered by Alexander the Great (possibly referred to in Zech. 9:3-8), but Sidon had already been destroyed in 343 by Artaxerxes III. Consequently, this passage would need to be dated before 343. If it is an addition even to what we have argued are the post-Joel oracles in this second part of the book, it can hardly be much older than the early fourth century, so we would be thinking of incidents that happened somewhere between about 400 and 350 B.C.E.

References to Greeks are uncommon in the Old Testament, but they are mentioned in some postexilic texts—for example, Isa. 66:19; Dan. 8:21; 10:20; 11:2; Zech. 9:13. Particularly interesting is Ezek. 27:13, which speaks about trade in human beings (i.e., slaves) between Tyre and Greece (*yāwān*), suggesting that the practice goes back into the sixth century (if this passage is genuinely by Ezekiel). The sorts of outrage mentioned here were not, however, restricted to the fourth century: 1 Macc. 3:41 recalls how forces from Syria and Philistia sought slaves from Israel in the second century B.C.E.

The Judaean slaves are being removed far from their own country by being sent into the Greek world; the tit-for-tat punishment on the Phoenician-Philistine coalition will be to see its own citizens sent to the Sabeans, the inhabitants of Sheba. Sheba is normally identified with ancient Saba in southern Arabia, more or less in the location of modern Yemen; the point is that, just as Judaeans were taken as slaves to the far north (Greece), so Phoenician and Philistine slaves will be taken to the far south. It is said that YHWH himself will "sell" the sons and daughters of the offenders to Judah, which will then sell them on to the Sabeans—it is not too clear what this means in practice.

In v. 4, "Are you paying me back for something? If you are paying me back, I will turn your deeds back upon your own heads" is clear enough but reads rather oddly. What might the coalition be "paying YHWH back" (*mĕšallĕmîm*) for? I can offer no suggestion. Whatever it was, Crenshaw suggests the writer must be sarcastic in implying that the coalition has some kind of *claim* on YHWH that they are invoking,[10] and this is no doubt true. Surely no prophet would suggest that there could really be any injury that foreign nations might legitimately be "paying YHWH back" for. But what is intended is wholly obscure.

In v. 5, *hêkĕlêkem* may be "temples," as in NRSV, or "palaces," as in NRSV footnote. Either is perfectly appropriate: those who have stolen the gold and silver

---

10. Crenshaw, *Joel*, p. 180.

from Jerusalem might use it to adorn temples or palaces. But the fact that we read "*their* palaces/temples" might slightly throw the probability onto "palaces"—otherwise we might expect something like "the temples of their gods." Certainly the Babylonians took away much silver and gold when they conquered Jerusalem in the sixth century, as we find in 2 Kings 25:13–17, and Daniel preserves a tradition that the Temple vessels were kept in Babylon and brought out on state occasions (see Dan. 5:2–4). But when was any Phoenician-Philistine coalition actually in a position to remove silver and gold from Jerusalem—and probably, since YHWH describes it as "my" silver and gold, from the Temple? This, too, is shrouded in obscurity. The author could be referring to a nonhistorical or legendary tradition, but if so, we have lost it.

5. Judgment on the Nations (3:9–13)

9 Proclaim this among the nations:
Sanctify a war,
    stir up the warriors.
Let all the soldiers draw near,
    let them come up.
10 Beat your plowshares into swords,
    and your pruning hooks into spears;
    let the weakling say, "I am a warrior."

11 Come quickly,[a]
    all you nations all around,
    gather yourselves there.

(Bring down your warriors, YHWH.)[b]

12 Let the nations rouse themselves and come up
    to the valley of Jehoshaphat;
for there I will sit to judge
    all the nations round about.

13 Put in the sickle,
    for the harvest is ripe.
Go in, tread,
    for the wine press is full.
The vats overflow,
    for their wickedness is great.

    a. In v. 11, NRSV "Come quickly," which I follow here, is an attempt to make sense of an otherwise unattested verb *'ûšû*. This could be a corruption of *ḥûšû* (hurry), and

Oracles of Salvation

some such reading (or conjecture) may lie behind the Vulgate's *erumpite*. BHS suggests *'ûrû*, "rouse yourselves." From the context it is clear that the command has something to do with getting ready for battle, even though the exact meaning must remain obscure.

b. It is possible that the line "Bring down your warriors, YHWH" is a later insertion, perhaps a prayer by a scribe that God would make haste and carry out his promise/threat.[11] However it is interpreted, it clearly breaks the frame of the verse by addressing YHWH. This has led some to suggest various emendations. The Vulgate reads *ibi occumbere faciet Dominus robustos tuos*, "there the Lord will make your mighty ones lie down," which may suggest that it read a different Hebrew original, possibly *wĕyāniaḥ* rather than MT *hanḥat*; by following this, one can avoid a sudden interpolation of an address to YHWH in the middle of a verse in which YHWH is addressing the nations. In that case the "mighty ones" are warriors in the foreign armies, not YHWH's own militia.

Commentary

It seems altogether probable that this oracle is a continuation of 3:1–3, interrupted by 3:4–8; it refers again to the "valley of Jehoshaphat" and continues the theme of judgment against the nations. What is not clear is where the unit ends. A case could be made for ending it at v. 12 ("for there I will sit to judge all the neighboring nations") and treating v. 13 as a fragment. Equally, one could see vv. 14–15 as an integral part of it, taking the "valley of decision" as an alternative name for the valley of Jehoshaphat. All that is clear is that a new section begins with 3:16. On balance, I prefer to see the unit as running to the end of v. 13, taking vv. 14–15 as a separate, fragmentary piece.

Two lines of interpretation are possible. On one reading, the addressees of the plural imperative in v. 9 are those who had the task of mustering the armies of Judah (perhaps a purely imaginary force by this time), who are exhorted to make the necessary preparations for a battle (a holy war, judging from the term *qaddĕšû*) that Judah will fight in YHWH's name against the foreign nations. For them to do so, old habits of peaceful life will have to be changed, and the prophecy of Isa. 2:4 (= Micah 4:3) will need to be reversed, as agricultural implements are turned into weapons for the fight. Then, in v. 11, the nations are summoned to gather together in the valley of Jehoshaphat, and YHWH himself is urged to bring his "warriors," that is, the armies of Israel. Instead of a battle, however, what happens is more a massacre, as Israel "harvests" the nations, metaphorically "putting in the sickle"—in other words, killing off the enemy for their wickedness.

An alternative interpretation, which is suggested, though not developed, by Crenshaw,[12] is that the imperative in v. 9 is addressed by YHWH to the members of his heavenly court (cf. Isa. 6:8; 40:1; 1 Kings 22:20), telling them to

---

11. Thus Crenshaw, *Joel*, p. 189.
12. Ibid., p. 187.

muster the army of the *nations,* in order that it can be destroyed. It is then the nations who are to "beat their plowshares into swords," in the (false) hope that they are about to win a great battle against Israel. Instead, YHWH summons them to the valley of Jehoshaphat where, rather than allowing them to fight and win a battle, YHWH himself enters into judgment with them. He does this by bringing down his "mighty ones" (*haggibbôrîm*), who are perhaps not soldiers but angelic beings who fight in his service (though this line is suspect—see below). And it is to these heavenly attendants that the task of "reaping" the earth is then committed in v. 13.

This would then be the source of the prophecy in Rev. 14:14–20, where the vintage of the earth is to be "reaped" by *angels,* with the result that "blood flowed from the wine press, as high as a horse's bridle, for a distance of about two hundred miles." Compare also Isa. 63:1–6, where it is YHWH himself, explicitly without any helpers, who treads the wine press:

> I have trodden the wine press alone,
>   and from the peoples no one was with me;
> I trod them in my anger
>   and trampled them in my wrath;
> their juice spattered on my garments,
>   and stained all my robes. . . .
> I trampled down peoples in my anger,
>   I crushed them in my wrath,
>   and I poured out their lifeblood on the earth.

On either interpretation there is a shift in the addressee of the imperative verbs, since Joel 3:11 clearly addresses the nations and Joel 3:13 cannot do so, so that the passage is somewhat awkward. On the whole I think that the second interpretation, in which YHWH decides the outcome in person or through his angelic representatives, is probably preferable. It is worth saying again that I do not think the passage comes from Joel, and there is therefore no reason why it should not reflect relatively late, apocalyptic ideas. If the authenticity of the oracle is defended, then it would probably be better to adopt the first interpretation; though even then the idea of judgment on all the nations in a quasi-mythical valley of Jehoshaphat seems to me rather distant from Joel's concern for the fate of a nation threatened by horrible but entirely mundane locusts.

As in 3:1–3, the summons is addressed to "all the nations (round about)," without distinction. Whether the author of this prophecy thought that all foreigners were to be judged equally and equally destroyed is not really clear. If pressed, he might have distinguished between better and worse cases. But the rhetoric of this kind of prophecy does not concern itself with shades of gray.

With these verses, we are in an extraordinarily bloodthirsty world, in which there is no mercy for foreigners: a million miles away from the hint in 2:28 that

Oracles of Salvation

YHWH might pour out the spirit on "all flesh." I cannot see how that oracle and this can come from the same hand. Joel 3:1–4, 9–13 inhabits the same mental universe as later "apocalyptic" texts such as Daniel 10–11, in which the fate of the nations is determined by YHWH with regard to his desire to bless his own people, and these nations are cardboard cutout figures who act out their fate as if in a pageant or tableau. There is no engagement, as in the words of the prophets themselves, with the political realities of international affairs.

6. The Day of YHWH (3:14–15)

14 Multitudes, multitudes,
    in the valley of decision!
  For the day of YHWH has drawn near
    in the valley of decision.
15 The sun and the moon are darkened,
    and the stars withdraw their shining.

Commentary

As already indicated, it is difficult to feel any confidence about the delineation of this unit. It may be a continuation of the previous oracle, but it seems to me also possible that it is an independent fragment. The "valley of decision" (*'ēmeq heḥārûṣ*) may be the same as the "valley of Jehoshaphat," but one cannot feel sure of this. (The Targum perhaps offers some support for this by translating *'ēmeq heḥārûṣ* in identically the same way as it renders *'ēmeq yĕhôšāpāṭ* in 3:2 and 12.) It could also conceivably mean "valley of threshing," in which case a reference back to the harvesting imagery of vv. 13–14 is entirely possible (cf. Micah 4:13).

As usual, it is unclear whether the day of YHWH has drawn near—that is, has come—or is drawing near—that is, has not yet (quite) come; and the fact that the verbs in "are darkened" and "withdraw their shining" are in the perfect (*qatal*) does not help us, since, as we have seen, prophets commonly speak of future events as already present. The multitudes in the valley of decision may be the foreign nations of the previous oracle, but they might also be Israelites/ Judaeans or, for that matter, angelic beings. Verse 15 is in any case a direct quotation from 2:10. This is a highly derivative oracle that tells us very little.

7. YHWH Roars from Zion (3:16)

16 And YHWH roars from Zion,
    and from Jerusalem he utters his voice,
    and the heavens and the earth shake.

> But YHWH is a refuge for his people,
> and a stronghold for the children of Israel.

Commentary

Crenshaw suggests that "the apparent contradiction between YHWH's sitting in the valley of Jehoshaphat to judge the nations and setting out from Zion to attack the same group need not indicate secondary tampering with the text."[13] It seems to me more likely, however, that this is simply a separate oracle unconnected with the foregoing one. This probability is increased by the fact that the first half of the verse occurs almost verbatim in Amos 1:2, so that it should be regarded as a piece of "floating" tradition—perhaps a liturgical formula. If it is original in either book, then presumably it originated in the older Amos, but it could have been introduced secondarily into both. The idea of YHWH "roaring" like a lion can also be found at Jer. 25:30. Whereas in Amos the verse continues by speaking of the withering of pasture land—part of the coming judgment on Israel—in Joel there is instead a reference to the shaking of heaven and earth, but then a piece of reassurance for Judah, which may be based on Isa. 25:4:

> For you have been a refuge to the poor,
> a refuge to the needy in their distress,
> a shelter from the rainstorm and a shade from the heat.

Compare also Ps. 46:1.

For the author of Joel 3:16, YHWH's roaring and the earthquake (which is probably what it amounts to in practice) are a sign of destruction for Israel's enemies but not for Israel itself, whom YHWH keeps in security. This is another theme common in the Isaiah apocalypse (Isaiah 24–27); compare also Hag. 2:6–7, where again YHWH makes the heavens and earth shake, but this portends the coming of foreign nations to pour wealth into Jerusalem, not any destruction for YHWH's own people. What for Amos had been the sign of YHWH's coming to judge Israel is in Joel an experience that passes Israel by, because YHWH is unequivocally on their side. Note that here (as in 2:27 and 3:2) "Israel" is used, in accordance with time-honored prophetic practice, even though it must really be only Judah that is in question: the term is by this time a purely theological one, denoting the people of YHWH. "Children of Israel" occurs only here in Joel.

8. The Holiness of Jerusalem (3:17)

17 So you shall know that I, YHWH your God,
    dwell in Zion, my holy mountain.

---

13. Ibid., p. 194.

> And Jerusalem shall be a sanctuary,
> and strangers shall never again pass through it.

Commentary

If much of the second part of the book of Joel promises dramatic divine intervention in the history of the world, this oracle, on the contrary, promises stability and peace on an enduring basis. The old promises to Jerusalem as the city of God are reaffirmed, as in the psalms of Zion (Psalms 46–48, 76, 87) and as in the oracles of Deutero-Isaiah (Isa. 52:1–2; 54:1–3). Zion is to be reestablished as the place where YHWH himself lives (*šōkēn*), as if it were God's own tent or house. This language is in the tradition of Zechariah, who had predicted that YHWH would return and dwell in the midst of Jerusalem:

> Thus says the LORD: I will return to Zion, and will dwell in the midst of Jerusalem; Jerusalem shall be called the faithful city, and the mountain of the LORD of hosts shall be called the holy mountain. (Zech. 8:3)

According to the influential theory of P. D. Hanson, there was a deep rift in Judaism in the Second Temple period between those like Zechariah—the "theocratic party"—who believed that YHWH had decided to make his dwelling forever in Jerusalem, so that no fresh intervention on his part was to be looked for, and the spiritual descendants of Trito-Isaiah, who kept alive the hope for a radical transformation of society by divine inspiration. It is difficult to align Joel with either of these alleged groups, since the book contains both the most radical hope for fresh prophecy (2:28–29) and this present oracle, which speaks in "theocratic" terms of YHWH taking up permanent abode on Mount Zion and therefore, by implication, giving his blessing to the people's cultic life. Wolff, indeed, seeks to distance Joel from too "cultic" a commitment:

> When Jerusalem is called a "sanctuary," this is meant to stress not so much its cultic purity . . . as rather its inviolable assignment to the God of the covenant. . . . In this way it is emphasized—over against the theocratic circles who saw the goal of the ways of God with his people in the already present cultus of Jerusalem—that the future day alone will truly bring Yahweh's reigning presence on Zion as the pledge that Israel can dwell undisturbed.[14]

Certainly the oracle speaks of the future; but there seems to me little in it to suggest a critique of the existing state of affairs in Jerusalem, and I think this is another place where Wolff is anxious to avoid approving of matters of cult or *torah* for reasons that go beyond the concerns of the text itself.

That strangers (i.e., foreigners) shall never again pass through Jerusalem

---

14. Wolff, *Joel and Amos*, p. 82.

expresses the same xenophobia as 3:1–3, 9–13. In one of the most detailed surveys of possible datings of Joel, M. Treves attempted to base a good deal on this verse, arguing that it implied an invasion had just occurred—hence the opposition to foreigners in Jerusalem. He thought that the only possible candidate for the invading force was that led in 312 B.C.E. by Ptolemy Soter (323–285), mentioned by Josephus in *Jewish Antiquities* 12:7, 26, 29 and by Appian, *Syriaca* 8:50.[15] While this is possible, and so late a date does not seem to me to be ruled out once we treat the second part of Joel as secondary to the work of the prophet himself, it is a slim basis for dating (though Treves adds other reasons from elsewhere in the book). The most obvious reference would be to the Babylonian invasion in 586 B.C.E., which indelibly marked the Jewish consciousness and made the whole idea of foreigners in Jerusalem a fraught issue. I doubt one can be any more specific than this.

9. Miraculous Fruitfulness (3:18)

18   And it shall happen on that day:

that the mountains shall drip sweet wine,
  the hills shall run with milk,
and all the watercourses of Judah
  shall flow with water;[a]
and a fountain shall come forth from the house of YHWH
  and water the Wadi Shittim.

a. Some MSS say "water of life"; cf. *BHS*.

Commentary

"On that day" is the most common of the formulas for joining fresh material on to prophetic oracles, and it justifies us in thinking that this, again, is a separate passage from what precedes it, though it continues the theme of YHWH's abode in Zion and especially in the Temple. The restoration of "sweet wine" (*'āsîs*) makes a connection with the beginning of the prophecy of Joel, where lack of sweet wine was one of the people's complaints (1:5), but the parallel may be accidental. The first half of the verse is again found also in Amos (9:13b), where it is widely suspected of being an addition to the words of Amos himself. This may be another piece of "floating" prophecy that was used by the editors of both books, though it is also possible that it is original in one or other case; we simply cannot tell. The language of miraculous fruitfulness is certainly

---

15. See Treves, "Date of Joel." Compare above, p. 16.

at home in postexilic prophecy, as can be seen also from Isa. 65:17-25 and Zech. 14:6-11.

The second half of the verse speaks, in language reminiscent of Ezek. 47:1-12 and Zech. 14:8, of fresh water flowing out from the Temple and watering the desert region to the south. The Wadi Shittim cannot be identified with any certainty, and it might (like the valley of Jehoshaphat) be a mythical or imaginary area, "the brook of the acacias," acacia wood being regarded as particularly valuable and used in the manufacture of Temple furniture (see Exod. 30:1). One candidate is the Wadi 'en-Nar, which continues the Kidron Valley and ends at the Dead Sea—this would make the similarity between the present verse and Ezekiel's vision very close, for his "living water" (cf. the reading "water of life" here, noted in *BHS*) also runs out into the Dead Sea, whose waters become sweet. Perhaps there was a whole mythology of the renewal of life-giving water through the establishment of the sanctuary, only small traces of which now remain in such texts as these.[16]

10. Judgment on Egypt and Edom (3:19-21)

19 Egypt shall become a desolation
     and Edom shall become a desolate wilderness,
   because of the violence done to the children of Judah,
     in whose land they have shed innocent blood,
20 But Judah shall be inhabited forever,
     and Jerusalem to generation after generation.
21 I will avenge their blood, and I will not clear the guilty,[a]
     for YHWH dwells in Zion.

a. In v. 21 there is a problem of interpretation. MT reads *wĕniqqêtî dāmām lōʾ-niqqêtî*, which, as the NRSV footnote has it, means something like "I will hold innocent their blood which I have not held innocent." Various suggestions have been made to improve the sense. The simplest is the proposal in *BHS* that the first *niqqêtî* should simply be omitted, producing "I will not hold their blood innocent," i.e., "I will not forgive them for their violence." LXX, however, seems to have read a text with two verbs and renders *kai ekzētēsō to haima autōn kai ou mē athōōsō*, "I will avenge their blood and will not put it away," which may suggest that the first *niqqêtî* should be read as *wĕniqqamtî*, "I will avenge," and the second *ʾănaqqeh*, "I will declare innocent," thereby yielding the NRSV rendering, which I follow (thus also Crenshaw).[17] The assumption of these emendations seems to be that it is the blood shed by the Egyptians and Edomites that is to be avenged in the new order, when YHWH takes up permanent residence in Zion. One could defend MT, however, and understand it to mean that YHWH will henceforth overlook the sins

16. Cf. Barker, *Gate of Heaven*, p. 69.
17. Crenshaw, *Joel*, pp. 202-203.

of *Judah*, which he previously used to avenge: "I will now declare them innocent of the bloody crimes for which I convicted them." This would be in keeping with the turn to an oracle of pure blessing in the last verse of the whole book.

More complicatedly, one could abide by NRSV's emendations but take the reference still to be to the sins of Judah; then the sense would be that YHWH will bless Judah by taking up his abode in Zion but will not leave them unpunished in the process. Compare Jer. 30:11:

> For I am with you, says the LORD, to save you;
> I will make an end of all the nations
>   among which I scattered you,
>   but of you I will not make an end.
> I will chastise you in just measure,
>   and I will by no means leave you unpunished.

More likely, however, the book ends on a note of unalloyed blessing for Judah, as YHWH promises henceforth to dwell in Zion forever.

Commentary

This oracle could be a continuation of 3:18, contrasting the fruitfulness of a renewed Judah with its miraculous water supply with the desolation threatened to Egypt and Edom, but again it seems to me more probably a fragment. Egypt and Edom are singled out from among what the book of Joel otherwise calls simply "the nations," perhaps as archetypal enemies of Israel. Egypt, as the place where the Israelites were enslaved, is an obvious candidate for this role, and Edom ever since the exile had been equally a byword for its ill treatment of Judah (see Obadiah *passim* and Ps. 137:7; also Mal. 1:3–4: the Edomites had apparently assisted materially in the Babylonian destruction of Jerusalem). But it is also possible that the prophet is here referring to more recent events, and Treves could be right in thinking that Ptolemy Soter's campaign against Jerusalem in 312 brought Egypt into play not just as the ancestral enemy but as a contemporary oppressor. This is made more likely by the fact that the text speaks of the Egyptians shedding blood "in their land," that is, the land of Judah, which would rule out a reference to Israel in Egypt. There were, however, also earlier invasions of Judah by Egyptian forces (cf. 1 Kings 14:25–26; 2 Kings 23:29–34).

My own impression is that a reference to "traditional" enemies might have led to the selection of Egypt and Assyria or Babylon, rather than, as here, to Egypt and Edom, and so I am inclined to think there may well be a reference here to contemporary events. Edom is still being cursed as late as Ben Sira (Sir. 50:26), surely also for some more up-to-date reason than what it did in the sixth century.

The prophet seems to envisage the complete extermination of the Egyptians

Oracles of Salvation

and Edomites, since by way of contrast he promises that Judah and Jerusalem will be perpetually inhabited. We may note again that in these oracles, even though they speak of an end time, there is no suggestion of any cosmic or universal disturbance. The earth continues in its course; only its inhabitants are destroyed or promoted. As in all the Prophets, the hope is entirely "this-worldly."

We have treated the second part of the book of Joel—Deutero-Joel, as I have half-seriously named it—as a miscellaneous collection of oracles from sometime in the postexilic period, possibly in some cases from the fourth century, if Treves is right about the connections with Ptolemy Soter. The oracles do not present us with a coherent set of expectations for the future but rather with a kind of anthology of late Hebrew prophecy. The predominant theme is the vindication of Judah, the establishment of YHWH forever in Zion, and the destruction of hostile nations, all to the accompaniment of disturbances in the heavens and through natural disaster on earth. In this context, the promise of the outpouring of the spirit on "all flesh" stands out as atypical of the material of which it forms a part. Otherwise there are no great surprises in Deutero-Joel: its themes are characteristic of prophecy in Second Temple Judaism.

The book of Joel can be regarded, indeed, as a good case study of what became of the words of earlier prophets as their books were redacted, revised, and incorporated into a prophetic "canon." Words that once had a bearing on particular circumstances—in Joel's case, a series of natural disasters—came to be supplemented by material bearing on the end of the present world order and the beginning of a new age of blessedness for Israel. In the process, the particularity of the original situation faced by the prophet was blurred, and his oracles came to be read if they were addressed to each successive community that read them, offering warning but also hope for the future. A common pattern emerged, of which all prophetic books were exemplars, in which calamity was followed by restoration and renewal.[18] Those who added oracles (sometimes drawn, perhaps, from a common "pool" of prophecies) to the original prophetic utterances were not necessarily second-rate thinkers, as has sometimes been implied when their words have been treated as "inauthentic" not only in the literal sense (secondary to the original prophecies) but also in the sense of "derivative" or "second class." In the case of Joel, one of the additional prophecies at least—2:28–29—is of the first importance for eschatology in both Judaism and Christianity. But there remains a certain sense in which all the completed books of the prophets say the same thing: that God "wounds, but he binds up; he strikes, but his hands heal" (Job 5:18).

---

18. Cf. Clements, "Patterns in the Prophetic Canon."

THE BOOK OF OBADIAH

INTRODUCTION

1. Contents of the Book

"The literary-critical problems are as great as the booklet is small," wrote T. C. Vriezen of Obadiah in 1948; "they cannot be solved with certainty."[1] And indeed, most commentators have remarked on the difficulty that such a short book manages to present to the reader, often quoting Jerome's tag *quanto brevis est, tanto difficilis*—glossed by Mason in the words "its difficulty is in inverse proportion to its length."[2] In the last few years, something similar could be said about the length of commentaries on Obadiah, for we now have two massive works, both from 1996: Paul R. Raabe's commentary in the Anchor Bible (310 pages)[3] and the monograph *A Historical-Critical Study of the Book of Obadiah*, by Ehud Ben Zvi (309 pages).[4]

Despite its brevity, however, the "booklet" contains a surprising number of important theological themes and makes a far-from-negligible contribution to Old Testament thought, as Raabe comments:

> This short book elegantly summarizes many of the great prophetic themes, such as divine judgment against Israel's enemies, the day of Yahweh, the *lex talionis* as the standard of judgment, the cup-of-wrath metaphor, Zion theology, Israel's possession of the land, and the kingship of Yahweh.[5]

No mean feat in the space of twenty-one verses! Obadiah does enshrine attitudes to foreign nations that many modern readers find distasteful, the writer seeing them primarily as the object of punishment by Israel's God; but it is far

---

1. "Zo klein als het boekje is, zo groot zijn de litterair-kritische vragen; zij zijn niet met zekerheid op te lossen"; T. C. Vriezen, *Oud-israëlitische geschriften*, in *Sevire's Encyclopaedie*, The Hague 1948, p. 192; cited in G. Fohrer, "Die Sprüche Obadjas," in *Studia Biblica et Semitica T. C. Vriezen Dedicata*, Wageningen 1966, pp. 81–93; the quotation is from p. 81.
2. R. Mason, *Micah, Nahum, Obadiah* (Old Testament Guides), Sheffield 1991, p. 87.
3. P. R. Raabe, *Obadiah: A New Translation with Introduction and Commentary* (AB 24D), New York 1996.
4. E. Ben Zvi, *A Historical-Critical Study of the Book of Obadiah* (BZAW 242), Berlin 1996.
5. Raabe, *Obadiah*, p. 3.

from being a mere rant. It is, on the contrary, a cleverly constructed text that develops quite a sophisticated theology.

The contents of the book are easily summarized. It describes a divine judgment on the Edomites, which is to be a punishment for the way in which Edom has behaved (or is behaving, or will behave—the tenses in vv. 12–14 are notoriously difficult to pinpoint) toward Judah, which is described as its "brother" (v. 12). It is predicted that Edom will suffer a tit-for-tat punishment: "As you have done, it shall be done to you" (v. 15). Then the book goes on to foretell a general judgment on all foreign nations on the "day of YHWH" but deliverance for Judah, or at least the holy remnant of the nation (v. 17). The people of Judah will possess the surrounding areas, and finally, "the kingdom shall be YHWH's" (v. 21). The pattern of judgment on a foreign nation for its offenses against the people of YHWH, God's vindication of his people, and a general day of judgment and vindication with ramifications all over the world is found in many of the Old Testament's prophetic books, and Obadiah represents the pattern in a miniature form.

2. Canon and Text

In the Hebrew Bible as represented by the Leningrad codex (L), reproduced in *BHS*, Obadiah stands next after Amos in the canon of the prophets, and it is not unlikely that this reflects the fact that it concerns Edom, which is mentioned in the last verses of Amos (Amos 9:11–15). It could then be seen as "a virtual commentary on Amos 9:12."[6] There are also links with Joel 3:2 and 14—"I will gather all the nations . . . for the day of YHWH is near"; compare Obad. 15, "The day of YHWH is near against all the nations"—and with Joel 3:19, where again Edom is mentioned as the particular object of YHWH's anger. H. W. Wolff accordingly suggests that "Obad. 1–14 would seem to be a commentary on Joel 3:19, and Obad. 15–21 a commentary on Amos 9:12."[7]

This kind of thinking had led some commentators to propose that the order of the twelve "minor" prophets is far from arbitrary, and that those who collected them meant them to be read as a coherent corpus, with themes and patterns running throughout the work. This is argued very strongly by J. Nogalski and P. R. House and, most recently, R. J. Coggins.[8] House even suggests that

---

6. L. C. Allen, *The Books of Joel, Obadiah, Jonah, and Micah* (NICOT 5), London and Grand Rapids 1976, p. 129.

7. H. W. Wolff, *Obadiah and Jonah: A Commentary*, Minneapolis 1986, p. 17 (English translation of *Obadja und Jona*, Neukirchen-Vluyn 1977).

8. See J. Nogalski, *Literary Precursors to the Book of the Twelve* (BZAW 217), Berlin 1993; idem, *Redactional Processes in the Book of the Twelve* (BZAW 218), Berlin 1993; P. R. House, *The Unity of the Twelve* (JSOTSup 97), Sheffield 1990; R. J. Coggins, "The Minor Prophets—One Book or Twelve?" in *Crossing the Boundaries: Essays in Biblical Interpretation in Honour of Michael D. Goulder*, ed. S. E. Porter, P. Joyce, and C. E. Orton, Leiden 1994, pp. 57–68.

Introduction

the "Book of the Twelve" exhibits the pattern of a "comedy" (disaster for Israel in the earlier books, salvation in the later ones). The argument has been rebutted by Ben Zvi,[9] who shows that the verbal echoes from one prophetic book to another are seldom such as to suggest intentional patterning. In Judaism it has certainly been normal to write all twelve minor prophets on a single scroll, but this has not generally led to a loss of the awareness that they are separate works. Qumran, for example, has no commentary on "the twelve" but separate commentaries on Habakkuk (1QpHab) and Nahum (4QpNah). At best, then, we should probably think of the positioning of Obadiah in the canon as a result of perceived similarities with the two books that precede it but not, with Nogalski, suppose the text has actually been reworked to make it fit better in its present position—still less that it was designed to function as merely one chapter in a longer work, "The Twelve."

In any case, the order of the canon of the Minor Prophets was not fixed in antiquity. Ben Zvi notes that four separate orders are attested: (1) the Masoretic tradition reproduced in *BHS*; (2) the LXX order, in which Obadiah follows Hosea, Amos, Micah, and Joel; (3) the order implied in the work called *The Ascension of Isaiah*, where Obadiah is the seventh book of the twelve and comes between Jonah and Habakkuk; and (4) the order in *The Lives of the Prophets*, which begins Hosea, Micah, Amos, Joel, Obadiah. It does not seem from this that there was a general consensus in ancient times on how the twelve were to be arranged. Though one could certainly notice some relationship between Obadiah and Joel, the connection with Amos is not made in these alternative orders. It is impossible to discover the basis, if any, for the variant orders, and we cannot rule out the possibility that some features of it are arbitrary. The only consensus appears to have been that the preexilic prophets should come at the beginning of the list and the postexilic at the end, but the placement fluctuates in the case of those books that give little clue as to their date, and Obadiah is precisely one such book.

The text of Obadiah is generally fairly well preserved, with relatively few major cruces. One problem is presented by the fact that a number of verses have parallels in Jeremiah 49 (see below), and a case could be made for reconciling minor variants between the two texts. If, however, they both derive from a common source but are independent of each other, we should do better not to eliminate differences between them. Six textual problems, in vv. 6, 7, 13, 17, 20, and 21, are discussed in the commentary below; in several cases, the ancient versions offer some helpful possibilities. There is a copy of parts of Obadiah among the Minor Prophets material found at Murabbaʻat (Mur XII 1–21),

---

9. Ben Zvi, *Obadiah;* and idem, "Twelve Prophetic Books or 'the Twelve': A Few Preliminary Considerations," in *Forming Prophetic Literature: Essays in Isaiah and the Twelve in Honour of John D. W. Watts*, ed. J. D. W. Watts and P. R. House (JSOTSup 235), Sheffield 1996, with extensive bibliography.

which has a variant reading in v. 17 that supports a widely proposed conjecture in that verse; otherwise the scroll in general supports the Masoretic text. There is also a Qumran text covering some verses (4Q 82 1–5, 8–12, 14–15), again with one significant variant. The Qumran community also preserved a *Psalm of Obadiah*, but only a fragmentary first line is extant (4Q 380 1 ii 8–9).

3. Unity and Structure

On the face of it, the structure of Obadiah is fairly simple. The book falls naturally into two parts: vv. 1–14, an attack on Edom for certain specified (though to us obscure) offenses against Judah, and vv. 15–21, a more generalized prediction of judgment on all foreign nations and the restoration of Judah. Whereas in vv. 1–14 the other nations are God's instrument for punishing Edom, in vv. 15–18 they themselves are judged.[10] Since J. Wellhausen,[11] it has been common to suggest that verses 15a and 15b should be reversed, with 15b serving as the final verse of the first section and 15a leading directly into 16. This simple rearrangement makes the distinction between the anti-Edom oracle of the first part and the more general oracles of the second sharper and more satisfactory.

If this is correct, then Obadiah replicates on a small scale the structure of many other prophetic books, with a second section developing the specifics of the first in a more general way and extending oracles originally intended for one particular crisis to cover a wider "eschatological" future. In particular, Obadiah would then have essentially the same structure as Joel (see the commentary above). One may hesitate to dub vv. 15a, 16–21 "Deutero-Obadiah" when the book as a whole is so very short, but ridiculous as such a name may sound, it may well do justice to the realities of the book's composition. Of course, we cannot tell that a single prophet may not have generalized his own oracles by adding the second part, especially as (see below) the date and setting of both parts are so difficult to establish for certain. Nevertheless, the distinction between the two parts does seem clear. The book consists, as G. Fohrer argues, of "the simple end-to-end arrangement of a certain number of sayings to form a little collection, which is then completed through the addition of a subsequent section of promise."[12]

But the expression "a certain number of sayings" covers a multitude of disagreements among commentators where the further analysis of the text, especially the first part, is concerned. Fohrer presents the state of the question in the

---

10. Compare the same transition in Isa. 10:5–19; and see W. Rudolph, "Obadja," *ZAW* 8 (= 49) (1931): 223–31, esp. p. 230.

11. J. Wellhausen, *Die Kleinen Propheten übersetzt und erklärt*, 4th ed., Berlin 1963 (3d ed. 1898).

12. "die einfache Aneinanderreihung einer gewissen Zahl von Sprüchen, die mit einer nachträglich angefügten Verheißung abgeschlossen worden ist"; Fohrer, "Die Sprüche Obadjas," p. 92.

Introduction

1960s, when commentators had proposed that the text should be divided into two, three, five, or seven individual sayings: Fohrer himself suggested there were six (1bβ–4; 5–7; 8–11; 12–14 + 15b; 15a + 16–18; and 19–21), all but the last being the work of Obadiah himself. For more recent work on the structure and unity of Obadiah, there is an exhaustive summary in Raabe's commentary. Some commentators, despairing of extracting any certain solutions to the problem of the book's structure, have argued that we have no choice but to read the text "holistically." Raabe himself writes, "All we can deal with is the book as we now have it,"[13] and adds that "the book's structure and linear style of thematic progression promotes a kind of reading that will treat it in a holistic way."[14] Similarly, S. D. Snyman, after his own survey of recent proposals, suggests that we can see the work as a unity by concentrating on its "macro-structure," using the following chart:

A1	Doom upon Edom (2–9)
A2	Edom's behavior to Judah (10–14, 15b)
B1	Judah and the nations on the day of YHWH (15a, 16–17)
B2	Judah and Edom on the day of YHWH (18)
C	Restoration and salvation for Judah (19–21)

A1 and C here form an *inclusio,* as do A2 and B2, with B1 as a central section.[15]

I am inclined to think it is sensible to read each main *part* of Obadiah holistically, in the sense that there is a progression of thought that subsumes the smaller units of which each part is composed. Fohrer's division into six units is form-critically sound, since in each case there is a clear marker of what in earlier prophecy we should think of as a separate "oracle." Thus 1–4 ends with the concluding formula "oracle of YHWH"; 8 begins with "on that day," normally the start of a fresh utterance; and so on. It may well be, however, that by the time Obadiah was written such formulas were expected in a prophetic book, so that they are no longer to be seen as evidence of originally separate, oral oracles. In the commentary we shall therefore, for convenience, follow Fohrer's divisions, but without implying that the book has been put together from fragments. It is quite possible that at least each of the two main parts formed a unity from the beginning. The alternative view, that Obadiah consists simply of "a pastiche of traditional and original oracles deriving from the fifth century B.C.,"[16] is probably held by few scholars.

---

13. Raabe, *Obadiah,* p. 18.
14. Ibid., p. 22.
15. S. D. Snyman, "Cohesion in the Book of Obadiah," *ZAW* 101 (1989): 59–71.
16. P. Kyle McCarter, "Obadiah 7 and the Fall of Edom," *BASOR* 221 (1976): 87–91.

4. Historical Context

1. Most readers of Obadiah who are familiar with the rest of the Old Testament are likely to think that vv. 10–14 are a reference to Edomite involvement in the Babylonian sack of Jerusalem in 587 B.C.E. This is reflected in Psalm 137:7—"Remember, YHWH, against the Edomites the day of Jerusalem's fall, how they said 'Tear it down! Tear it down! Down to its foundations!'"—and is widely held to be implied in Lam. 5:9, "We get our bread at the peril of our lives, because of the sword in the wilderness." Edomites, it is thought, infiltrated the south of Judah and assisted the Babylonians when Jerusalem fell, thereafter continuing to make life difficult for those left in the ruins of Jerusalem once the walls had been destroyed. "The day that strangers carried off his wealth, and foreigners entered his gates and cast lots for Jerusalem" (Obad. 11) seems obviously to refer to the events of the Babylonian conquest. There is thus a fairly widespread consensus that at least the first part (vv. 1–14, 15b) of Obadiah comes from the aftermath of these events and is therefore an exilic work—contemporary with Ezekiel, the later oracles of Jeremiah, and the book of Lamentations. This (already suggested by both Luther and Calvin) seems to me the most probable solution to the question of the book's historical setting, though for the second part (vv. 15a, 16–21) a later date is entirely possible.

This accords with the account given by H. W. Wolff.[17] Wolff argues that no other historical context is remotely so probable as 587, and that the book of Obadiah was probably intended to be used in the ceremonies of lamentation that went on in the ruined Temple (cf. Zech. 7:3, 5; 8:19), for which Lamentations was probably written. He cites Ezek. 35:1–9 as the closest Old Testament parallel to Obadiah, reflecting precisely the same historical experience:

> The word of YHWH came to me: Mortal, set your face against Mount Seir, and prophesy against it, and say to it, Thus says the Lord YHWH:
>
> I am against you, Mount Seir;
> I stretch out my hand against you
> to make you a desolation and a waste.
> I lay your towns in ruins;
> you shall become a desolation,
> and you shall know that I am YHWH.
>
> *Because you cherished an ancient enmity, and gave over the people of Israel to the power of the sword at the time of their calamity, at the time of their final punishment*; therefore, as I live, says the LORD YHWH, I will prepare you for blood, and blood shall pursue you; since you did not hate bloodshed, bloodshed shall pursue you. I will make Mount Seir a waste and a desolation; and I will cut off

---

17. See Wolff, *Obadiah and Jonah*; and idem, "Obadja—Ein Kultprophet als Interpret," *EvTh* 37 (1977): 273–84.

from it all who come and go. I will fill its mountains with the slain; on your hills and in your valleys and in all your watercourses those killed with the sword shall fall. I will make you a perpetual desolation, and your cities shall never be inhabited. Then you shall know that I am YHWH.

Obadiah would thus fit well into the midexilic period, when Judaeans reflected angrily on the treachery, as they saw it, of the "brother" nation of Edom. (Edom's brotherhood with Israel is clearly marked in the patriarchal stories in Genesis 27 and 32 and in the law of Deut. 23:7-8, which distinguishes Edomites sharply from Israel's other neighbors, the Ammonites and Moabites [cf. Deut. 23:3-6], and describes them as "kin" to Israel.)

2. Nevertheless, commentators have by no means agreed on this dating for the first part of Obadiah. It is fair to point out, as J. R. Bartlett has done in two important articles, that there is no direct evidence in the Old Testament (1 Esdras 4:45, which says that Edomites burned the Temple, is hardly a sound historical source) or from archaeological discovery that there was in fact an Edomite invasion in the sixth century.[18] It is a hypothesis for which, in fact, Obadiah is often cited as one of the primary sources, thus involving a degree of circularity in argument.

The passage in Obad. 12-14, according to Bartlett, is not a description of what Edom in fact did and should not have done but is imperative in force, envisaging a *possible* invasion and urging Edom not to take part in it (see the commentary on this possibility): "The Edomites are dramatically urged to avoid the savage behaviour of a conquering army"; "These verses in Obadiah should not be understood as an historian's description of Edom's behaviour in 587 B.C. The poet derives his picture largely from his imagination."[19] For Bartlett, Edom is a kind of cipher for all Israel's enemies, and consequently the oracles in Obadiah cannot be dated securely at all.

The same view is espoused by Ben Zvi in his large monograph, who speaks of Edom as a "code word" for all the enemies of Israel.[20] It appears from Jeremiah 27 that Edom was actually allied with Judah and the other small states of Palestine in 594, the fourth year of the reign of Hezekiah, and it may be argued that this makes Edomite involvement in the Babylonian sack of Jerusalem

---

18. See J. R. Bartlett, "The Brotherhood of Edom," *JSOT* 4 (1977): 2-27; idem, "Edom and the Fall of Jerusalem," *PEQ* 114 (1982): 13-24. But see now I. Beit-Arieh, "New Data on the Relationship between Judah and Edom toward the End of the Iron Age," in *Recent Excavations in Israel: Studies in Iron Age Archaeology*, ed. S. Gitin and W. G. Dever (AASOR 49), Winona Lake 1989, pp. 125-31.

19. Bartlett, "Edom and the Fall of Jerusalem," p. 21.

20. Ben Zvi, *Obadiah*; cf. also M. Bič, "Zur Problematik des Buches Obadja," *Congress Volume Copenhagen 1953*, VTSup 1 (1953): 11-25; R. J. Coggins, "Obadiah," in R. J. Coggins and S. Paul, *Israel among the Nations (Nahum, Obadiah, Esther)* (International Theological Commentary), Grand Rapids and Edinburgh 1985.

unlikely; furthermore, Edomites are not mentioned alongside the "Chaldeans, Arameans, Moabites, and Ammonites" who joined in the attack on Jerusalem in the third or fourth year of Jehoiakim (2 Kings 24:2). It is possible that there was a shift in Edomite policy between then and the Babylonian invasion of 587,[21] and even that the Edomites might have felt it necessary to demonstrate their own loyalty to Babylon precisely because they had so recently been allied against it;[22] but this must remain very speculative.

While recognizing that Edom may have become a symbol for all nations or powers opposed to Israel, I am still inclined to think that Obadiah is engaging with real events. Even if Bartlett were correct in thinking that 12–14 is a warning about the future rather than a description of the past (which I doubt—see the commentary, below), there is nothing conditional about Obadiah's oracles of judgment on Edom. It seems that the Edomites must already have done *something* to incur the prophet's wrath. (As B. Glazier-McDonald points out, it is not adequate to say that Edom came to represent the type of the age-old enemy if—as Bartlett tends to suggest—it had never done Israel wrong on any occasion!)[23] Are there alternatives to the exilic setting for such oracles? Older commentators often proposed a preexilic date for Obadiah and saw a reflection here of the battles between Edom and the kings of Judah, for example, the campaign of Jehoram in the mid–ninth century (see 2 Kings 8:20–22).[24] In Jewish tradition, there tends to be an identification of our Obadiah with Ahab's chamberlain (1 Kings 18), but this has no basis apart from their having the same name—which occurs twelve times in the Old Testament.

3. A stronger case can be made out for a later dating of Obadiah. If we accept that an Edomite attack on Jerusalem in 587 is hypothetical, then we might look for a later period in which there is evidence of hostility between Judah and Edom. Wellhausen found this in the fifth century around the time of Malachi (who is strongly anti-Edomite; see Mal. 1:2–5), when the Nabateans were beginning to settle to the south of Judah—the reason it came, by New Testament times, to be known as Idumaea, "Edomite territory."[25] Obadiah could be

---

21. Thus J. M. Myers, "Edom and Judah in the Sixth–Fifth Centuries B.C.," in *Near Eastern Studies in Honor of W. F. Albright*, ed. H. Goedicke, Maryland 1971, pp. 377–92.

22. Thus B. C. Cresson, "The Condemnation of Edom in Post-Exilic Judaism," in *The Uses of the Old Testament in the New and Other Essays (Studies in Honor of William Franklin Stinespring)*, ed. J. M. Efird, Durham, N.C. 1972, pp. 125–48.

23. B. Glazier-McDonald, "Edom in the Prophetical Corpus," in *You Shall Not Abhor an Edomite for He Is Your Brother: Edom and Seir in History and Tradition*, ed. D. V. Edelman (Archaeology and Biblical Studies 3), Atlanta 1995, pp. 23–32.

24. This is still defended by the rather conservative T. McComiskey, *Obadiah*, in T. McComiskey, ed., *The Minor Prophets: An Exegetical and Expository Commentary*, vol. 2: *Obadiah, Jonah, Micah, Nahum, and Habakkuk*, Grand Rapids 1993.

25. Wellhausen, *Die Kleinen Propheten*, pp. 213–14; cf. McCarter, "Obadiah 7."

Introduction 123

read coherently as a contemporary of Malachi and would then come from much the same date as we have argued above for the first part of Joel.[26]

There remains, however, a problem: Obad. 11 refers to the sack of Jerusalem by some *other* power, which the Edomites did nothing to prevent ("you stood aside") and in which, indeed, they joined (13–14). This would not make Nabatean invasions a good "fit." To my mind, the early exilic date remains the easiest to defend. Of course, one may simply succumb to a counsel of despair and argue, with P. R. Ackroyd ("Obadiah"), that the historical context is unrecoverable. But some time soon after 587 still seems to me the best defensible dating for the first part of the book.

4. The second part of the book (15a, 16–21—Deutero-Obadiah) is another matter. As with Joel 2:28–3:21, we have here a generalized eschatological prophecy of the "day of YHWH," in which the cup of wrath imposed on Edom is to be drunk by *all* the nations around (16), and Judah and Israel are to be restored to their former territories and those territories, indeed, enlarged by the takeover of adjoining land (19–20). The expression "the exiles of Jerusalem who are in Sepharad" (20) probably implies a Jewish diaspora in Asia Minor (see the commentary), and this would lead us to think of a date considerably later than 587. Obadiah seems to be no exception to the general tendency in the later Persian or Hellenistic period to add eschatological passages to older prophecies; the reader is referred to the commentary on Joel, above, for a more extended discussion of this.[27]

5. Obadiah as a Prophet

1. General considerations about the nature and development of Old Testament prophecy are as applicable to Obadiah as they are to Joel, and for this the reader is referred to the discussion above, under the heading "Joel as a Prophet."[28] There is a widespread consensus that Obadiah, like Joel, was essentially a "cultic prophet." Where the great preexilic prophets whose books we have spoke mainly against Israel itself, denouncing its sins and foretelling national calamity, prophets such as Obadiah fit better into the mold of prophecy as an institution linked to court and Temple, their role being to denounce the enemies of Israel and to declare God's salvation to Israel itself.

As with Joel, it may be pressing this point too far to see the text of Obadiah as, in effect, the libretto for a liturgy. In the case of Obadiah, such a position has been maintained chiefly by M. Bič. Bič thought that Obadiah was "completely

---

26. This dating is defended by J. A. Thompson, "The Book of Obadiah," in *IB* 6, New York 1956, pp. 855–67.
27. See above, pp. 92–93.
28. See above, pp. 18–22.

ahistorical"[29] and designed for constant reuse in a Temple liturgy at which the enemies of Israel were ritually cursed. In his hands even the most concrete historical references in the book turn out to be timeless notions: thus "Sepharad" in v. 20 is understood not as a specific place to which Judaeans have been exiled but as a nonspecific phrase meaning "the end of wandering" (*swp rwd*). Few, if any, scholars have followed Bič in this, but his position may serve conveniently as one extreme possibility in interpreting the book.

2. Other scholars, even when they have stressed the book's cultic links,[30] have continued to see it as deriving from some specific historical context, as we have seen. They have simply suggested, "It is safer to conclude that Obadiah borrowed cultic and traditional themes in developing his prophecy."[31] Certainly Obadiah was a prophet of "weal," not woe, for Judah and is far removed from any incipient "universalism" such as we might find in the preexilic prophets or in Deutero-Isaiah; he comprehensively condemns the Edomites. The added second part of the book by no means moderates this attack on the enemies of Israel but extends it to cover all the surrounding nations. The ancient tradition of cultic prophecy, which many think already underlies Amos 1:1–2:3, here survives in all its xenophobic fervor. Whether Obadiah actually delivered his oracle at a public gathering, and specifically at a religious festival, we cannot tell, but it is from such events that his language is probably drawn. Raabe even suggests that the Edomites were meant to hear the oracles, presumably by some paranormal means or else by report. This raises a general point about oracles against foreign nations in the Prophets: Were they intended for domestic consumption, or was it seriously thought that the foreign nations being denounced would hear them? It is hard to see how this question can be decided.

3. A special feature of Obadiah, which also links him with Joel, has been highlighted by Wolff,[32] namely, that the text seems to take up older prophecies and reuse them, so that Obadiah is, to use Bergler's expression for Joel, a "learned" prophet—Wolff calls him "an interpreter." In this, perhaps like other cultic prophets, both Joel and Obadiah picked up older oracles and updated them to fit a new crisis. What was to be done to Obadiah's original oracles of vv. 1–14, 15b by the addition of vv. 15a, 16–21, Obadiah himself had probably done to older oracles by other prophets. Obadiah 17 may quote Joel 2:32—but also, of course, vice versa. The main evidence for Obadiah's use of older prophecy, however, is his relationship to Jeremiah 49, discussed below.

---

29. "ganz ahistorisch"; Bič, "Zur Problematik," p. 15.
30. See R. J. Coggins, "An Alternative Prophetic Tradition?" in *Israel's Prophetic Tradition: Essays in Honour of Peter Ackroyd*, ed. R. J. Coggins, M. A. Knibb, and A. Phillips, Cambridge 1982, pp. 77–94.
31. Allen, *Books of Joel, Obadiah*, p. 137.
32. See Wolff, "Obadja—Ein Kultprophet als Interpret."

But Wolff thinks this is also what has happened in the case of vv. 1b–4, which begin: "We have *heard a report* from YHWH, and a messenger has been sent among the nations." Here Obadiah is quoting a prophecy the community had already received at some earlier time from another prophet (perhaps even a non-Israelite?), and he then develops this further for his own audience, much as a preacher in Christian or Jewish tradition might take a quotation from the Bible as the text for a sermon. On this understanding, there was already an anti-Edomite oracle (or even many such oracles) in general circulation, and Obadiah chose to make it the basis for his own message, which intensifies the message of doom on Edom. Edom is no longer to become merely "the least among the nations," as in the source text (v. 2), but will be "cut off forever" (v. 10). Wolff suggests that quotations from older sources may extend as far as v. 10, though it is hard to see why this should be so—the oracle beginning "We have heard" (v. 1) seems to end in v. 4 ("oracle of YHWH").

4. Obadiah's relationship to Jer. 49:7-22 is a particular example of possible indebtedness to older material. There can be no doubt that the passages are related in some way. Jeremiah 49:7-11 parallels Obad. 5-7; Jer. 49:14-16 parallels Obad. 1-4, the most salient difference being that Jeremiah says "I have heard" for Obadiah's "We have heard"; and Jer. 49:12 uses the image of the cup of wrath, which recurs in Obad. 16, though in a rather different way.

There are obviously three possible explanations of the parallels: Obadiah borrowed from Jeremiah; Jeremiah borrowed from Obadiah; or both depend on a common source.[33] It is notoriously difficult to resolve such questions, as may be seen by comparing discussions of Isa. 2:2-5 // Micah 4:1-4. If the material could be shown to come from the prophet Jeremiah himself, then, given that Obadiah comes from a later period, that would settle the question in favor of Obadiah's having borrowed it from Jeremiah. But the Jeremiah passage has little about it that is particularly "Jeremianic," so few would defend its authenticity.[34] Whether it is distinctively "Obadianic" can hardly be said, since we have only twenty-one verses attributed to that prophet.

Most commentators have settled for the conclusion that the material is anonymous and has been taken over independently by the authors of Jeremiah and Obadiah.[35] Probably in the case of both books we are dealing with the reuse of a venerated older oracle (though whether it is "extremely ancient" [*uralt*] as Bič maintains, may be doubted).[36] Wolff suggests the material in these oracles may have been transmitted orally rather than in written form. An exception to the recent consensus can be found in Raabe, who argues that the oracles are

---

33. See Ben Zvi, *Obadiah*, pp. 99-114, for a full discussion of the possibilities.
34. See the discussion in R. P. Carroll, *Jeremiah: A Commentary* (OTL), London 1986, pp. 802-807. Carroll thinks the passage in Jeremiah is an expansion of the verses from Obadiah.
35. See Mason, *Micah, Nahum, Obadiah*, pp. 89-90; Ben Zvi, *Obadiah*, pp. 102-103.
36. Bič, "Zur Problematik," p. 15.

indeed more "at home" in their context in Jeremiah 49 than in Obadiah, and that Obad. 5c means that the oracle in Jeremiah has been fulfilled in the events of the exilic period.[37] But I cannot see this myself. My own impression is that the use of shared material in Jeremiah 49 and Obadiah is of a piece with the general tendency of postexilic prophecy to become derivative, reusing and reshaping earlier material to its own ends.

6. Theology

> It seems but a dark surge staining the stream of revelation, as if to exhibit through what a muddy channel these sacred waters have been poured upon the world.
> George Adam Smith[38]

Obadiah is hard to love. It seems to contain very little beyond a xenophobic hatred of other nations and of Edom in particular; as Wolff puts it, "If we subject Obadiah to the moral judgment of a superior idealistic or materialistic stance, what we find is pure, primitive hate."[39] Wolff, however, like many other commentators, is disposed to think that we should not apply such judgments but should look for the good in Obadiah's message and try to understand that his circumstances must have been such as to explain his xenophobia. In any case, he is a witness to the "punitive justice of God," which Wolff evidently regards as a good thing. And after all, the alternative to such punitive justice might be divine indifference to the good and evil that happen on earth; and that would not be so attractive, either.

Monotheism as Jews and Christians have received it certainly contains the idea that God is passionately concerned with what happens on earth, not indifferent to it. One way of expressing the concern God is believed to feel is to portray God as judge of the world, and that is one of the Hebrew Bible's most common images of divinity. The prophets worked out what this might mean in practice. In the preexilic situation, they diagnosed complacency and injustice in Israel itself and foretold imminent disaster as a divine punishment for these ills. After the exile, when what remained of Israel was fragmented and vulnerable, prophets such as Deutero-Isaiah brought new hope to a disheartened people by predicting the fall of their oppressors—primarily Babylon—and the glorious restoration of the preexilic state, perhaps even in an enhanced form. In doing so, they expressed considerable savagery toward the enemies of Israel: see, for example, Isa. 47:1-3, 8-11.

---

37. See Raabe, *Obadiah*, pp. 22-23, following the detailed study of J. Wehrle, *Prophetie und Textanalyse: Die Komposition Obadja 1-21 interpretiert auf der Basis textlinguistischer und semiotischer Konzeptionen* (ATAT 28), St Ottilien 1987.
38. Cited in Allen, *Books of Joel, Obadiah*, p. 138.
39. Wolff, *Obadiah and Jonah*, p. 22.

Introduction

Obadiah belongs in this latter tradition and deserves no more (also, perhaps, no less) condemnation than Deutero-Isaiah, who is widely thought of as a sublime poet of love and beauty. There is a vindictive strain in all Old Testament prophecy. Whether we justify it in light of the extremity of suffering the people of Israel and Judah had to undergo or distance ourselves from it in the name of some higher insight into divine forgiveness, there is no point in denying that it is there. Obadiah is in this respect neither better nor worse than the generality of the prophets: he simply presents the belief in divine judgment on wicked foreign nations in a rather pure form. It is the other side of the coin from a passionate belief in YHWH's love for his people—and, it should be added, for justice in international affairs, which had been a prophetic theme since the days of Amos.

As the New Testament forcibly reminds us, the God who "exalts the humble and meek" can do so only by "putting down the mighty from their thrones" (cf. Luke 1:52). The violence of Obadiah's language may appall us, but it may be wishful thinking to suppose that an ethical monotheism can altogether avoid contemplating the judgment of the just God.

In fact, Obadiah contains more than mere invective against Edom and other foreign nations, as is pointed out in the passage from Raabe cited at the beginning of this introduction. Judgment on the enemies of Israel is obviously a principal theme. But there is also its counterpart: YHWH's care for Israel and good purposes for them. This is expressed in vv. 17–21, which foretell the restoration of a remnant of Judah that will overflow the former boundaries of the Israelite state (cf. Isa. 54:1–3) and rule over other nations (cf. Isa. 55:5). There is no implication that this rule will be harsh or unjust, and probably the reverse, since in the end the kingdom will belong not to Judah but to YHWH (v. 21).

Here is a standard postexilic hope for a kind of renewed empire, but one founded on justice and peace—one in which foreign nations can participate once they have been judged in their turn, as Judah was judged through its destruction by the Babylonians. The Edomites, admittedly, will have no share in this new state of affairs, since "there shall be no survivor of the house of Esau" (v. 18). If Bartlett is correct in thinking that Edomite hostility to Judah was largely a prophetic myth, this will, of course, have been unjustified. But as we have seen, not everyone agrees with Bartlett about this.

YHWH's judgment on Edom is presented in Obadiah not as the result of unmotivated anger but as well deserved. Just as earlier prophetic predictions of disaster for Israel itself always point to actions on the nation's part that justify God in attacking it, so in postexilic times oracles against other nations are accounted for by identifying "sins" that deserve punishment. Most commonly the sin in question is hubris, seen in the foreign nation's thinking it has the right to act as though there were no God. This was already the classic picture in Isa. 10:5–11, against the Assyrians, and it is taken up in what Deutero-Isaiah has to say about the Babylonians in Isa. 47:7–11. Obadiah touches on the same theme in v. 3: "Your proud heart has deceived you. . . . You say in your heart, 'Who will bring me down to the ground?'"

But Obadiah goes further than this and produces a quite sophisticated account of the sin of the Edomites and its punishment, which draws on a "tit-for-tat" pattern of thought also well attested in earlier prophecy.[40] In this way of thinking, the punishment is designed to fit the crime—classically expressed in the so-called *lex talionis*, found in Exod. 21:23–24 and elsewhere. "Poetic justice" is the normal English phrase for such punishment, and it is summed up in Obad. 15b (probably originally the conclusion of the authentic words of Obadiah):

> As you have done, it shall be done to you;
> your deeds shall return on your own head.

The proud nation which says, "Who will bring me down to the ground?" (v. 3) will be made "least among the nations" (v. 2); the one who "soars aloft like an eagle" will be brought down (v. 4); the one who assisted in the fall of his "brother" (vv. 10, 12) will be deserted and deceived by his own allies (v. 7); the one who "gloated" over the fall of Judah (vv. 12–13) will be "despised" among the nations (vv. 1–2, 10); the one who stole and looted (vv. 5, 13) will be plundered (vv. 5–6). The pattern extends into the second part of the book, where the one who "cut off the fugitives" of Judah and "handed over the survivors" (v. 14) will himself have no survivors (v. 18).[41] Thus the prophet takes care to indicate the justice of the coming divine judgment on Edom: it is not the result of a divine whim.

Underlying such condemnations is an idea that one nation ought not to treat another as Edom has treated Judah; but this is not simply a general principle applicable to all international relations (as is probably the case in Amos 1 and 2)[42] but rests on the perception of a *blood tie* between Judah and Edom. As Cresson puts it, "The damnation of Edom is based upon the writer's idea of divine retributive justice: supposed blood-kin and neighbours who behave in such a way are certainly in line for terrible punishment."[43] The prophet's outrage reflects not just the belief that foreigners ought not to attack YHWH's chosen people but a sense of shock that it was specifically the *Edomites*, Israel's "kith and kin," who had perpetrated such crimes: closer even than the psalmist's "companion and familiar friend" who had betrayed him (Ps. 55:13). This makes

---

40. Cf. J. Barton, "Natural Law and Poetic Justice in the Old Testament," *JTS* 30 (1979): 1–14; H. B. Huffmon, "Lex Talionis," *ABD* 4 (1992): 321–22.

41. For this analysis, see Raabe, *Obadiah*, pp. 58–59, and Wolff, *Obadiah and Jonah*, pp. 276–77.

42. Cf. J. Barton, *Amos' Oracles against the Nations* (SOTSM 6), Cambridge 1980.

43. Cresson, "Condemnation of Edom," p. 135.

it wholly appropriate that they should, in turn, be dumped by "those who ate their bread" (v. 7; see commentary for the textual crux here). Obadiah is thus not saying merely that the Edomites will be destroyed but that they "have it coming to them." His glee at the imminent role reversal is understandable.

Obadiah's message makes sense only against the background of a Zion theology, in which YHWH's chosen mountain, the site of the Temple, is particularly close to his heart. The attack, we may say, was not by just any nation but by Israel's brother; and it affected not just any place but the "place which YHWH had chosen out of all the tribes as his habitation to put his name there" (cf. Deut. 12:5): Jerusalem, the holy city. Foreigners had "cast lots for Jerusalem" (Obad. 11), and this was an unforgivable crime because of all that Jerusalem had meant within the religious thought of preexilic Judah. Lamentations expresses the same agony at the destruction of the holy city, and Obadiah 1–14 + 15b, which we have argued is contemporary with Lamentations, strikes the same note. Zion theology continues in the later addition, 15a + 16–21, where Zion is the place of refuge for the survivors of the disaster and is reconsecrated to become the focal point for YHWH's rule over all the nations (vv. 17, 21) in a new dispensation. This is close to the picture of restored Zion in Isa. 2:2–5 (Mic. 4:1–4) as the center from which instruction goes out and to which the nations flock to be ruled by YHWH.

Obadiah is thus perfectly at home within the prophetic corpus of the Old Testament and inherits and develops a number of major central themes. While it would be eccentric, to say the least, to present it as containing all the best ideas of the Old Testament, it does not deserve the opprobrium heaped on it by George Adam Smith.

COMMENTARY ON OBADIAH

Superscription
Obadiah 1a

1 The vision of Obadiah.

This is the shortest superscription in any prophetic book and gives the minimum possible information. Obadiah is not identified by patronymic or given any place of origin, as is common in other prophetic books. The name, as pointed in MT, means "worshiper of YHWH" and occurs as the name of twelve people altogether in the Hebrew Bible—most famously, Ahab's chamberlain in 1 Kings 18. The name also occurs in the Samarian ostraca (50:2) and at Kuntillet Ajrud, as well as in the ostraca from Arad (10:4).[1] It is possible that LXX *Abdiou* or *Abdeiaou* implies that the name was (sometimes?) read as Abdiyahu, equivalent to *'ebed-yhwh,* "servant of YHWH." Clearly, the sense is very little different, and it is possible that someone might be called variously by both names: thus someone called Obadiah (*'ōbadyâ*) in 1 Chron. 9:16 appears in Neh. 11:17 as Abda (*'abdā'*).

It is conceivable that the word is a common noun, "servant/worshiper of YHWH,"[2] just as some think that Malachi is a title ("my messenger") rather than a name. But other prophetic books begin with the name of the prophet, and since this is a common name, there seems little reason to doubt it was the real name of the author of the following oracles. Bič's theory[3] that the expression refers to a worshiper of YHWH who is about to participate in a cultic ceremony of cursing Edom simply lacks the necessary evidence.

Though there is no reason to believe that the Obadiah who produced these prophecies was the chamberlain of Ahab cited in 1 Kings, as Jewish tradition has tended to think, it is possible that the later editor who attached the superscription intended it to be taken in that way. Postexilic scribes liked to associate prophecy with individuals known from the historical books (cf. Jonah, and also the link made between Micaiah ben Imlah and the prophet Micah in 1 Kings 22:28).

The prophecy is described as the "vision" (*ḥāzôn*) of Obadiah, rather than, for example, the "word" that came to him. But this does not necessarily mean that Obadiah received his prophetic revelation in a way different from that of

---

1. See the discussion in Ben Zvi, *Obadiah*, pp. 13–15.
2. See P. R. Ackroyd, "Obadiah," *ABD* 5 (1992): 2–4.
3. Bič, "Zur Problematik"; see the discussion in Allen, *Books of Joel, Obadiah*, p. 137.

other prophets. In 1 Sam. 3:1 we read that "the word of YHWH was rare in those days; visions were not widespread," as though visions would be the normal means by which the word of YHWH would be appropriated.[4] Other prophetic books seem similarly content to use language of seeing and hearing interchangeably for the prophetic experience. Thus the book of Isaiah is "the *vision* of Isaiah son of Amoz, which he saw" according to 1:1 but "the *word* that Isaiah son of Amoz saw" in 2:1.

It is possible that there was a transition from hearing to seeing as prophecy developed (Daniel, for example, contributes twelve of the thirty-five cases of *ḥăzôn* in the Old Testament), and in that case the superscriptions to prophetic books—being postexilic additions to the oracles themselves—might be expected to reflect this shift. But Joel still speaks of "the word of YHWH that came to Joel" (cf. Zech. 9:1 and 12:1). Conversely, vision is already an important channel for receiving prophetic revelations in the first of the classical prophets, Amos (7:1, 4, 7; 8:1; 9:1). We understand little about the "mechanism" of prophetic insight, and it may be that the prophets themselves could not say clearly how they came by it: hearing and seeing are two natural metaphors for receiving a message from outside oneself.

First Oracle against Edom
Obadiah 1b–4

1 Thus says the Lord YHWH concerning Edom:
   We have heard a report from YHWH,
       and a messenger has been sent among the nations:
   "Rise up! Let us rise against it in battle!"
2 Behold, I will make you the smallest among the nations;
       you will be greatly despised.
3 The pride of your heart has deceived you,
       you that live in the clefts of the rock,
       whose dwelling is in the heights.[a]
   You say in your heart,
       "Who will bring me down to the ground?"
4 Though you soar aloft like the eagle,
       though you set your nest among the stars,
       thence I will bring you down—
           oracle of YHWH.

---

4. Cf. Raabe, *Obadiah*, p. 95.

First Oracle against Edom

a. "Whose dwelling is in the heights," *mĕrôm šibtô* (literally, "the height of his seat"), is a textual crux. LXX has *hupsōn* (and Vulgate *exaltantem*), the participle providing a better parallel to the other participles in this verse. This could suggest that we should read *mērîm*, the *hiphil* participle, "you who exalt"; but the Jeremiah parallel (49:16) has the same word as the MT of Obadiah here, though in the easier phrase *tōpĕśî mĕrôm gibʿâ*, "(you) who hold the height of the hill." The versions may simply represent an attempt to smooth over the somewhat rough Hebrew.

Commentary

We are justified in treating this passage as a single oracle by the fact that it begins and ends with the clear markers "Thus says YHWH" and "oracle of YHWH." This is not to say, however, that it was necessarily delivered on an occasion separate from that for the oracles that follow. Indeed, in the postexilic period to which we have dated Obadiah there may have been a sense—gained from studying the already collected prophetic books, such as Amos or parts of Isaiah—that any self-respecting prophetic text would be punctuated in this way; hence a "learned" prophet such as Obadiah might well construct his text, even if it was literary rather than oral in character from the beginning, so that it included these markers. Still, 1b–4 is a convenient unit for comment.[1]

[1] "The Lord YHWH": "the Lord GOD" is the standard way in English translations of conveying Hebrew *'dny yhwh*, which occurs many times in the Hebrew Bible, especially in Ezekiel (211 occurrences). It is unproblematic in Hebrew, and indeed, it may have been the common juxtaposition of the title "Lord" with the divine name that eventually led to the tendency to read YHWH as *'ădōnāy* and, in due course, to point it accordingly. Once this had occurred, "the Lord YHWH" was conventionally read *'ădōnāy 'ĕlōhîm*, to avoid repetition of *'ădōnāy*. This is signaled in English translations by capitalizing GOD instead of LORD.

Commentators are generally agreed that "We have heard a report from YHWH" ("*I* have heard" in the parallel verse Jer. 49:14) refers to an earlier oracle the prophet is citing—evidence of the learned character of Obadiah's prophecy, though it could have been taken from oral tradition, not necessarily from a written source. The quotation seems (as indicated in the translation) to consist simply of the words "Rise up! Let us rise against it in battle!"—"it" being Edom. (The Hebrew *le'ĕdôm*, "to Edom," is generally taken to mean "concerning Edom," using a "*lamedh* of specification.")

These words are said to have been delivered by a *ṣîr*, a messenger or envoy (an international ambassador in Isa. 18:2 and 57:9) who has been sent "among the nations." Who is this messenger, and who is the subject of the imperatives in "Rise up! . . ."? In my view, Raabe is probably right to think that an angelic

---

1. Our division of the text follows Fohrer, "Die Sprüche Obadjas."

or heavenly messenger is meant, whom YHWH sends to incite the nations to battle against Edom.[2] But of course, sometimes a human prophet can take the place of the angelic emissary (as in Isa. 6:8), and that may be the case here: Obadiah may be referring to some earlier prophet who was deemed to be carrying the divine word.

If cursing foreign nations was a regular part of the cult in Jerusalem, then this prophecy might have been uttered in such a setting—not really reaching anyone except the worshiping community but deemed to be winging its way out into the wider world. It was commonly believed in the ancient Near East that foreign nations could be tools in the hand of a god in bringing destruction on other nations.

Here YHWH calls on foreign nations to punish Edom. The anonymous writer who added the second part of the book saw these nations as being punished in their turn—much as Isaiah thought that the Assyrians, having discharged their commission to punish Judah but then having exceeded it, would in turn fall victim to YHWH's vengeance (Isa. 10:12; cf. Zech. 1:15).

[2–4] Here we have Obadiah's own prophecy against the Edomites, building on what the earlier prophetic voice said. At least, this is so if (as I think we should) we construe the perfect verb *nĕttatîkā,* "I have given/made you least among the nations," as a so-called prophetic perfect, meaning "I will make you"[3] or perhaps "I hereby make you" (a performative sense). (Then *bāzûy 'attâ* means "you are to be despised" rather than "you are [already] despised.") If the verb is taken to refer to the past, it would have to relate to some earlier humiliation of the Edomites that, according to Obadiah, is going to be extended in the future.

A possible candidate for such an event is the Edomite withdrawal from the anti-Babylonian coalition sometime between 594 and 587 (see above on "Historical Context"), as a result of which it may well have been "despised" by its erstwhile allies. Obadiah is then predicting that Edom will be still further humiliated. But it seems to me altogether more likely that the whole of this passage concerns the future; Edom is not yet "the smallest among the nations" or widely "despised," but it will be so once YHWH has carried out his acts of vengeance upon it.

[3–4] These verses develop a theme dear to the hearts of many of the prophets, that of human hubris—the pride in one's own status that presents a challenge to the sole supremacy of God. It is a regular feature in oracles against the nations in the Old Testament:[4] classic examples are Isaiah's attack on the Assyrians (Isa. 10:5–19) and Ezekiel's diatribe against the prince of Tyre (Ezek.

---

2. Raabe, *Obadiah,* p. 114.
3. Thus Wellhausen, Rudolph, and many other commentators.
4. And, indeed, elsewhere in the ancient Near East; cf. Ben Zvi, *Obadiah.*

28:1-10, 17-19). Whether the Edomites were notably more full of arrogance than other nations or even more prone to congratulate themselves on their exalted status than the Judaeans whom Obadiah was addressing we are in no position to say; the prophets assume that foreigners are all arrogant and proud. Reflecting on Edom's mountainous terrain, Obadiah describes Edom as a bird living in a lofty crag, setting its nest "among the stars" (thus challenging the divine court?). The sense of security this brings is a false one, which will soon cease once YHWH gets to work in humiliating its arrogance.

Edom is said to dwell "in the clefts of the rock," *běḥagwê-ssela'* (*sic*: the *samekh* is doubled). It is tempting to find in *sela'* a reference to the city of Petra: compare Isa. 42:11, where the reference is again to people living on the other side of the Jordan. However (*pace* Wolff), there is no evidence that Petra was named "rock city" in this period. The same phrase occurs in the Song of Songs (2:14), referring to the niches and holes in steep rocks where doves nest, there parallel to *běsēter hammadrēgâ*, "in the covert of the cliffs." Ben Zvi in *Obadiah* thinks that *sela'* does here refer to a specific place but that the place is Khirbet es-sil' near Buseirah. My own view is that the term is here a common noun, which gives a better parallelism.

qinnekâ certainly refers to the Edomites' dwelling in the rocks as being similar to an eagle dwelling in its nest, though Barr has argued that this use of *qn* is probably in origin a metaphor, the word having originally meant "home": Semitic languages may well not have possessed a word for nest, as many other languages do not.[5] The word does not demonstrably connote "nest" here or elsewhere, though plainly an eagle's "abode" is what we call a nest.

One of the closest parallels to this passage is in another prophecy widely held to be postexilic, Isa. 26:5 in the so-called Isaiah apocalypse, which reads:

> For he has brought low
>   the inhabitants of the height;
>   the lofty city he lays low.
> He lays it low to the ground,
>   casts it to the dust.

Divine opposition to all that is "haughty" or "lofty" is a recurring theme in the book of Isaiah[6] (cf. also Isa. 2:12–18, where high trees and mountains are at risk from God's judgment, as symbols of overweening human pride). In Obadiah it is easy to dismiss this theme as merely a convenient stick with which to

---

5. J. Barr, "Is Hebrew קן 'nest' a Metaphor?" in *Semitic Studies in Honor of Wolf Leslau*, ed. A. S. Kaye, Wiesbaden 1991, vol. 1, pp. 150–61.

6. J. Barton, "Ethics in Isaiah of Jerusalem," *JTS* 32 (1981): 1–18; idem, *Isaiah 1—39* (Old Testament Guides), Sheffield 1995; idem, "Ethics in the Book of Isaiah," in *Writing and Reading the Scroll of Isaiah: Studies of an Interpretive Tradition*, ed. C. C. Broyles and C. A. Evans (VTSup 70; 2 vols.), Leiden 1997, vol. 1, pp. 67–77.

beat the hated Edomites: they are so proud, they even prefer "high" places to live in! But the theme has wider resonance than this, as its treatment in Isaiah shows. It belongs to the Old Testament's perception of the relative status of God and humanity, and its absolute conviction that no one must for a moment challenge the supremacy of YHWH. That the Edomites have set their dwelling "among the stars" should ring warning bells, if one has read (as perhaps the author of this oracle had) Isa. 14:12–14.

What is the practical effect of believing this? The modern developed world has become skeptical of any belief that requires "humility" of human beings, rightly seeing that such a belief can become a tool for enforcing subservience to what is not God at all but a human tyranny. Furthermore, most modern people have come to believe that there is a perfectly proper "pride" that human flourishing needs to cultivate: a sense of one's own (God-given) place in the world that affirms one's achievements and evaluates them justly. This attitude is not "overweening" pride in the sense that was denounced as hubris in the classical world and as "haughtiness" in the Old Testament but involves treating oneself with the same respect that many religions enjoin as proper in our relations with others. Few people believe in a God before whom human beings should simply grovel.

But the Old Testament condemnation of pride is seldom really a psychological matter. Even if the Assyrians or, here, the Edomites are condemned for what they "say in their heart" (Obad. 3), it is by the practical consequences of this that they are to be judged. The Edomites' sense of security and self-sufficiency, as diagnosed by Obadiah, is objectionable because of what it makes them *do*: behaving disloyally to their "brother" nation, Judah, and feeling free to rob and pillage. Granted that Christianity in particular has sometimes, through its doctrine of sin, encouraged an unhealthy self-abnegation and failed to respect the fact that humankind is the work of God and therefore not to be regarded as utterly corrupt, however flawed it may be, human pride of the kind attacked by the prophets remains a blight. They are not talking on a microcosmic level, about the more subtle spiritual distortions that Christian ethicists have sometimes been thinking of in condemning pride, but on the broad canvas of the ambition and ruthlessness of nations who think nothing of liquidating their neighbors. At that level, the prophetic condemnation of hubris remains highly pertinent and deflates the pretensions of tyrannous regimes. The prophets would have appreciated Percy Bysshe Shelley's sonnet "Ozymandias":

> I met a traveller from an antique land
> Who said: Two vast and trunkless legs of stone
> Stand in the desert . . . Near them, on the sand,
> Half sunk, a shattered visage lies, whose frown,
> And wrinkled lip, and sneer of cold command,

Tell that its sculptor well those passions read
Which yet survive, stamped on those lifeless things,
The hand that mocked them, and the heart that fed:
And on the pedestal these words appear:
"My name is Ozymandias, king of kings:
Look on my works, ye Mighty, and despair!"
Nothing beside remains. Round the decay
Of that colossal wreck, boundless and bare
The lone and level sands stretch far away.

Second Oracle against Edom
Obadiah 5–7

5   If thieves came to you,
      if plunderers by night
      —how you have been destroyed!—
      would they not steal only what was enough for them?
    If grape-gatherers came to you,
      would they not leave behind some gleanings?
6   How Esau has been pillaged,
      his treasures searched out!
7   All your allies have driven you to the border,
      your confederates have deceived and prevailed against you;
    those who ate your bread[a] have set a trap[b] for you—
      there is no understanding in it.[c]

   a. The text reads "they have forced you to the border, all the men of your covenant; your bread; they have set a trap beneath you." The problem of the isolated phrase "your bread" has been solved satisfactorily by G. I. Davies.[1] Taking a cue from A. B. Ehrlich, who proposed in 1912 that *'ōkĕlû*, "those who eat (ate)" has fallen out in front of "your bread," Davies proposes a reading *lōḥĕmê*. This would have the same meaning, but its similarity to *laḥmĕkâ* would explain how the omission occurred, by haplography. This makes a perfect parallel with "the men of your covenant"—that is, people with whom the Edomites were bound by treaty (not necessarily a "religious" covenant, as Coggins suggests); and it recalls Ps. 41:9, "Even my bosom friend in whom I trusted, who ate of my bread, has lifted the heel against me."

   b. *māzôr* is usually taken to mean "snare," as evident by the versions: LXX *enedra*, Vulgate *insidias*, Targum *tql'*, Peshitta *km'n'* (ambush). *BHS* suggests an emendation to *māṣôd*, "siege," which would capture approximately this sense; perhaps the versions assumed that *māzôr* was an alternative spelling of this word, or perhaps they saw it as

1. G. I. Davies, "A New Solution to a Crux in Obadiah 7," *VT* 27 (1977): 484–87.

linked with the verb *mzr*, "to twist, weave," which would yield a sense something like "plot." McCarter notes that *māzôr* means "wound" in its three other appearances in MT but suggests that here it may come from *zwr*, "to be a stranger," and proposes a rendering of the whole verse as follows:

> Your allies have sent you to the border,
> Your confederates have deceived you in order to overpower you.
> They have established a *place of foreigners* in your stead [for *taḥteykâ*]:
> there is no understanding in it.[2]

This implies the displacement of Edom and its replacement by foreigners, a fate similar to that which met the Northern Kingdom of Israel after 721 B.C.E. McCarter's rendering is accepted by Raabe.[3] On the whole, however, the sense "trap"—whether or not the text is emended—seems preferable to hypothesizing an otherwise unknown word and then allowing this to lead to a completely fresh interpretation of the threat to Edom as resettlement of the territory by foreigners. The verse does not occur in Jeremiah 49, so we can get no help from there. (Jeremiah 38:22 offers a partial parallel.) Ben Zvi interprets "they have driven you to the border" as referring not to the ejection of Edomites from their own land but rather to Edomite refugees being expelled by their allies, with whom they have sought refuge. This seems to me to make better sense than the "resettlement" idea, especially as it corresponds to what Edom is said to have done to Judah in v. 14 in refusing succor to fugitives.

c. The concluding line of the oracle, *'ēn tĕbûnâ bô*, should mean "there is no understanding *in* it" rather than "*of* it" (NRSV; this point is made by Raabe). The meaning is probably that there is no understanding *in Edom* (or Esau)—a pointed remark since, according to the next verse (v. 8) Edom claimed to contain "wise" people and "understanding" and in any case was well known in the ancient Near East as a place from which "wise men" came (Job being an obvious example). The line seems rather inconsequential in this location, however, and we should perhaps follow *BHS* and assign it to the end of v. 8, though then it produces a repetition of the word *tĕbûnâ* within the same verse, which is also not very satisfactory. Maybe it, too, is an interjection by a later writer.

Commentary

What is being said about the Edomites in this oracle is clear enough. Ordinary thieves steal only what they need and leave the rest (a little optimistic, perhaps); grape-gatherers leave gleanings, not stripping the vines of every single grape. But what is to happen (or has happened; see below) to Edom goes beyond the bounds of all normal activity, even of all normal crime: it will amount to a total destruction. This, we learn in the next oracle, is because Edom itself showed no pity to Judah but went beyond the normal bounds of human conduct. In line with Obadiah's general appeal to a "tit-for-tat" or talionic principle of justice,

---

2. McCarter, "Obadiah 7," p. 88.
3. Raabe, *Obadiah,* p. 155.

Second Oracle against Edom

the atrocities committed against Judah deserve a punishment that similarly goes beyond all normal "civilized" bounds. Wolff suggests that the comments about thieves and grape-gatherers are in fact not prophecies but well-known sayings of a semiproverbial kind, quoted here by the prophet to point up the contrast with the impending fate of Edom.

The crucial question in interpreting the oracle is again whether the verbs are to be understood as referring to the past or the future. If they genuinely refer to the past, then once again events shortly before the capture of Jerusalem by the Babylonians in 587 must be implied—or some other, unknown events, if the prophecy is dated later in the postexiilic period. Even if Edom did leave the anti-Babylonian coalition in the years leading up to the invasion of 587, however, there is no evidence that its former allies took any extreme forms of revenge for this. On the whole, with most commentators, I believe it is better to take these verbs as "prophetic perfects," speaking of coming events as already a complete certainty. This is rendered the more likely by the fact that the fate of Edom in v. 7 is so similar to what Edom is said to have done to Judah in vv. 11–14, helping to force the inhabitants of Jerusalem out of their homes and thereby betraying those with whom they stood in a relationship of brotherly covenant.

[5] The verse contains an interjection, "How you have been destroyed!" which is not in the Jeremiah parallel. This could contain a play on words, since *nidmêtâ* might in principle come from either of two roots: *dmh* II, "to be silent," yielding a *niphal* meaning "be destroyed," which is the usual interpretation; or *dmh* I, "to be like." Then the interjection might read "How you have been similar!" that is, how much plundering and destruction *you* have caused, and in that case the point is not that Edom will be plundered but that Edom has itself plundered Judah, anticipating what is said in the next oracle. My own impression is that the usual rendering is probably preferable, and I doubt whether Raabe and Ben Zvi are correct in suggesting there is a deliberate ambiguity. But in any case, the line falls outside the structure of the oracle and is probably a comment on it rather than part of it: a scribal interpolation, reflecting on Obadiah's words, perhaps after Edom had, in fact, been destroyed.

Like the traditions in Genesis 27–28 and Mal. 1:2–5, Obadiah identifies Edom with the patriarch Esau, the brother of Jacob; the theme of brotherhood then comes to the fore in the following oracles, vv. 8–11 and 12–14 (15b). Edom is presented as being destroyed by its confederates because it did not itself recognize its covenantal obligations, presumably to Israel/Judah, its "brother." There is an interesting parallel in Amos 1:11–12, where again Edom is condemned for violence shown toward its "brother":

> Thus says YHWH:
> For three transgressions of Edom,
>   and for four, I will not revoke the punishment;

    because he pursued his brother with the sword
        and cast off all pity;
    he maintained his anger perpetually,
        and kept his wrath for ever.
    So I will send a fire on Teman,
        and it shall devour the strongholds of Bozrah.

This oracle is widely regarded as a later addition to the authentic words of Amos and could well come from the same period as Obadiah.[4] This, together with the parallels to Obadiah in Jeremiah 49, makes one think there may have been a "pool" of anti-Edomite oracles, which may have formed in the immediate aftermath of the events of 587, on which later prophets drew. It reminds us that what we see in the extant Old Testament prophecies may well be only the tip of the iceberg: many sayings probably circulated anonymously and were taken up and reissued, sometimes in a reworked form, by "learned" prophets or scribes who had access to them.

The Old Testament is, in general, harsh in its judgments on those who break obligations that depend on ties of either kinship or sworn loyalty, and Edom is here presented as guilty on both counts and so liable to condign punishment. The ancient Near East was familiar with conventions about international relations, and faithfulness to treaties, for example, was regarded as the *sine qua non* of good international order. When the treaties concerned were vassal treaties, the disobedient vassal could expect no mercy; when they were parity treaties, unfaithfulness amounted to a declaration of war and was construed as such.[5] Ideas inherited by us from the classical world about the laws of nations are rooted in older traditions that go back into Mesopotamian and Syro-Palestinian civilizations, though this is not widely realized today.

Third Oracle against Edom
Obadiah 8–11

8   Surely on that day (oracle of YHWH)
        I will destroy the wise men from Edom,
        and understanding from Mount Esau.
9   And your warriors shall be shattered, O Teman,
        so that everyone may be cut off from Mount Esau by slaughter.[a]

---

4. Thus also Bartlett, "Brotherhood of Edom."
5. See Barton, *Amos' Oracles against the Nations*, for a discussion of such international conventions.

Third Oracle against Edom

10   For the violence done to your brother Jacob,
     shame shall cover you,
     and you shall be cut off for ever.
11   On the day you stood aside,
     on the day strangers carried off his wealth,
     and foreigners entered his gates
     and cast lots for Jerusalem,
     you too were like one of them.

    a. As the Hebrew text is punctuated in MT, it reads "so that everyone from Mount Esau may be cut off by slaughter. For the violence done to your brother Jacob . . . ," that is, *miqqāṭel* is marked with *soph pasûq*. I have followed this, against NRSV, in my translation. BHS suggests that one of the two words for "violence" is a gloss on the other; I suppose that *ḥāmās* is likely to be the gloss, given that *qāṭel* is *hapax*, though it is hard to think that anyone would have been in doubt as to its meaning. English translations, supported by the versions, generally ignore the Masoretic verse division: thus NRSV "will be cut off. For the slaughter and violence done to your brother Jacob . . ." Raabe, however, defends MT, arguing that v. 9 means "everyone will be cut off *by slaughter*" (rather than, say, by exile), drawing attention to a parallel in the flood narrative, where "all flesh will never be cut off again *by the waters of the flood* [*mimmê hammabbûl*]" (Gen. 9:11). RSV also supports this reading. Nonetheless, the word does seem to overload the meter of v. 9 (not that Obadiah suggests much regularity in the use of meter). If Raabe is correct, however, then there would again be an emphasis on the talionic character of Edom's punishment: violence will be repaid with slaughter.

Commentary

Fohrer makes a case for treating v. 8 as beginning a fresh oracle, namely that it begins with the phrase "on that day." Often[1] this is a marker of an "eschatological" addition to an earlier oracle collection. But here this does not seem to be the case, since the reference is to an imminent act of divine vengeance on the Edomites for their ill treatment of Judah. Only two other passages in the Old Testament have "on that/the day" preceded by *hălô'* ("will it not happen/be the case that . . . ?," i.e., "surely")—Ezek. 24:25 ("surely on the day when I take from them their stronghold . . .") and Ezek. 38:14 ("surely on the day when my people are living securely . . .")—and in neither case is the phrase exactly "in *that* day," absolutely, as here. Normally, "in that day" is followed by a verb in the imperfect (*yiqtol*); here we find a "consecutive perfect" (*weqatal*) form, but this is well within the range of acceptable usage.[2]

    The "day" referred to is the day on which Edom will be punished for its actions in 587 (if we are right to take that as the period referred to in Obadiah).

---

1. See the discussion in the commentary on Joel, pp. 93–94 above.
2. Cf. the discussion in Ben Zvi, *Obadiah*.

The prophet seems to envisage this as happening soon enough for the "tit-for-tat" character of the disaster to be clear, though there is no reason to think he had any specific, already foreseeable event in mind. In fact, disaster did not overtake the Edomites in the aftermath of the Babylonian invasion. Trouble probably came to Edom some decades later, when Nabonidus decided on his move into Edomite territory.

But it is possible that Obadiah has in mind an invasion of Edom by Nebuchadnezzar in about 582, when he may have captured Bozrah.[3] Of course, the idea that such an attack on Edom was a divine revenge for what the Edomites had done to Judah is the prophet's theological construction, not a straightforward fact of history like the invasion itself: the Babylonians would not consciously have punished Edom for assisting them in the sack of Jerusalem. Possibly, however, this attack on Edom was the occasion for Obadiah's oracles. Just as national disaster for Judah was assumed to be YHWH's punishment and led the prophets to look for possible moral reasons why YHWH should be angry with the people, so the news that an Edomite town had fallen might well have led Obadiah similarly to reflect on possible reasons for such a fate. Given the already existing tradition of oracles against foreign nations, it would not have taken him long to decide that some national sin on Edom's part was the reason for its plight, and no time at all to draw the conclusion that it was Edom's ill treatment of Judah that constituted that sin.

The phrase "Mount Esau" occurs only here in the Old Testament. Teman (Tawilan) is frequently referred to as a major Edomite city; it lay some five miles east of Petra,[4] though Wolff, following R. de Vaux,[5] thinks it was the name of a region rather than a single town. There are several Old Testament references to its reputation as a center for "wisdom": Job's "comforter" Eliphaz was a Temanite (Job himself was supposed to be from Edom, "Uz"); and consider Jer. 49:7, "Is there no longer wisdom in Teman?" a verse that introduces one of the oracles parallel to Obadiah. The much later Bar. 3:23 denies that wisdom can be found anywhere on earth except in Israel, but it mentions Teman as one of the places one might look—in vain: "She has not been heard of in Canaan, or seen in Teman."

The kind of "wisdom" Obadiah has in mind is probably political wisdom, rather than the "insight" into the ways of God that Baruch is thinking of. This oracle is thus similar to Isaiah's condemnations of the vaunted "wisdom" of the counselors of Pharaoh (Isa. 19:11–15), and probably implies, in the same way, that people in Teman are not really very wise anyway, since they have not foreseen Edom's downfall.

---

3. See Bartlett, "Brotherhood of Edom."
4. See N. Glueck, *The Other Side of the Jordan*, New Haven 1940.
5. R. de Vaux, "Téman, ville ou région d'Edom?" *RB* 76 (1969): 379–85.

Third Oracle against Edom

The sin of Edom is here spelled out: it lies in how the Edomites assisted in the fall of Jerusalem.[6] It is not necessarily implied that Edom had a formal relationship to the Babylonians (for example, by way of treaty), which is almost certainly not the case. As Wolff puts it, "What Obadiah probably had in mind ... were freebooter Edomite reconnaissance patrols, who were friendly towards the Babylonians and hostile towards the people of Jerusalem."[7] In this oracle the prophet does not specify in much detail what the Edomites had actually done: "slaughter" (*qāṭel*) is *hapax legomenon* but clearly from the root *q-ṭ-l*, well known to all students of Hebrew grammar; "violence" (*ḥāmās*) is a very general word that, referring originally to killing, is often used by the prophets to denote any kind of violent crime. The Edomites simply joined in whatever the Babylonians did by way of violent atrocities against the inhabitants of Jerusalem.

Bartlett, as we have seen, is very skeptical about the claim that Obadiah's accusations are well founded. He argues that there is no archaeological evidence of any Edomite presence in the Negeb nearly as early as 587.[8] Jeremiah 13:19, "The towns of the Negeb are shut up with no one to open them; all Judah is taken into exile, wholly taken into exile," is in Bartlett's view a prediction rather than a description of what has occurred. "It took another two or three hundred years for the region between Arad and Bethzur to become known as Idumaea."[9]

Even if this is taken to rule out large-scale or "official" Edomite involvement in the sack of Jerusalem, however—and it should be noted that Obadiah nowhere claims that Edom has sacked *other* towns—it does not seem to have much force against Wolff's "freebooters," who might represent the "sword from the desert" of Lam. 5:9. In other words, Bartlett could be right in denying blame to the official Edomite leadership without us thereby ruling out an involvement of Edomites sufficient to attract the opprobrium of Obadiah. The prophet may not have been well informed about how much support the Edomite offenders had from the government.

In fact, v. 11 taken literally implies chiefly that Edom sinned by "standing aside" (*'āmādēkā minneged*); it became "like one of" those sacking the city because it did nothing to *prevent* the sack. "Thus Obadiah condemns personified Edom for standing directly in front of Jacob as an indifferent or hostile observer instead of coming to the side of its brother Jacob when strangers and foreigners attacked."[10] Neither here nor in the next oracle does the prophet imply that the Edomites themselves killed the people of Jerusalem or breached

---

6. See the discussion above, pp. 120–23.
7. Wolff, *Obadiah and Jonah*, p. 54.
8. See Bartlett, "Edom and the Fall of Jerusalem," which has detailed comments on individual sites.
9. Ibid., p. 18.
10. Raabe, *Obadiah*, p. 172.

Jerusalem or any other city. They were like hyenas, taking the pickings after a death caused by some other animal.

That those who sacked Jerusalem "cast lots" (*yaddû gôrāl*) for it is an accusation found elsewhere in the Old Testament's account of the sack of cities; compare Nahum 3:10, "lots were cast for her [Thebes'] nobles," and Ps. 22:18, "for my clothing they cast lots," if the psalm is understood as a communal lament so that the "clothing" is metaphorical. In Joel 3:3 the nations have "cast lots for my people"—to see who should take whom as a slave. Probably the reference here in Obadiah is also to distributing the people of Jerusalem as slaves of this or that soldier taking part in the attack, though other accounts of the fall of Jerusalem imply a more general capture of the people (especially the leadership) by the commanding officer of the Babylonian army (cf. 2 Kings 25:11).

It is more than likely, however, that people as well as objects were regarded as legitimate booty, and the idea that soldiers threw dice to decide the distribution is not far-fetched. There seems no reason to suppose that Obadiah has borrowed this idea from Joel.[11] The Edomites who were present evidently decided to get in on the act when it came to the distribution of prisoners.

For the general sentiments of this oracle, we cannot do better than to refer to Ps. 55:12-14:

> It is not enemies who taunt me—
>   I could bear that;
> it is not adversaries who deal insolently with me—
>   I could hide from them.
> But it is you, my equal,
>   my companion, my familiar friend,
> with whom I kept pleasant company;
>   we walked in the house of God with the throng.

Edomites had been "companions" to Judah; if Deut. 23:7 is older than Obadiah, it implies that they might indeed "walk in the house of God" with Israelites as their kin. As Allen aptly observes in summarizing Obadiah's oracle: *et tu, Brute!*

Even at this distance in time we can sympathize with Obadiah, if Edom was indeed allied with Judah at the level he suggests and did indeed connive at the destruction of Jerusalem. How far the "kinship" between Edom and Judah was embraced in Edom, however, we cannot tell. We do not know whether there were Edomite versions of the stories of Jacob and Esau; if there were, they might well have included Edomite reactions not unlike Obadiah's, to the treacherous behavior Jacob had showed to his brother on more than one occasion, and might have suggested that Israelites had not in this respect changed their spots.

---

11. Against Raabe; ibid., p. 176.

Perhaps the Edomites who gloated over the fall of Jerusalem believed they were settling old scores. Even if Bartlett has been a rather partial supporter of the Edomites against the way in which they are described in the prophetic literature, he has been right to remind us that we have heard only one side of the story. We need to be as alert to the possibility of bias in reading the Prophets as we are (or should be) in reading modern newspaper reports emanating from only one side of a conflict. It is fatally easy for readers of the Bible to identify with the "Israel" of the text and to assume that Israel, which is thus ultimately ourselves, is always in the right.

Fourth Oracle against Edom
Obadiah 12–14, 15b

12 But you should not have gloated over your brother
       on the day of his trouble;
    you should not have rejoiced over the children of Judah
       on the day of their ruin;
    you should not have opened your mouth wide
       on the day of distress.

13 You should not have entered the gate of my people
       on the day of their calamity;
    you should not have joined in the gloating over their disaster
       on the day of their calamity;
    you should not have reached out to take his goods[a]
       on the day of his calamity.

14 You should not have stood at the fork[b]
       to cut off his fugitives;
    you should not have handed over his survivors
       on the day of distress.

15b As you have done, it shall be done to you;
       your deed shall return on your own head.

    a. In v. 13b, *'al-tišlaḥnâ* is odd, being apparently in the feminine plural where we expect a masculine singular, as with the other verbs in the section. Various proposals have been made to deal with this, the simplest being that of *BHS*, *'al-tišlaḥ yād*, "you should not have *stretched out your hand* upon its wealth." As it stands, there is no object for the verb, so this seems a satisfying solution. Another suggestion is that we should read *'al-tišlaḥ nā'*, "please do not stretch out (your hand)." More sophisticated, but looking more like special pleading, is Raabe's proposal[1] that the form is a second masculine singular energic, to be read as *tišlaḥanna* (cf. Judg. 5:26, where the same verb occurs in a similar form). MT has the support of Mur XII 1–21.

b. Verse 14 contains the unusual word *pereq*. Its only other occurrence is at Nahum 3:1, where it seems to mean "plunder" (in parallelism with *ṭerep*, "prey"). From the context in Obadiah, however, it must mean the place where the fugitives are caught; hence LXX *diekbolas* and Vulgate *exitibus*, both possibly aware of the similar word *pereṣ*, "breach." Whatever the exact meaning ("fork" is the suggestion of BDB), the general sense is clear: the Edomites have policed some point where fugitives might expect to be able to make their getaway. (The other prophetic passage that refers to a "fork" in the road is Ezek. 21:21 [Heb. 26], which has *'el-'ēm hadderek bĕrō'š šĕnê haddĕrākîm*.)

Commentary

The main exegetical question in this section is how to understand the verbs in vv. 12–14. The obvious way to take them is as imperative imperfects: "do not gloat, rejoice, boast," and so forth. But this produces an odd effect, since until now the prophecy has clearly referred to what the Edomites have *already* done. It is possible that the present oracle is to be seen as older than the first three and that it represents what Obadiah had said to Edom (i.e., to a Judaean audience but intending to be "overheard" by the Edomites) before the fall of Jerusalem. Apart from the general implausibility of the prophet's uttering such instructions to an absent audience, they are curiously detailed for such a scenario—forbidding, for example, standing at a crossing point to cut off fugitives' escape. The prophet would hardly have had in mind such a detailed blueprint for the Edomites' actions.

The usual solution has been to read these imperfects as referring to what Edom *should not have done*. There are few examples of such a use of the imperfect in the Old Testament, but it was recognized by GK §107 (a) (1), though not with reference to this passage: "so also, in the first pers., to express a wish which is asserted subsequently with reference to a fixed point of time in the past, e.g. Jb 10 18 אגוע *I ought to . . . have . . . given up the ghost*; cf. verse 19 אהיה and אוכל Lev 10 18, Nu 35 28." In fact, there is no necessary connection with the first person in such a use (and in Lev. 10:18, as far as I can see, the form is actually second person, *tō'kĕlû*, "you should have eaten," while Num. 35:28 does not seem to contain the use at all). This interpretation gives a satisfactory sense. It may be thought far-fetched; but if one stops to ask how, in biblical Hebrew, such an *irrealis* could be expressed, it is hard to see any solution other than to use the imperfect, which is regularly the form in modal and counterfactual sentences. (Cf. also Ps. 81:13–15, which similarly describes what YHWH *would have done* on certain conditions.) Most English translations have followed this

---

1. Also found in Allen, *Books of Joel, Obadiah, ad loc.*

approach. LXX and Vulgate use subjunctives to render the verbs throughout the passage.

Thus we have quite a detailed account of what the Edomites had done at the time ("on the day") when Jerusalem fell to the Babylonian army. It is this passage that makes me doubt whether Bartlett can be right to think that "these verses in Obadiah should not be understood as an historian's description of Edom's behaviour in 587 B.C. The poet derives his picture largely from his imagination";[2] or Carroll, when he writes that whereas

> some even read the book as the work of an eye-witness to the events of Jerusalem's destruction and Edomite involvement in that catastrophe.... The formal nature of the language and the stereotypical "oracle against the nations" pattern militate against this understanding of what is essentially anonymous material. The deep hatred of Edom (Esau) displayed in Obadiah is characteristic of the Hebrew Bible... and is rationalized by reference to Edomite participation in the Babylonian destruction of Jerusalem.[3]

Both scholars are presenting the claim to historicity here in too strong a form, so as to make it easy to refute; but it is a straw man. No one, probably, would claim that what we have in Obadiah is "a historian's description," and probably few that it is literally "the work of an eyewitness." But between such claims and the conclusion that the description is entirely imaginary is a considerable gap! The most one needs to assert is that Obadiah seems to be reasonably well informed about some events that actually occurred, not that he is either an impartial observer or an eyewitness. And the detail of the presentation, involving entering the city, taking booty, gloating over the defeated inhabitants, and then preventing them from escaping, does not strike me as very likely to be pure imagination. It seems there is a sense that the prophet must somehow be speaking unfairly of the Edomites, and I cannot see how we can know this. Why was Edom hated so much? Perhaps because it had actually done some cruel things—after all, most nations do.

We follow Wellhausen in attaching v. 15b to the end of the oracle, making explicit the implication of listing all these atrocities committed by the Edomites: "As you have done, it shall be done to you." The sentiment is exactly that expressed in Psalm 137 in the concluding verses against Babylon, immediately after its condemnation of Edom, which perfectly fits in with the accusations leveled by Obadiah:

> Remember, YHWH, against the Edomites
> the day of Jerusalem's fall,

---

2. Bartlett, "Edom and the Fall of Jerusalem," p. 21.
3. R. P. Carroll, "Obadiah," in *A Dictionary of Biblical Interpretation*, ed. R. J. Coggins and J. L. Houlden, London 1990, pp. 496–97.

> how they said, "Tear it down! Tear it down!
> Down to its foundations!"
> O daughter Babylon, you devastator!
> Happy shall they be who pay you back
> what you have done to us!
> Happy shall they be who take your little ones
> and dash them against the rock!
> (Ps. 137:7–9)

Equal retribution is what is demanded here, and just as much is promised in Obad. 15b. To say that the prophet or the psalmist is being "vindictive" is to make an obvious, and obviously true, point, but it does not much help the modern believer cope with finding such material in the Bible. If one assumes that everything in scripture is intended (by God?) to act as an example and an inspiration to us, then there is a problem in reconciling what is said here either with New Testament teaching about forgiveness or with the Old Testament's frequent acknowledgment that not only foreigners but also God's chosen people have a past littered with atrocities (cf. Amos!). But, especially if Obadiah is a contemporary or near contemporary of the events he describes, there is no difficulty in understanding the desire for revenge, which is a universal human desire. It need not be commendable to be comprehensible. The insight that peace among nations can never come about if all insist on equal retribution is seldom expressed in the Old Testament, but there are passages that speak of the reconciliation of old enmities, which need to be set alongside more xenophobic texts such as Obadiah (cf. Isa. 19:19–25).

An Oracle against the Nations
Obadiah 15a, 16–18

15a For a day of YHWH has drawn near
       against all the nations.
16   For as you have drunk on my holy mountain,
       all the nations around you[a] will drink;
     they will drink and gulp down,[b]
       and will be as though they had never been,

17   But on Mount Zion there shall be a group who escape,
       and it shall be holy;
     and the house of Jacob shall take
       possession of those who dispossessed them.[c]
18   And the house of Jacob shall be a fire,
       the house of Joseph a flame,

An Oracle against the Nations 151

and the house of Esau stubble;
they shall burn among them and consume them,
and there shall be no survivor of the house of Esau;
because YHWH has spoken.

a. *tāmîd*, "continually," is commonly emended to *sābîb* to give the sense "all the nations around you," cf. NRSV. The proposal is supported by some manuscripts, though it may be an assimilation to Zech. 14:14.

b. *wĕlā'û* is *hapax legomenon* but perhaps from *l"* II, "gulp down," or a hollow form, *lw'*. BHS proposes an emendation to *wĕnā'û*.

c. *môrāšêhem* means "their possessions," and this can be taken to mean that "the house of Jacob" will repossess their own land (thus Raabe). There is a variant reading in Mur XII 1–21, *mwryšyhm*, which could be vocalized as *môrîšêhem*, "those who dispossessed them" (i.e., the Edomites or the Edomites and Babylonians). This appears to be supported by LXX and Vulgate; the Targum reads "those of the house of Jacob will possess the property of the peoples who dispossessed them," apparently combining both readings. Raabe and M. B. Dick[1] both support MT. In favor of the Murabba'at reading (which I have adopted from NRSV) might be the fact that this section is largely about vengeance on enemies; in favor of MT, we might note that the next section concerns the repossession of lost land by various sections of the Israelite and Judaean people.

Commentary

With this oracle we move into "Deutero-Obadiah," a short section added to the oracles of the prophet by a writer of the later, postexilic age—the exact date cannot even be guessed at. Again we have followed the proposal of reversing v. 15a and v. 15b, so that v. 15a is the introduction to this oracle against foreign nations. Ben Zvi defends the order in MT, arguing that the oscillation between one nation and all the nations is common enough in the Old Testament and that Edom has here become a symbol of all the nations that are opposed to Judah and regarded as the enemies of YHWH.

There are two possible interpretations of v. 16. On one reading, the addressee of this oracle is Edom ("as *you* have drunk on my holy mountain"), though the oracle *concerns* "the nations" in general; Edom is here being treated as a witness to the fate that will befall others rather than being itself the predicted victim of YHWH's anger. The oracle then makes sense best if the judgment pronounced on Edom in the preceding oracles *has now taken place*, in other words, if this oracle is considerably later than vv. 1–14, 15b and is a reflection on a disaster that has now befallen the Edomites. This, in turn, would make it likelier, in my view, that v. 15b ought after all to be assigned to the preceding oracle, as in our translation above (and see the section heading).

1. M. B. Dick, "A Syntactic Study of the Book of Obadiah," *Semitics* 9 (1964): 1–29.

On this view, the fate that has befallen the Edomites, whenever exactly this occurred, will now overtake all the nations, considered as enemies of Israel/Judah and hence also of YHWH. The writer, whom we take to be a later contributor to the oracles of Obadiah, uses the common image of the "chalice of wrath" (cf. Job 21:19-20; Pss. 60:3; 75:8; Isa. 51:17-23; 63:6; Jer. 25:15-29; 48:26-27; 49:12; 51:7-8, 39; Lam. 4:21, where it is again Edom who drinks from the cup; Ezek. 23:31-34; Hab. 2:15-16). There is a very long excursus on this image in Raabe,[2] to which the reader is referred. The meaning of the metaphor is clear enough: YHWH has judgment to mete out on the nations he hates, and each experiences YHWH's wrath in its turn, just as a loving cup (of which the chalice of wrath is a cruel parody) passes from one guest to the next at a banquet.

There is perhaps an incipient historical determinism here, not far from the image of the succession of world empires we find in texts such as Dan. 2:36-45: each nation or kingdom has its day, then succumbs to defeat and devastation—an idea based not on theological theory but on observation of the rise and fall of nations. Just as Edom "drank" from the chalice as a punishment for the way in which it attacked Judah, so now the other nations will find the cup of wrath at their own lips and have no choice but to drink.

An alternative explanation, preferred by most commentators, is that the "you" (plural) of v. 16 refers to the inhabitants of Jerusalem. It is they who have drunk the wine from God's chalice of wrath and from them that this cup will now pass to other nations, including Edom. This interpretation certainly necessitates moving v. 15b to be the conclusion of the previous oracle, since "you" (singular) there is clearly Edom. This second interpretation is supported by the fact that "your" drinking has occurred "on my holy mountain," that is, in Jerusalem, which is hard to explain if Edom is being addressed. On the whole, the second interpretation seems to me better, but neither can be called certain.

In either case, we have here a picture of the nations coming together to Zion, but for judgment rather than for instruction in YHWH's Torah as in Isa. 2:2-4. (A closer parallel here would be Isa. 45:14-17.) But the greatest similarity is with Zechariah 14, where YHWH's judgment on the nations is focused in the divine presence on the Mount of Olives, and it seems probable that this oracle is roughly contemporary with Deutero-Zechariah, some time later than the years of the return from exile. Zion, the place of salvation for Israel, is the place from which judgment will be visited on the nations:

> On that day a great panic from YHWH shall fall on them, so that each will seize the hand of a neighbor, and the hand of one will be raised against the hand of the other; even Judah will fight at Jerusalem. And the wealth of all the surrounding nations shall be collected. (Zech. 14:13-14)

2. Raabe, *Obadiah*, pp. 206-42.

There is also some relationship with the prophecies of Joel in this oracle. Verse 15a, "for a day of YHWH has drawn near," occurs also at Joel 3:14, and the expression in Obad. 17, "on Mount Zion there shall be those who escape," occurs in Joel 2:32. In the second case (see commentary), the Joel text adds "as YHWH has said," which may mean that its author knew Obad. 17 and wanted to reaffirm that it would indeed come about. If so, we should have relative dates for *this section* of Obadiah and for *that verse* in Joel—which is not to say that we should be any clearer about the dates of the finished books. As with the parallels in Jeremiah 49, so here both the Joel poet and the writer of Obadiah 17 could be drawing on an earlier, anonymous oracle.

The phrase "and it [i.e., Mount Zion] shall be holy" is found also in Joel 3:17 ("and Jerusalem shall be holy") and could be a gloss or an assimilation here in Obadiah, as argued by Allen. Allen also proposes that v. 21 in Obadiah should be inserted between vv. 17 and 18. All in all, the history of these verses may be quite complex, and we cannot be sure that we are reading anything more than one possible arrangement of bits of postexilic oracles, citing other texts but also cited by other texts in turn. One gets the impression that, in the Second Temple period, there were many fragmentary oracles circulating widely and getting themselves attached to existing prophetic collections, such as Joel and Obadiah, without much thought or planning.

Verse 18 returns to an attack on Edom (cf. Joel 3:19), presenting "the house of Jacob" and "the house of Joseph" as the agents that will wreak desolation on the Edomites. This oracle, too, might be a separate fragment that once circulated on its own, though (following Fohrer and *BHS*) we have included it with the present oracle; equally, it could belong with the next oracle, indicating that the territory of Edom will be cleared to make the various redistributions of land in Obad. 19–20 possible. Against this is the fact that it concludes with "because YHWH has spoken," normally marking the end of an oracle, and also that it seems to pick up the theme of v. 17: "*on Mount Zion* there shall be a group who escape . . . but there shall be no survivor of the house of Esau." (As noted by Raabe, the theme that Esau will have no survivors can be found in Balaam's oracle in Num. 24:18–19, which might also be from this period.)

The language is unusual, especially if the referent of "house of Jacob" and "house of Joseph" is in fact Judah, as seems quite likely. "House of Joseph" would more naturally be taken to refer to the Northern Kingdom (cf. 2 Sam. 19:20; Amos 5:6; Zech. 10:6, which places the phrase in parallel with "house of Judah"), in which case "house of Jacob" might have to mean Judah, which is strange. "House of Esau," necessitated by the parallelism, occurs only here in the Old Testament.

Unlike some other postexilic prophecies, these verses of Obadiah do not include any material about the eventual blessing of the nations that are to be punished, and the image of the chalice of wrath does not encourage any such idea. Obadiah belongs to the more xenophobic stream of thought in postexilic prophecy, in which the nations come to Jerusalem only to be destroyed: "they shall be as though they had not been" (*wĕhāyû kĕlō' hāyû*, v. 16); they will be removed from the area, leaving Judah free to take over their lands. This is unlike the rather more benign empire that had been envisaged by Deutero-Isaiah (Isa. 55:3-5; though compare Isa. 54:3, "you will spread out to the right and to the left, and your descendants will possess the nations, and will settle the desolate towns," which is not unlike Obadiah's idea).

Theologically, it may be asked what, if anything, we can make of these images of the destruction of Israel's enemies and the settlement by Judaeans of the towns and areas where the surrounding nations had lived. Almost all the "morals" one might draw from such prophecies are either platitudinous ("God hates sin and will avenge it") or unacceptable to many modern believers ("God will smash our enemies"). The chalice of wrath is a particularly difficult though highly evocative image, suggesting that though God's justice may seem hard to discern in the short term, in a longer perspective each nation (and person?) receives the due reward for their sin—a theme that is also present in a more sophisticated form throughout much of the literature of the exilic and postexilic periods.

An Oracle about the Restoration of Israel Obadiah 19–21

19 The Negeb shall possess Mount Esau, and the Shephelah the Philistines; they shall possess the land of Ephraim and the land of Samaria; and Benjamin, Gilead. **20** The exiles of the Israelites who are in Halah[a] shall possess[b] the Canaanites as far as Zarephath; and the exiles of Jerusalem who are in Sepharad shall possess the towns of the Negeb. **21** Those who have been saved[c] shall go up to Mount Zion to rule Mount Esau; and the kingdom shall be YHWH's.

 a. "Halah" in v. 20 is arrived at by emending *hahēl-hazzeh* (itself obscure, but possibly to be read as "this army," *haḥayil hazzeh*—Vulgate *exercitus huius*) to *ḥālaḥ zeh* (thus *BHS*) or *ḥālah zeh*, which then becomes a gloss meaning "this refers to Halah."
 b. Reading perhaps *yiršû* for *'ăšer* before *kĕna'ănîm*.
 c. MT has "saviors" (*môši'îm*, doubly defective), and this is defended by Coggins and Ben Zvi, but most commentators, with *BHS*, emend to a passive: *mûšā'îm*, "those who are saved"; though since the people referred to are going up to "rule" Mount Esau, one could think of them as the leaders (and therefore "saviors") of the restored Israel. LXX interprets the word as passive (*andres sesōsmenoi*), though the Vulgate has *salvatores* (cf. Symmachus, *sōzontes*).

Commentary

Some transpositions have been suggested within this oracle. Allen, as we saw above, favors moving the passage back into the previous oracle to precede v. 18, while Wolff suggests that the original oracle consisted of vv. 18 and 21, with vv. 19-20 added by a (still) later hand, or else that v. 21 has been added to the otherwise completed book as an appropriate coda. In addition to these changes, commentators take varying stances on whether the oracle is in verse or prose. There is certainly evidence of parallelism:

> The Negeb shall possess Mount Esau,
> and the Shephelah the land of the Philistines. (v. 19a)

> The exiles of the Israelites who are in Halah
> shall possess the Canaanites as far as Zarephath;
> and the exiles of Jerusalem who are in Sepharad
> shall possess the towns of the Negeb. (v. 20)

On the other hand, the lines are longer than verse usually permits, and there are aspects of the diction that suggest prose: *'ăšer* occurs only here in Obadiah, as does the accusative marker *'et*. On the whole, it seems to me that the oracle should probably be regarded as rhythmic prose—"tortuous prose" according to Allen;[1] "a parallelistic style of prose" according to Raabe.[2] Of course, our knowledge of Hebrew prosody is extremely meager. If the various suggestions about removing this or that phrase are adopted, it may be possible to reconstruct a verse oracle underlying the passage, but I feel little confidence in this. In v. 19, Wellhausen, for example, proposed the deletion of "Mount Esau," "the Philistines," and "the region of Samaria," which yields the much simpler oracle "Those of the Negeb shall possess the Shephelah, they shall possess the land of Ephraim." Since Duhm, it has been thought likely that the "Benjaminites" of the same verse should be "the Ammonites" (reading *bĕnê 'ammôn* for *binyāmin*) to produce "Gilead shall possess the Ammonites," though the accusative marker in front of "Gilead" then has to be explained as a nominative marker, which does occasionally occur.

The identity of most of the place-names is well known. "The Canaanites" indicates Phoenicia. "Sepharad" has been the subject of much discussion. Because of its use in later times, there is naturally a temptation to read it as meaning Spain (thus the Syriac and the Targum).[3] But there is general agreement that this is implausible, however late the oracle is dated. Other proposals

---

1. Allen, *Books of Joel, Obadiah*, p. 166.
2. Raabe, *Joel*, p. 272.
3. See D. Neiman, "Sefarad: The Name of Spain," *JNES* 22 (1963): 128-32.

have been Shuparda in southwest Media (G. A. Smith) and Hesperides near Benghazi.[4] But the majority opinion now follows Kornfeld, who argues for the Lydian capital Sardes (Sardis), on the basis that a bilingual Lydian-Aramaic text shows there was a Jewish colony there in the tenth year of Artaxerxes III, 349 B.C.E.[5] Lipiński adds evidence for Jewish settlers in this area as early as the mid–fifth century.[6]

This is enough to force a dating of these verses of Obadiah later than the time of the prophet himself, which we have seen to be probable in any case, since Jewish exiles would hardly have reached Lydia in the very early years of the exilic period. Nevertheless, Deutero-Isaiah attests the presence of dispersed people from Jerusalem at all four points of the compass (Isa. 43:5–6), assuming that we can take his words literally, so that by the end of the exilic age, in the 540s, there must have been a considerable number of Jews living in many places far from Jerusalem.

The exegetical puzzles of this oracle are many and various. The general sense is fairly clear: Jewish exiles will return and resettle the land of Israel, and the inhabitants of various regions will take control of adjoining territory belonging to other nations, who will be expelled to make room for them. But the detail is baffling.

If we adopt minimal textual emendations and do not remove whole phrases as glosses (which may nevertheless be the correct solution!), the picture we get is this. People exiled from the Negeb will return to inhabit not just the Negeb but the bordering territory of Edom (Mount Esau): fittingly for an addition to Obadiah, who was so concerned with Edom, this group is named first. Those from the Shephelah will add to it the land of the Philistines to the west. Then some group (the name is missing—perhaps Judah?) will inhabit the land of Ephraim ("and the land of Samaria" might be deleted as a gloss on "Ephraim"). Here we have, as in some other late exilic or postexilic oracles, a hope for the restoration of the old Northern Kingdom through its resettlement by the Jewish exiles (cf. Jer. 30:15–20; 50:17–20). Benjaminites will regain their ancestral holdings but also spread across the Jordan to take over Gilead; or, if we follow the plausible textual suggestions above, Gileadites will take over the territory of Ammon, which adjoins their own land. Those exiled to Halah in Syria will return to take over (the far north of Israel, i.e., Galilee, and) the territory of the Canaanites as far as Zarephath, north of traditional Israelite territory. And those exiled from Jerusalem to Sardis will take over the towns in the Negeb once they are back in the holy city.

---

4. Thus J. Gray, "The Diaspora of Israel and Judah in Obad. 20," *ZAW* 65 (1953): 53–59, who thinks that the logic of the passage requires a location south of Judah.

5. See W. Kornfeld, "Die jüdische Diaspora in Ab., 20," in *Mélanges bibliques rédigés en l'honneur de André Robert,* Paris 1957, pp. 180–86.

6. E. Lipiński, "Obadiah 20," *VT* 23 (1973): 368–70.

An Oracle about the Restoration of Israel

This makes a tolerably consistent and intelligible oracle, foretelling the glorious restoration of the preexilic (even pre-721) "land of Israel" and its annexation of neighboring territories to produce a kind of "Greater Israel," whose boundaries would correspond roughly to those supposed in the Old Testament to have existed in the age of David. The oracle thus spells out in detail the hopes probably implied in Isa. 55:4–5 and Amos 9:11–12. One could see Obad. 19–20 as a kind of commentary on or detailed working out of the underlying oracle that appears toward the end of the book of Amos (itself regarded by most commentators as a postexilic addition to the words of Amos):

> On that day I will raise up
> the booth of David that is fallen,
> and repair its breaches,
> and raise up its ruins,
> and rebuild it as in the days of old;
> in order that they may possess the remnant of Edom
> and all the nations who are called by my name [literally, "over whom my name is called," i.e. "whom I own"],
> says YHWH who does this.

With Rudolph, I believe that this is a "realistic" prophecy—not in the sense that it was at all likely to be fulfilled but in the sense that it was conceived as a genuine and specific hope, not as a kind of "utopian" dream.[7] Like other oracles of the early postexilic period, it is not speaking of some distant time when Israel would rule the entire world but simply hoping for a new Davidic age, when the Jews might turn the tables on their enemies and regain the territories over which they had once claimed jurisdiction. It is much less vague than many of the prophecies in "Deutero-Joel" and is, in fact, more like Deutero-Isaiah in foreseeing a wholly concrete, this-worldly, political Israel that would govern the surrounding areas. Nothing is implied about Persian rule, which is simply not in focus; certainly there is no suggestion that Israel will take over the Persian Empire or even be wholly independent of Persian authority, though the latter would no doubt have been a highly attractive prospect.

Verse 21 forms a fitting climax both to this oracle and to the book. The rule that is to be established over foreign territories is ultimately the reign of YHWH rather than that of any earthly king. It is striking that no renewal of the monarchy is predicted, any more than it is in Deutero-Isaiah or Jeremiah 50–51. Whether this represents political realism or a theological insistence that only YHWH is to be the king of the renewed Israel cannot be determined.

Commentators generally agree that the last verse is a kind of key to the theological stance of the book of Obadiah,[8] which is thus not as bad as it seems.

---

7. See Rudolph, "Obadja."
8. Cf. Ackroyd, "Obadiah."

The prophet and those who added to his message were concerned above all that YHWH's rule over the world should be reestablished, after it had appeared to totter because of the events of the exilic period. As Raabe argues, Obadiah is a kind of response to the message of Lamentations, with its fear that YHWH has abandoned his people. It reaffirms that it is truly YHWH who is in charge of what occurs on earth, and who will, in the long run, take steps to reestablish his sovereignty. God is not to be evaded, but his intention is ultimately to establish a new world order characterized by peace, though also by the predominance of his chosen people, Israel.

INDEX OF OTHER ANCIENT TEXTS

1QpHab	117	**Appian**	
4QpNah	117	*Syriaca* 8:50	108
4Q78	5, 58		
4Q82	5, 118	**Josephus**	
4Q380	118	*Jewish Antiquities*	
Mur XII	117, 148, 151	12:7	26, 29, 16, 108
Mur88	5	*Lives of the Prophets*	117
8HevXIIgr	5	*Ascension of Isaiah*	117

INDEX OF BIBLICAL PASSAGES

Old Testament		**Numbers**		**1 Samuel**	
Genesis		6:15	53	3:1	134
2–3	73	11:25	95	8:2	39
2:7	94	11:29	95	10:10	95
3:24	73	14:18	25, 81	14:24	56
7:16	96	15:24	53		
9:11	143	24:18–19	153	**2 Samuel**	
20:3	95	28:3–9	53	3:31	55
22:22–23	39	29:11	53	12:16	55
24:15	39	29:16–39	53	19:20	153
24:24	39	35:28	148		
24:47	39			**1 Kings**	
24:50	39	**Deuteronomy**		4:25	52
27–28	141	4:11	72	6:3	82
27	121	12:5	129	9:1–9	71
28:14	73	22:22–24	52	14:25–26	110
1	21	23:3–6	121		122, 133
37–48	95	23:7–8	121	19:13	39–40
		23:7	146	22:20	103
		28:20–44	64	22:28	133
Exodus		30:2	77		
6:3	62	30:10	77	**2 Kings**	
19:16	72			8:20–22	122
20:3–5	88	**Joshua**		18:31	52
21:23–24	128	8:22	98	23:25	77
29:38–42	53	10:13	74	23:29–34	110
30:1	109			24:2	122
34:6–7	20, 25, 32	**Judges**		25:11	146
34:6	23, 81	5:3	41	25:13–17	102
		5:26	148		
		6:5	43	**1 Chronicles**	
Leviticus		7:12	43	4:35	39
10:18	148	11:29	95	5:4	39
16:29	79	13:19	90	5:8	39
23:13	53	14:19	95	5:12	39
23:18	53	20:26	56		

Index of Biblical Passages 161

6:33	39	46:1	106	**Song Of Songs**	
6:36	39	48:1–2	70	1:4	82
7:3	39	48:4–8	70	2:14	137
9:16	133	49:1	41		
11:38	39	51:17	19	**Isaiah**	
15:7	39	55:12–14	146	1:1	40, 134
15:11	39	55:13	128	1:2	41
15:17	39	11	86	1:11–15	80
23:8	39	60:3	152	1:13	55
26:22	39	12	46	1:13b	19
27:20	39	75:8	152	2:1	40, 134
		12	107	2:2–5	125, 129
2 Chronicles		78:1	41	2:2–4	152
20:16	17	78:3–6	41	2:2	94
23:10	17	78:43	97	2:4	23, 103
26:10	54	78:63	82	2:12–18	137
29:12	39	79:10	23, 25	2:12	59, 60
		81:13–15	148	3:18	94
Ezra		84:6	85	3:26	53
10:8	41	86:15	25. 81	4:2	94
10:43	39	13	107	5:11–13	50
		97:2–5	72	6:8	103, 136
Nehemiah		103:8	25, 81	7:4	89
4:17	17, 68	105:5	97	8:6	68
4:23	68	105:27	97	8:18	97
9:17	25, 81	115:2	21, 25	9:7	88
11:9	39	126:2–3	89	10:5–19	118, 136
11:17	133	126:3	23	10:5–11	127
		127:3–5	54	10:12	136
Job		135:9	97	10:20	94
5:18	111	137:7–9	49–50	11:10	94
10:18	148	137:7	110, 120	11:11	94
21:19–20	152	145:8	25, 81	13–23	34
33:18	17	148:12	82	15	24, 65, 74
36:12	17	149:2	89	13:6	23, 24, 59
				13:9	59
Psalms		**Proverbs**		13:10	74, 98
19:5	82	5:18	52	14:12–14	138
20	21, 86	20:1	50	17:7	94
8	46	23:29–35	50	17:9	94
22:18	146	30:27	51, 73	18:2	135
41:9	139			18:7	94
42:1	63	**Ecclesiastes**		19:11–15	144
10	21, 78	3:11	17	19:16	94
44:9–16	83	7:2	17	19:18	94
46–48	107	12:13	17	19:19–25	96, 150

Isaiah (continued)		51:15	25	25:30	106
19:19	94	51:17–23	152	27	121
19:23	94	52:1–2	107	30:11	110
19:24	94	54:1–3	107, 127	30:15–20	156
20:3	97	54:3	154	31:1	94
22:1–14	60	54:6	52	31:27	94
22:20	94	55:3–5	154	31:31	94
24–27	106	55:4–5	157	31:38	94
25:4	106	55:5	127	33:15	23, 94
26:1	94	57:9	135	38:22	140
26:5	137	58:1–14	56	42:17	98
27:1	94	58:1–9	80	44:14	98
27:2	94	61:5	54	45:5	96
27:12	94	63:1–6	104	46–51	34
28:1–8	50	63:6	152	46:2–12	60
29:1–4	71	65:17–25	109	47:4	101
30:7	89	66:18	23, 99	48:12	94
32:15	94	66:19	101	48:26–27	152
33:4	68			16	117, 126
34:1	16	**Jeremiah**		49:7–22	125
34:4	74, 98	1:1	40	49:7–11	125
34:9–15	74	1:11–12	47	49:7	144
38:18–19	63	4:8	55	49:12	125, 152
40–55	25	4:9	94	49:14–16	125
40:25	25	4:11	94	49:14	135
42:6	25	4:23–28	74	50–51	157
42:8	25	4:23	98	50:4	23, 94
42:11	137	5:39	152	50:17–20	156
43:3	25	6:14	19	50:20	23, 94
43:5–6	156	7:34	82	51:7–8	152
43:11	25	8:11	19	51:14	43
43:15	25	9:21	74	**Lamentations**	
44:6	25	12:10–11	53	1–2	60
44:20–22	83	13:19	145	1:4	53
44:24	25	14:12	55	1:12	59
45:5	23, 25, 90	14:17–22	58, 76	2:1	59
45:6	23	14:17	52	2:8	53
45:14–17	152	15:3	45	2:21	59
45:17	90	16:9	82	3:1	63
45:18	23	23:5	94	3:19–33	32
45:21–22	25	23:7	94	4:21	152
47:1–3, 8–11	126	23:25–32	33, 95	5:9	120, 145
47:7–11	128	23:28	40	**Ezekiel**	
48:12	25	24:9	83	1:1	40
48:17	25	25:10	82	8:16	82
51:3	23, 73	25:15–29	152		

Index of Biblical Passages

13:1–9	60	5:1	41	1:12	5, 52, 54, 63
13:5	59			1:12ab	8
14:21	45	**Joel**		1:12c	8
18:32	33	1–2	6, 10, 11, 15, 44,	1:13–20	8
23:31–34	152		45, 46, 60,	1:13–14	6
24:25	143		70, 86, 89,	1:13	15, 44, 76
25–39	34	1:1–2:27	3, 6, 7, 8, 9,	1:14	16, 55, 56, 65, 82
27:13	101		12, 13, 15, 16,	1:14b	56
28	73		17, 20, 21, 22, 28,	1:15–20	6, 14, 57–66
28:1–10	136–37		32, 34, 61, 92, 93,	1:15–16	58–63
28:13	73	1	51, 65, 68,	1:15	9, 24, 35, 52,
28:17–19	136–37		69, 82, 89		59, 61, 62
29	89	1:1–20	5	1:15a	6, 13
30	65	1:1–12	5	1:16b	8
30:2	23, 58	1:1–7	42	1:16c	8
30:3	59	1:1–4	10	1:17–18	62, 63
32	74	1:1	10, 12, 39–40	1:17	17, 46, 58
32:7–8	74, 98	1:2–20	8, 10, 13,	1:17b	58
32:7	16		14, 40–66	1:18	46, 63
35:1–9	120	1:2–4	9, 14, 28, 40–48	1:19–20	62, 63, 72
36:11	23	1:2–3	14, 41–42	1:19	40
36:20	25, 83	1:2	8, 56, 72	1:20	54
36:21	78	1:2b	72	2	47, 51, 69, 77,
36:35	23, 73	1:3	8		80, 82, 83
19	95	1:4–2:27	42	2:1–32	5
38–39	8	1:4–20	10	2:1–27	5
38:14	143	1:4–7	12 n.25, 46	2:1–17	8, 10, 13, 14,
39:28–29	91	1:4	8, 42–48, 63, 87, 89		66–84, 89
39:29	16	1:5–2:27	28	2:1–11	6, 8, 10, 11,
39:29	23	1:5–2:17	10		14, 66–75
34		1:5–20	10	2:1–2	8, 70–72
47:1–12	109	1:5–14	14, 48–57, 76	2:1	15, 42, 59, 61
		1:5–7	12 n.24, 49,	2:1b–3	75 n.14
Daniel			50–52	2:1b–2a	9
2:36–45	152	1:5	8, 49, 53, 56, 108	2:1b	9, 47
5:2–4	102	1:6–7	40, 51, 52	2:1c	6, 13
8:21	101	1:6	8, 44, 55	2:2–11	42, 46, 48
10–11	105	1:7	8	2:2–10	12 n.24
10:20	101	1:8–10	52	2:2	24, 51, 67, 72
11:2	101	1:8	8, 17, 49, 50	2:2b	72
		1:9	8, 44, 49, 55, 76	2:4–9	44
Hosea		1:9a	49	2:4–5	73
1:1	40	1:9b	49, 50	2:6–9	51, 70, 73–74
2:16	94	1:10	5, 8, 49, 54	2:7	17
2:21	94	1:11–12	49, 54–55	2:8	17, 68
4:11	51	1:11	8, 49	2:9–10	75

Index of Biblical Passages

Joel (*continued*)
2:9 — 15, 68
2:10–11 — 69, 74, 75, 75 n.14, 77
2:10 — 28, 98, 105
2:11 — 59, 61, 74, 75
2:11b — 9, 13
2:11c — 6
2:12–17 — 6, 10, 11
2:12–17a — 14, 75–82
2:12–14 — 35, 78
2:12–13 — 78
2:12 — 10, 69, 80, 98
2:13 — 19, 20, 25, 32, 80, 92
2:14 — 15, 35, 70, 76, 81
2:15–17 — 82
2:15 — 70
2:17–18 — 10, 86
2:17 — 6, 15, 21, 25, 88
2:17a — 82
2:17bc — 14, 58
2:17b — 82–84
2:18–27 — 6, 8, 10, 13, 14, 84–92
2:18–20 — 11
2:18–19 — 88
2:18–19a — 102
2:18 — 9, 14, 46, 69, 86, 87, 88
2:19–26 — 30
2:19 — 88
2:20 — 6, 17, 47, 48, 70
2:21–27 — 11
2:21–24 — 89
2:21c — 85
2:23–27 — 26
2:23 — 40, 69, 85
2:24 — 90
2:25 — 42, 44, 47, 68, 89
2:26–27 — 27, 90
2:26 — 90
2:27 — 13, 25, 91, 106
2:27b — 90
2:27c — 86

2:28–3:21 — 3, 6, 7–9, 12, 15, 16, 18, 20–22, 26–30, 31, 45, 46, 61, 70, 92–111, 123
2:28–32 — 5, 7, 10, 11, 30
2:28–31 — 76
2:28–29 — 14, 29, 33, 93–96, 97, 107, 111
2:28 — 3, 5, 6, 13, 14, 26, 61, 90–92, 94, 104
2:30–32 — 14, 29, 97–98, 99
2:30–31 — 6
2:31 — 17, 28, 59, 61
2:32 — 6, 7, 30, 31, 96, 98, 124, 153
3–4 — 6, 91
3:1–21 — 5, 7, 10
3:1–14 — 6
3:1–5 — 5
3:1–4 — 105
3:1–3 — 11, 14, 15, 29, 98–100, 103, 104, 108
3:1 — 94
3:2–6 — 98
3:2 — 15, 105, 106, 116
3:3 — 100, 146
3:4–8 — 10, 12, 14, 16, 29, 92, 100–102, 103
3:6 — 16
3:9–17 — 11
3:9–13 — 14, 100, 102–5, 108
3:9–12 — 29
3:9 — 100
3:11 — 102, 104
3:12 — 103, 105
3:1:3 — 29, 103, 104
3:14–15 — 14, 29, 103, 105
3:14 — 59, 116, 153
3:15 — 6
3:16–18 — 6

3:16 — 14, 25, 29, 103, 105–6
3:16a — 4
3:17 — 14, 16, 17, 29, 106–8, 153
3:18 — 4, 6, 14, 26, 34, 61, 108–9, 110
3:19–21 — 6, 14, 109–111
3:19 — 16, 29, 116, 153
3:20–21 — 29
3:21 — 109

Amos
1–2 — 128
1:1–2:3 — 124
1:1 — 39, 40
1:2 — 23, 25, 29, 106
1:2a — 4
1:5 — 41
1:8 — 41
1:11–12 — 141
2:6 — 99
2:9 — 99
3:4 — 26
3:12 — 26
4:4 — 22, 56
4:6–11 — 63, 77
5:2 — 51
5:6 — 153
5:8 — 59
5:14–15 — 77
5:16 — 54
5:18 — 59, 60, 72
5:19 — 26, 60
5:20 — 59
5:21–24 — 80
5:21 — 55
6:6 — 50
7:1 — 54, 134
7:4 — 54, 134
7:7 — 54, 134
8:1–3 — 47
8:1 — 134
8:9 — 98
9:1 — 134
9:11–15 — 116

Index of Biblical Passages

9:11–12	157	16–21	118, 120, 123, 124, 129	1:7	23
9:11	94			1:14–18	24, 59
9:12	116	16–18	119	1:14–16	72
9:13	4, 23, 94	16	118, 125, 151, 154	1:14–15	73
9:13b	108	17–21	127	1:14	59
		17	23, 98, 116, 118, 124, 129, 153	1:15	72
Obadiah				3:8	99
1–14, 15b	151	18	23, 127, 128, 153, 155	3:11	94
1–14	116, 118, 120, 124, 129	19–21	119, 154–58	**Haggai**	
1–4	119, 125	19–20	153, 155, 157, 133–34	1:1	40
1b–4	119, 125, 134–39			2:6–7	106
		20	117, 124, 154, 156 nn. 4, 5	2:23	94
2	125, 128				
3	128, 138	21	116, 117, 127, 153, 155	**Zechariah**	
4	128			1:1	40
5–7	119, 125, 139–42			1:15	136
5–6	128	**Jonah**		7:3–5	55
6	117	1:1	40	7:3	120
7	117, 122 n.25, 129, 139 n.1, 141	3:9	23, 81	7:5–7	56
		4:2	23, 25, 81	7:5	120
8–11	119, 141, 142–47			8:3	107
8	119, 143	**Micah**		8:18–19	55
9	143	1:1	40	8:19	120
10–14	120	1:2	41	9–14	17, 26
10	125, 128	3:9	41	9:1	134
11–14	141	4:1–4	125, 129	9:3–8	101
11	99, 120, 123, 129, 145	4:1	94	9:13	16, 101
		4:3	23, 103	10:1	26
12–14, 15b	147–50	4:4	51	12:1–13:6	26
12–14	116, 119, 121, 122, 141, 148			12:1	134
		Nahum		12:10–13:1	26
12–13	128	1:1	40	12:10	26
12	128	1:3	25, 81	13:1	94
13–14	123	2:10	23	13:2	94
13	117	3:1–3	73	13:4	94
13b	147	3:1	148	14	26, 152
14	148	3:10	100, 146	14:1	59
15–21	116, 118			14:2	23
15a, 16–18	150–54	**Habakkuk**		14:6–11	109
15	23, 59, 60, 116	2:3	31	14:6	94
15a	118, 119, 124, 129, 151, 153	2:15–16	152	14:8	94, 109
				14:13–14	152
15b	118, 119, 128, 129, 141, 149, 150, 151	**Zephaniah**		14:13	94
		1:1	40	14:14	151
		1:4	59	14:20	94

Malachi
1:1	39, 40
1:2–5	122, 141
1:3–4	110
2:14–15	52
3:16–17	87
3:23	59
4:5	23

Apocrypha
1 Esdras
4:45	121

Judith
8:5	52
9:1	52

Sirach
11:12	17
49:10	16
50:26	110

Baruch
2:23	144

1 Maccabees
3:41	101

New Testament
Luke
1:52	127

Acts
2:1–21	3
2:16–21	94

Revelation
9:3–6	46
9:7	73
14:14–20	104

INDEX OF MODERN AUTHORS

Abegg, M., 5
Ackroyd, P. R., 123, 133, 157
Ahlström, G., 7, 11, 21, 78
Albertz, R., 94
Allen, L. C., 7, 124, 126, 133, 146, 148, 153, 155
Andiñach, P. R., 42, 43

Barker, M., 73, 109
Barr, J., 137
Bartlett, J., 121, 122, 127, 142, 144, 145, 147, 149
Barton, J., 28, 31, 33, 40, 96, 128, 137, 142
Baumgärtel, F., 77
Baumgartner, W., 12
Beit-Arieh, I., 121
Ben Zvi, E., 115, 117, 121, 125, 133, 136, 137, 143, 151
Bergler, S., 12, 19, 24, 45, 92, 124
Bergman, J., 52
Bewer, J. A., 6, 39, 50
Bic, M., 15, 121, 123, 124, 125, 133
Blenkinsopp, J. A., 6
Bourke, J., 10, 13, 60
Brongers, H. A., 79
Buber, M., 62

Carroll, R. P., 9, 21, 31, 59, 125, 149
Cathcart, K., 59
Childs, B. S., 45
Clements, R. E., 36, 71, 111
Clifford, R. J., 70
Clines, D. J. A., 53
Coggins, R. J., 4, 20, 21, 26, 116, 121, 124
Credner, K. A., 42
Crenshaw, J. L., 4, 17, 22, 35, 41, 42, 43, 50, 51, 54, 56, 62, 63, 68, 73, 74, 77, 79, 80, 81, 82, 85, 86, 91, 96, 97, 101, 103, 106, 109
Cresson, B. C., 122, 128

Davies, G. I., 139
Deist, F. E., 20, 30, 45

Dennefeld, L., 7
Dentan, R. C., 25, 32, 35
Deutsch, R. R., 43
de Vaux, R., 144
Dick, M. B., 151
Dozeman, T. B., 35
Driver, G. R., 53, 68
Duhm, B., 6, 8, 9, 10, 13, 15, 16, 26, 51, 67
Duval, Y.-M., 43

Ehrlich, A. B., 139
Eissfeldt, O., 6
Elliger, K., 101
Ellul, D., 10
Engnell, I., 21
Everson, J., 60-61

Flint, P., 5
Fohrer, G., 115, 118-19, 135, 153
Fox, M. V., 24
Frankfort, T., 55
Fuller, R. E., 5

Glazier-McDonald, B., 122
Glueck, N., 144
Goldfajn, T., 75
Grabbe, L. L., 41
Gray, J., 156

Hanson, P. D., 7, 29, 31, 107
Horst, F., 83
House, P. R., 4, 116
Hulst, A. R., 96
Hurowitz, V. A., 44

Jacobsen, T., 43
Jeppesen, K., 59
Jepsen, A., 7
Johnson, A. R., 20

Kapelrud, A. S., 7, 11, 15, 52, 53
Kaiser, O., 24

Keller, C. A., 7
Koch, K., 15
Kornfeld, W., 156
Kutsch, E., 55

Lipinski, E., 156
Loretz, O., 12, 21

Mason, R. A., 26, 115, 125
McCarter, P. K.yle, 119, 122, 140
McComiskey, T., 122
Merx, A., 3, 13, 16, 18, 19, 24, 29, 34, 42, 87, 93
Mowinckel, S., 59
Müller, H.-P., 9, 10, 12, 13, 20, 21, 28, 30
Myers, J. M., 16, 122

Neiman, D., 155
Nogalski, J., 4, 116, 117

Ogden, G. S., 21, 43

Plöger, O., 6, 7, 9, 22, 31, 80
Prinsloo, W. S., 18, 34

Raabe, P.R., 115, 119, 124, 125, 126, 127, 128, 134, 136, 140, 141, 143, 145, 148, 151, 152, 153, 155, 157
Redditt, P. L., 10, 18, 80
Reimer, D. J., 47-48
Ringgren, H., 52
Robinson, T. H., 6
Rosenzweig, F., 62
Roth, C., 86
Rothstein, J. W., 6
Rudolph, W., 118, 136, 157

Schmalohr, J., 15
Schmemann, A., 65-66
Schmidt, W. H., 48
Sellin, E., 43
Simkins, R., 11, 13, 15, 42, 46, 51, 54, 79
Smith, G. A., 126, 129, 156
Snyman, S. D., 119
Soggin, J. A., 78
Stephenson, F. R., 17

Thompson, J. A., 12, 44, 51, 123
Tov, E., 5
Treves, M., 10, 15, 108
Tzevat, M., 52

Ulrich, E., 5

van Leeuwen, R. C.., 4
Vatke, W., 14-15
Vernes, M., 6, 9, 13
von Rad, G., 59
Vriezen, T. C., 115

Wanke, G., 80, 83
Watts, J. D. W., 54
Weiser, A., 7, 96
Wellhausen, J., 18, 19, 26, 41, 68, 118, 122, 136, 149
Wenham, G., 52
Westermann, C., 94
Wolff, H. W., 4, 7, 8, 10, 11, 13, 15, 16, 17, 20, 21, 22, 26, 30, 41, 42, 45, 46, 47, 49, 50, 51, 52, 53, 54, 55, 56, 62, 65, 68, 69, 72, 73, 75, 77, 80, 83, 86, 90-1, 92, 95, 96, 97, 107, 120, 124, 125, 126, 137, 141, 144, 145, 155

CPSIA information can be obtained at www.ICGtesting.com
Printed in the USA
LVOW10*2101121015

457926LV00016B/833/P